ICTs and Development in India

India and Asia in the Global Economy

Anthem's **India and Asia in the Global Economy** series invites
scholars and researchers to undertake bold projects exploring the internal
and external dimensions of a 'new' India, and its economic and political
interactions with contemporary global systems. Titles in this series examine
India's economic development and social change in global and Asian
contexts, and topics include the politics of globalization, Indian middle class
revolution, the politics of caste, India-US relations, India in Asia, emigrants
and diaspora, economic policy and poverty, and changing gender relations.

Series Editor
Anthony P. D'Costa, Copenhagen Business School, Denmark

Editorial Board
Govindan Parayil, United Nations University, Japan
E. Sridharan, UPIASI, India
Kunal Sen, Manchester University, UK
Aseema Sinha, University of Wisconsin at Madison, USA

ICTs and Development in India

Perspectives on the Rural Network Society

T. T. Sreekumar

ANTHEM PRESS
LONDON · NEW YORK · DELHI

Anthem Press
An imprint of Wimbledon Publishing Company
www.anthempress.com

This edition first published in UK and USA 2011
by ANTHEM PRESS
75-76 Blackfriars Road, London SE1 8HA, UK
or PO Box 9779, London SW19 7ZG, UK
and
244 Madison Ave. #116, New York, NY 10016, USA

British Library Cataloguing in Publication Data
A catalogue record for this book is available from the British Library.

Library of Congress Cataloging-in-Publication Data
Sreekumar, T. T.
ICTs and development in India : perspectives on the rural network society /
T.T. Sreekumar.
p. cm. – (India and Asia in the global economy)
Includes bibliographical references and index.
Summary: "ICTs and development in India is a unique attempt to study the nature and
consequences of the growing presence of information technology in development projects
in India, focusing particularly on e-governance and information & communication
technologies (ICT) development programs initiated by civil society organizations (CSOs).
Sreekumar persuasively argues that there is in fact a wide chasm between the expectations
and the actual benefits of CSO initiatives in rural India, and that recognising this crucial
fact yields important lessons in conceptualizing development and social action in rural
areas."—Publisher's description.
ISBN 978-1-84331-843-9 (hardcover : alk. paper)
1. Information technology–India. 2. Communication in rural development–India.
3. Rural development projects–India. I. Title. II. Series: India and Asia in the global
economy.
HC440.I55S74 2011
303.48'330954–dc22
2011012835

ISBN-13: 978 1 84331 843 9 (Hbk)
ISBN-10: 1 84331 843 1 (Hbk)

This title is also available as an eBook.

CONTENTS

List of Figures and Tables   vii

Preface   ix

1. Introduction: Exploring the Rural Network Society   1
Two Rural Vignettes and the Beginning of a Story   1
ICTs, ICT4D and the Neo-Liberal Discourse   6
ICTs and the Civil Society Argument   13
Research Questions, Contexts and Conceptual Framework   19
Analytical Issues for Discussion   24
Methodology and Sources of Information   27
Organization and Focus   30

2. Civil Society and Cyber–Libertarian Developmentalism   33
The Cyber–Libertarian Turn   33
ICTs and Neo-Liberal Developmentalism: The Rise
of the Social Enterprise Model   35
Information Village Research Project (IVRP)   40
TARAkendras   45
Expectations and Outcomes   48
State–CSO Relations: Emerging Contradictions   56
Narratives of Success and the Sustainability Puzzle   58
Lessons and Non-Lessons   63

3. Decrypting E-Governance   67
Technology and Governance   67
The Beginnings of E-Governance in India   68
Gyandoot: Organization and Technology   72
E-Governance and the Kiosks: The Social Dynamics   74
E-Governance and the Network Society: Deciphering
the Narratives of Success   82
QUANGOs, Civil Society and the Private Sector   91
Beyond Technocratic Definitions   93

4. Cyber-Kiosks and Dilemmas of Social Inclusion 97
ICTs and Social Change 97
Gender and Information Technology 98
Women and ICTs: Rhetoric and Reality of Participation 101
Gyandoot: Tribal Women at Large 103
TARAkendras: Accepting Gender Divisions 106
Knowledge Centres and Women's Participation 109
Social Enterprises as Social Movements 112
Participation in Net-Based Social Action 116
ICTs and Limits of Developmental CSOs 122

5. Innovating for the Rural Network Society 125
The Appropriate Technology for the Masses 125
Innovation and CSOs in Rural ICT Interventions 128
CSOs and the Triple Helix Model 130
The Simputer: 'Gandhi's Invention, Steve Jobs' Ad Campaign' 134
The Case of CorDECT WLL: 'The MIDAS Touch' 144
ICT Innovations, CSO and the State 149

6. ICT and Development: Critical Issues 151
Civil Society, Community and ICTs 151
Structure and Agency 155
Technology and Sustainability 161
Rural Network Society: The Politics of Transformation 168

Notes 175

Bibliography 187

Index 207

LIST OF FIGURES AND TABLES

Figures

Figure 1.1   Researcher with some youngsters in Veraampattinam
              fishing village. Pondicherry   22

Figure 2.1   Protected by the caste Hindu Pantheon –
              The Embalam kiosk   42

Figure 2.2   The Thirukanchi kiosk notice board displaying
              local news and names of sponsoring agencies   57

Figure 2.3   Sivanandapuram village veterinary hospital
              (It is located only 3–4 kilometres from Kizhoor).   60

Figure 3.1   Gyandoot's promotional material showing how
              kiosks provide matrimonial assistance   76

Figure 3.2   Gyandoot's promotional material on how kiosks
              solve rural credit problems   84

Figure 4.1   Gyandoot's promotional material offering small
              monetary rewards for reporting illegal activities
              in the village to the kiosk   103

Figure 4.2   IVRP's offline newspaper *Namma ooru Seythi*
              (Our Local News)   114

Figure 4.3   The 'two doors' and the Embalam kiosk   116

Figure 5.1   The hype cycle of innovations   143

Tables

Table 2.1   Management of MSSRF kiosks   43

Table 2.2   Unevenness in basic infrastructure facilities
              in selected IVRP centres   49

Table 2.3   Projections for TARAkendras 2002–2006   53

Table 2.4   Sustainability matrix of rural Internet kiosks   62

Table 3.1   Sector-wise installation of computers in India
             1965–1980   69

Table 3.2   Infrastructure, ownership, earnings and expenses:
             A comparative picture of selected Gyandoot centres   79

Table 3.3   Narratives in contexts: Understanding the tales
             from Gyandoot villages   86

Table 4.1   Users of Gyandoot by gender and age
             during 2000–2002   105

Table 4.2   Categories of users of knowledge centres
             in Pondicherry   111

Table 4.3   Users by gender at the Veerampatinam kiosk
             in March 1999   112

Table 4.4   Users by gender and age at the Veerampatinam
             kiosk in June 2002   112

Table 4.5   Telecentres and their activities   113

Table 4.6   Ideological milieu of civil society-based
             ICT initiatives   120

Table 5.1   ICT requirements of early CSO interventions   126

Table 5.2   Amida Simputers: Comparison of the
             marketed models   136

Table 5.3   Comparison of DECT, PHS and CDMA   145

PREFACE

When I began this study on the state, civil society and information communication technologies (ICTs) nearly a decade ago, the area now identified as ICT4D (Information and Communication Technologies for Development) or ICTD (Information and Communication Technologies and Development) had not evolved into a full-fledged discipline. Nevertheless, the last two decades of the twentieth century had seen the emergence of perceptive studies on the social and economic impacts of ICTs and it was only a matter of time that the field acquired a name of its own. ICT4D, or ICTD, is now an advanced field of research and teaching in Science, Technology and Society Studies (STS). My study, keeping a critical distance from the mainstream concerns and methods of research in ICT4D or ICTD, draws on multiple theoretical, ideological and political perspectives that attempt to examine ICT–society interfaces in diverse social and economic landscapes.

Nevertheless, I share the idea that there are understated distinctions between ICT4D and ICTD, and that they cannot be used interchangeably. The difference, as far as I understand, is not just one of semantics, and it goes beyond a mere objection to the assertiveness of the implied linearity represented by the numeral 4 in the former acronym and preference for the ambivalence brought in by removing the numeral in the latter. Epistemologically speaking, in its methods and convictions, ICTD should be representative of studies that look at ICT deployment in developing countries from the multiple perspectives of North–South relations, social and class divisions that mediate technology adoption in rural settings, and subaltern approaches that carefully understand the micropolitics of power relations in postcolonial societies.

I have set out my research in terms of the paradigms and methods that challenge the fallacy of unmediated computer literacy and ICT deployment leading to 'e-topian' futures of social and economic development. Moreover, such a position refuses to problematize the notions of both 'technology' and 'development'. Another significant issue in the contemporary history of ICT diffusion is the central role played by civil society organizations (CSOs) in carrying forward the message and mission of the e-topia that characterizes most of the ICT-based developmental initiatives. Traditional players in fostering innovations such as states, markets and universities had reasons to forge alliances with these organizations, as they supposedly possessed higher degrees of credibility and acceptability in postcolonial societies. The notion that civil society, by default, is a virtuous domain, since the state and the market are 'evil', needs to be challenged. Although my study does not cover all relevant areas in this emerging field, I have tried to provide an overview of some of the key critical themes and ideas that help to understand the complex interrelationship between state, market and civil society in the context of the widely known new technology-based development initiatives in India. What I have critically examined are the potential and (im)possibilities of the emergent 'rural network society'.

I understand that there will be a deficit of gratitude that I can actually express to people and institutions for the favours received while writing this book. Nevertheless, it is a pleasure and privilege to remember and acknowledge the support and encouragement that made the work possible. This book project evolved out of my doctoral study at the Division of Social Science, Hong University of Science and Technology (HKUST), Hong Kong. My deep-felt thanks are due my supervisor Prof. Erik Baark, and my committee members Dr Greg Felker and Dr Agnes Ku, who were always ready to share their views, opinions and ideas with me. I also thank Prof. Govindan Parayil and Dr Robert Fergusson, former faculty members of the division, for many meaningful intellectual interactions. Prof. Parayil, (Vice Rector of the United Nations University, Tokyo, Japan) has been a collaborator and coauthor whose experience and expertise have benefited me personally, much beyond the writing of this modest book. I also benefited from discussions with Prof. Andrew Walder (Denise O'Leary and Kent Thiry Professor of Sociology, Stanford University), during his visiting professorship at HKUST, whose teaching and critiques have always been valuable. Besides being able to interact with a great teacher and author of our times, teaching and seminars by Prof. Gayatri Chakravorty Spivak during her Y. K. Pao Distinguished Visiting Professorship in Cultural Studies at HKUST (Spring, 2001), have also helped me clarify several theoretical and epistemological confusions. The fellowship and the travel grant from the School of Humanities and Social Sciences, HKUST, provided the financial support for my stay in Hong Kong and fieldwork in India. The staff of the General Office and the Social Science lab at the Division of Social Sciences have always been helpful and supportive.

I am indebted to a number of friends and colleagues who, through discussions and exchanges, helped me revise my ideas and expand and enrich my work in various ways in the past few years. I would like to thank professors and peers Wesley Shrum, Harmeet Sawhney, Milagros Rivera Sánchez, Paula Chakravartty, Marcus Ynalvez, V. V. Krishna, Tojo Tachankary, Ashwini Saith, Asok Junjunwala, Anthony D'Costa, Payal Arora, Richard Ling, Denise Cogo, Heather Horst, Mark Thompson, Balaji Parthasarathy, Anke Schwittay, Jonathan Donner, Heather Hudson, Erwin Alampay, Gregory Clancy, , Kong

Chong Ho, Sriramesh Krishnamurthy, Mohan Dutta, Meera Tiwari and Antony Palackal for stimulating interactions, online and/or offline. I may also thank Soraj Hongladarom, Chris Coward, Colin MacLay, John Kelly, Qinjiu Zhao, Lee Lee Loh, Kelly Hutchinson, Donny Budhi Utoyo, Uma Sarmistha, Pattarasinee Bhattarakosol, Mridul Chowdhury, Francisco Magno, Nguyan Tuan Anh, and Pamela Koch – the team members of the research project "The Role of Universities in Information Technology for Development in Asia (U-ICT4D)" for several rounds of rigorous meetings and discussions. I am also grateful to the participants of the "International workshop on ICTs and Development, Experiences from Asia," which I co-organized with Rivera Sánchez at the Communication and New Media Programme, National University of Singapore, for their contributions. The workshop and its spinoff, the special issue of *Science Technology & Society*, 13 (2) that I co-edited with Rivera Sánchez, along with the U-ICT4D project, have been useful in providing insights into varied Asian experiences with ICTD experiments.

Many of my friends in India have been a major source of strength during times of crisis. They have helped me to manage the logistics of fieldwork. Gayatri Vasudevan and Prof. Alakh Sharma, Director, Institute of Human Development, New Delhi, provided the much-needed help in arranging the fieldwork in Pondicherry, Dhar and Bhatinda. Prof. Jaya Mehta in Indore and Prof. Ramachandra in Pondicherry helped me find suitable persons for translation and research assistance. Pravin Raju in Pondicherry and Asit in Madhya Pradesh helped me with translations during interviews. I thank all of them for their invaluable assistance. Thanks are also due some of the most committed and insightful practitioners of the ICTD experiments in India with whom I had the pleasure and privilege to engage in meaningful discussions – Satish Jha (Drishti), Subbaiah Arunachalam (MSSRF), Sanjay Dubey, Naveen Prakash (Gyandoot), Ranjith Khosla (TARAhaat) Vinay Deshpande (The Simputer Trust) and Victor Raj (HOPE) to name a few. It was vital to talk to them, and they granted me time and showed willingness to share their vision, concern and anxieties. Obviously, their intellectual and social contributions and expertise are not limited to the projects on which I was interested in interacting with them. I will remember and cherish their generous and open-minded engagement with the critical issues that I have discussed with them. My friends Gopakumar Thampi (Institute of Governance Studies, BRAC University, Dhaka), Basheerhamad Shadrach (telecentre.org Foundation, Manila, Philippines) Ravi Gupta (Centre for Science Development and Media Studies, New Delhi, India) Frederic Noronha (co-founder of BytesForAll, Goa, India) Anita Gurumurthy (IT for Change, Bangalore, India) and Anivar Aravind (Moving Republic, Bangalore, India) have done important work in the area of ICTD in India. Associating with them in some of their initiatives has been a source of joy and learning.

    I thank the villagers and grassroots-level workers and volunteers whose cooperation and support made the fieldwork a pleasurable learning experience. This book is written with the knowledge and insights they have shared with me. The overwhelming warmth and hospitality that I received in the villages will always be fondly cherished.

    I would also like to thank Laurent Elder and Chaitali Sinha, International Development Research Centre (IDRC), Canada, for their interest in my work and the kind invitations to contribute to some of the ICT4D Research Methodology workshops they organized. I also thank, Cheryll Soriano Ruth, Anuradha Rao, Rachel Amtziz, Eugene Chen, Teh Pei Li, Shib Shankar Dasgupta, Nandini Prashad, Manjari Kishore and Pratichi Joshi, for showing keen interest in discussions on issues relating to technology and development and for sharing their views and observations on ICT4D research.

    I wish to put on record my gratitude and appreciation for Tej P. S. Sood and Janka Romero of Anthem Press. Their patience, involvement and friendly pressures helped to speed up the completion of the book.

    If this book has been completed, most of the credit goes to my colleagues at the Communications and New Media Programme (CNM), National University of Singapore, Singapore, whose collegiality and generosity know no bounds. I thank all of them for their unfailing support and cooperation. I particularly thank Adeline Loi and Kanaga Muthuvelu (Retna) of the CNM General Office for their patience, care and concern.

    Some of the chapters are revised versions of articles I have previously published. I am grateful to the publishers for their copyright policies and permissions that enabled me to reuse the following material: 'ICTs for the Rural Poor: Civil Society and Cyber-libertarian Developmentalism in India' in Parayil, G (ed.), *Political Economy and Informational Capitalism in India* (New York: Palgrave Macmillan, 2006), pp. 61–67, for chapter 2; 'Decrypting E-Governance: Narratives, Power play and Participation in the Gyandoot Intranet' in *Electronic Journal of Information Systems for Developing Countries* 32 (94) 1–24, for chapter 3; and 'Cyber kiosks and dilemmas of social inclusion in rural India' in *Media, Culture and Society* 29 (6): 869–889, for chapter 4.

    I also take this opportunity to say a word of thanks to my family, although in India, it is 'culturally inappropriate' to thank your own kith and kin, since their love flows to you for no quid pro quo, including formal expressions of gratitude. My parents, my wife and my daughter showed remarkable understanding. They had to manage the household responsibilities all by themselves during my long absences. I particularly thank my wife Sobha and my daughter Kalyani for their love and emotional support. I am aware that the personal and intellectual debts in writing a book are huge and could never be fully acknowledged. I apologize if due to inadvertence, I missed anyone.

                                                              T. T. Sreekumar

Chapter 1

INTRODUCTION: EXPLORING THE RURAL NETWORK SOCIETY

Two Rural Vignettes and the Beginning of a Story

The following introductory paragraphs appeared in an article published in the *Canadian Journal of Educational Communication* in 1987:

> In the small Swedish village of Vemdalen, the visitor can witness an unexpected sight. On the first floor of the building containing the local general store, a considerable number of modem computers and other equipment are being used diligently by local people from eight o'clock in the morning until ten o'clock in the evening. The equipment is worth a closer look: PC ATs, 15 personal computers from the United States and Japan, word processors and teletexts from Holland, Telefax, Videotex; in short, lots of high technology in the heart of a sparsely populated mountainous part of Sweden (Vemdalen today boasts having more computers per capita than any other part of Sweden).
>
> The first Scandinavian telecottage, Härjedalens Telestuga, was opened here on 13 September 1985, and shortly after its inception, all this equipment was being used by 15 per cent of the people in the village, with everyone from 10-year-old children to pensioners represented. The funds for establishing the telecottage came from the County Government Board as part of a project for the propagation of modern technology in sparsely populated areas, Swedish Telecom and the municipal board. The aim of the telecottage was to open up the vast opportunities of the information age to the people in this remote part of Sweden (where there is less than one inhabitant per square kilometre) by providing access to a variety of computers and modern telecommunications equipment for anyone willing to invest time and energy in learning how to use the hardware and software.
>
> Modern information technology has, for the first time in history, given people in remote regions of the earth the opportunity to overcome

their worst handicap: their distance from the centres of learning and development. The new information technology may lead to further centralization and to the development of a comparatively small elite, worldwide and in each country. However, if used properly, it may also further decentralization and the development of local democracy. In the Nordic countries, governments are eager to prevent the cities from growing too large, and the grassroots drive towards local democracy is very strong indeed. (Albrechtsen 1987, 327–28)

At the time of writing this article, the author was the Chairman of the Board of the Association of Nordic Telecottages (FILIN), and of the International Union of Telecottages (IUTC). Established in 1986, FILIN was the world's first telecentre association. It launched a newsletter, *FILINFO*, conducted the first survey of telecentres, and became instrumental in popularizing the telecentre movement in Scandinavian countries in the 1980s (Murray et al. 2001). In a short span of ten years since the inception of the first telecentre, it became quite popular in Europe. As noted by Colin Campbell:

Telecottages have existed…since 1985. The concept apparently was first implemented in Sweden, where their official names are Community Tele-service Centers. These centers have central locations in isolated rural communities and typically have personal computers, printers, a modem, a fax machine, and a consultant. The telecottage idea has spread to a large number of countries. The Telecottage Association, a British organization, counts 120 telecottages in the United Kingdom, 49 in Finland, 40 in Australia, and 23 in Sweden. It also lists telecottages in Germany, Portugal, Ireland, Denmark, Canada, Norway, and Brazil Typical Nordic and British telecottages offer many similar kinds of services, though sometimes they are classified somewhat differently. (Campbell 1995)

Approximately 15 years later, after the first telecentre was established in Sweden, and when the telecentre movement became popular across Europe, the following news report appeared in the *New York Times*:

Embalam, India – In this village at the southern tip of India, the century-old temple has two doors.

Through one lies tradition. People from the lowest castes and menstruating women cannot pass its threshold. Inside, the devout perform daily pujas, offering prayers. Through the second door lies the Information Age, and anyone may enter.

In a rare social experiment, the village elders have allowed one side of the temple to house two solar-powered computers that give this poor village a wealth of data, from the price of rice to the day's most auspicious hours.

'If I can get a job through this, I'll be happy,' said V. Aruna, 14, who pestered her father, a farmer, until he agreed that she could come here each day to peck at a computer keyboard, where she learned Word and PowerPoint. 'I want to work instead of sitting in [the] house.'

At a time of growing unease about global gap between technology knows and knows-nots, India is fast becoming a laboratory of small experiments like this one at the temple that aim to link isolated rural pockets to the borderless world of knowledge. Local governments and nonprofit groups are testing new approaches to provide villages where barely anyone can afford a telephone with computer centers that are accessible to all. (Dugger 2000)

Both reports have some striking similarities and dissimilarities. Both are talking about computers installed in rural telecentres where children through the elderly use them. Both articles see this development as an important achievement in linking the rural countryside with the outside world. Both talk about the opportunities that it offers to villagers. Both accounts share an optimism and enthusiasm with regard to the benefits of the projects. Nevertheless, separated by space and a gap of 13 years, the former account about a social experiment with Information and Communication Technologies (ICTs) in a developed country and the latter about a similar project in rural South Asia have, unsurprisingly, obvious differences in the backdrop, organizational settings, sources of funding, mode of working and the socioeconomic impacts. Participants in the telecentre movement in Europe, as citizens of the social democratic welfare state, arguably enjoyed better access to personal resources, economic opportunities and social equality within a liberal democratic political framework that ensured constitutional and civic rights and workable mechanisms to contain societal fissures and tensions.[1] So the telecentre movement itself was initiated as part of a larger state and private sector involvement in reducing regional technological gaps through social experiments using ICTs. These experiments aimed to establish new forms of social organization using information technology in various sectors like agriculture, health care and education and involving local communities (Qvortrup et al. 1987).[2] The state and its agencies, including sub-regional local governments such as counties, and powerful national and international telecommunication organizations played a significant role in facilitating these technology-based social experiments. While the movement became popular to a certain extent in Europe,[3] there was some discrete interest in using ICTs for social and economic development in the developing world also. Albrechtsen, for example, notes in the profile of the telecottage in Vemdalen that:

> [T]he developing world has followed the Nordic experiments closely and with considerable interest. Plans are being made to establish telecottages in Papua New Guinea, Sri Lanka, India, Indonesia, Benin and Nigeria, and in several countries in South America. (Albrechtsen 1987)

Although India showed an early interest in telecentres as reported by Albrechtsen, the first telecentres in India did not appear until the late 1990s. These telecentres were set up by state and civil society organizations (CSOs) with widely differing agendas, motivations and ideological proclivities.[4] The initiatives, in their media exposure as well as in the publicity materials and in-house research articles, however, shared a similar rhetoric that marks the undertone of Albrechtsen's description of the telecottage in Vemdalen, Sweden. While Albrechtsen's 1987 article, written two years after the experiment was actually initiated, mostly makes futuristic predictions that the telecottages hold significant promise for strengthening local democracy, learning and development 'if used in the proper way', the Indian initiatives were catapulted into instant fame as harbingers of social transformation and economic development in rural areas where such telecentres were set up, as reflected in the passage by Dugger quoted above.

Contemporary cyber-libertarian development orthodoxy identifies deployment of ICTs as a dominant factor in eliminating vestiges of feudal social organization and its iniquities and hierarchies in Asia, by envisioning a techno-development paradigm of social change inherited from the industrial era (Mansell and Wehn 1998; UNDP 2000; Wade 2002; Sreekumar 2003 and 2006).[5] Consequently, myriad government-sponsored agencies and nongovernmental organizations (NGOs) in South Asia have initiated a host of ICT-based development projects to demonstrate ICT's potential to provide unprecedented social and economic opportunities for vulnerable groups such as women and marginalized communities (Bhatnagar and Sechware 2000; Kanungo 2004; Pringle and Subramaniam 2004; Singh 2004; Peizer 2005; Ng and Mitter 2005). Arguably, the inclusion of marginalized communities in the emerging rural network society would enhance their participation in democratic processes on the one hand, and provide access to expanding social and economic opportunities on the other hand (Rajora 2002; Hafkin and Taggart 2001; Hafkin 2002; Gajjala 2002; Sharma 2003). Nevertheless, it is necessary to recognize that the complex ensemble of social reality in South Asia makes it difficult to find simple solutions to developmental maladies.

By the turn of the new millennium, the phenomenon of village cyber-kiosks, which began to appear in India only in the late 1990s, had already come to be identified as a major form of development experiment involving the deployment of ICTs for social and economic transformation in rural India. Three major projects in India, the Village Knowledge Centres (VKCs) set up by the M. S. Swaminathan Research Foundation (MSSRF) in Pondicherry, TARAkendras initiated by Development Alternatives (DA) in Bhatinda (Punjab) and Bundlekhund (Uttar Pradesh), and Gyandoot Soochanalayas (information centres) set up by the District Administration of Dhar (Madhya Pradesh), won international awards in a short span of two years following their inception. The city of Stockholm instituted the 'Stockholm Challenge Award' in separate categories in the mid-1990s in the wake of Sweden's entry into the European Union, initially to introduce Stockholm as a leader in ICT and to challenge other European cities to highlight their contributions in bridging the deeply felt technological gap between Europe and the United States. Later, the competition was thrown open to entries from non-European countries for projects attempting to bridge the global digital divide. The projects from India, which were established mostly in the late 1990s, bagged prizes in several categories in 1999 and 2000 as initiatives with huge potential for bringing about social and economic changes. International and national media began to give wide coverage to the projects, and several anecdotes of radical changes that these projects were bringing about circulated to the domestic publics, assuring them that an ICT revolution has been unleashed in rural India. These projects were promising, through effective use of ICTs, the creation of jobs, food security, better health, alleviation of poverty, eradication of illiteracy and democratic participation and empowerment of the socially and economically disadvantaged groups and communities in Indian villages. The CSOs mainly initiate developmental action through the deployment of ICTs, while Quasi-Autonomous Non-Governmental Organizations (QUANGOs) emphasize providing e-governance, both with the potential of creating a network of information flows and one-way and two-way exchanges facilitating the emergence of what could be called rural network societies. Does the rural subject get initiated into cyberspace, paving the way for the formation of a rural network society, when the kiosks get interlinked through wired and wireless technologies?

Independent evaluations or academic studies on the ways in which tele-kiosks are set up in villages and who benefit from them and how are almost nonexistent. The introduction of ICTs through the telecentres or kiosks is a sociotechnological process that requires closer attention and systematic analysis. The present study is a modest attempt to offer a preliminary engagement with the myriad issues that this unprecedented technological intervention in rural India has engendered. There are several structural and analytical levels where questions concerning technology-human interaction become significant in the context of the socialization of ICTs through the kiosks. How true is the story of the formation of a protoform of a rural network society realized through interlinked ICT kiosks where villagers transcend social hierarchies of caste, gender and class in a community of modernizing subjectivities for harmony and progress? Is there a sociopolitical constraint in the form of reinforced conflicts between local elites and the poor leading to the capture of the control as well as the benefits of the projects by the elites when the new technology is introduced in the rural areas? Is there a resource constraint in terms of shrinking possibilities for generating internal funds for the sustenance of the projects leading to an increase in external dependence for running the projects?

ICTs, ICT4D and the Neo-Liberal Discourse

ICTD (Information Communication Technologies and Development) emerged as an interdisciplinary approach to understand the multidimensional impacts of ICT diffusion, resistance and acceptance in developing societies challenging varying presumptions of ICT4D (Information Communication Technologies for Development).[6] ICT4D as a discipline has helped to provide competing interpretative frameworks to understand and analyse the drastic changes that transformed of the nature and pattern of ICT diffusion and adoption in rural India. Mazzarella (2010) discusses my adaptation of Linden and Fenn's hype-cycle model (Sreekumar 2003; see also Chapter 5), and acknowledges that the early phase of ICT diffusion can be categorized as an early 'peak of inflated expectations', followed by a downward curve of 'disillusionment' and then drawing on an 'increasing realism' to ultimately settle down on a 'plateau of productivity'. He also argues that the discourse of ICT4D at the peak of the hype cycle was deeply ideological. Nevertheless,

> [T]he hype was not just empty; rather, it brought about its own concrete social effects 'on the ground.' These social effects might not have been neatly measurable by the yardsticks of ICT4D discourse; in fact, they were perhaps even often unintelligible within its terms. Nevertheless ICT4D discourse, as an object of collective desire, helped to enable them. (Mazzarella 2010, 784)

Perceptive reviews of ICT4D literature (O'Neil 2002; Walsham and Sahay 2006; Heeks and Bailur 2007; Hedström and Grönlund 2008; Donner 2008; Patra, et al. 2009, and Walsham 2010) recognize the contentious nature of the trajectories of ICT diffusion in rural areas. O'Neil's review can be considered a pioneering analysis of, arguably, the most problematic subgenre of ICT4D literature evaluations of ICT/community-related projects. Focussing on an examination of over 30 evaluations of primarily US-based ICT/community projects during 1994–2001, O'Neil argues that most of them failed to 'meet academic requirements for evaluative objectivity' (O'Niel 2002, 78). Nevertheless, the study identified five key emerging areas that evaluation of ICT-based projects ought to provide serious scholarly attention: strong democracy, social capital, individual empowerment and sense of community, and economic development opportunities (ibid., 78–79). Heeks and Bailur (2007) also surveyed articles mostly focussing on the Euro-American contexts published during the initial years of the twenty-first century appearing in the journals *Information Polity* (2002–2004, volumes 7–9), *Government Information Quarterly* (2001–2005, volumes 18–22) and conference proceedings for the *European Conference on e-Government* (2001–2005). They argue that a greater awareness about the perspectives, approaches, implications and limitations, use of a broad range of research traditions, explicit engagement with information systems, political science and other social science theories, greater engagement with frameworks and models, use of a broader range of research have emerged within the e-government literature. Review by Hedström and Grönlund (2008) covered all articles in the journal *Information Technology for Development* and *the Electronic Journal on Information Systems in Developing Countries* between the years 2004 and 2008. Walsham (2010) examined all peer-reviewed academic articles published in *Information Technologies & International Development, Information Technology for Development* and the *Electronic Journal of Information Systems in Developing Countries*. They also chose articles that appeared in eight mainstream journals. Both reviews had a focus on e-government but could provide indications that the emerging field of ICT4D studies is, ostensibly, marked by diverse methodological and epistemological concerns and frameworks.

However, mainstream ICT4D is permeated by technocratic and instrumental approaches that posit a unidirectional relationship between new media technologies and development. ICT4D discourse has accented developmental impacts of ICTs privileging civil society-based initiatives with private partnerships over dirigistic models of technology diffusion. ICT4D has correctly been criticized for its techno-utopian assumptions. *The Incommunicado Network* (Lovink and Zehle 2005) almost pioneered a sustained critique of the role of an info-developmental NGO world view that emphasized the need for a shift away from global policy making toward more decentralized citizen-to-citizen networks 'where collaboration, not aid, is the central driver' (Lovink 2007, 177). ICT4D has been considered as a strategic part of ICT expansion.

Pierterse (2005, 19) has argued that ICT4D is pressing for deepening the market through increased liberalization and opening up of spaces for competition and investment. It serves as a new ideological weapon for bypassing regulations or devising or legitimating new sets of future regulations. It is further pointed out that ICT4D 'is a prism in which key profiles and problems of neoliberal globalization are refracted' and it represents a welter of interests including 'major forces in private, public and social spheres: telecoms, international institutions, states and civil society groups and cyber activists' (ibid., 20). ICTD, on the other hand, raises practical and theoretical questions relating to state-civil society-market relationships and interactions in the domain of ICT-based development interventions. The approach attempts to understand the advent of new technologies in the rural landscape of developing countries as a sociotechnical process of great import and multiple meanings. While ICT4D undermines the historical as well as political economic dimensions of technology transfer and diffusion, ICTD foregrounds the awareness that these technologies are arriving in rural Asia, Africa and elsewhere after a decade or more of experimentation in rural Europe and other so-called developed regions. It is important to point out that the backdrop, lived experiences, and the historical, sociocultural and economic impacts of the phenomenon as a techno-social innovation would vary widely in these differing spatial-temporal coordinates. The differences are in many ways fundamental in terms of technological contours, resource mobilization, achievements, organizations and impacts. At the same time, there is a common thread of rhetoric of the hope, aspirations, motivations, ideological ramifications and expectations that unites these efforts. A unilateral emphasis on the supply side has further diminished the analytical power of ICT4D discourses. Wade identifies the neglect of demand-side dimensions of ICTs as a fundamental aspect of ICT4D literature and approach:

> The ICT-for-development literature is biased toward the supply side and gives scant attention to demand. It is striking that at a time when the digital divide has become a buzzword among researchers, we have little knowledge of the relationship between, for example, human development indicators and ICT indicators, over time. Such knowledge would help to make investment decisions about ICT that do not simply assume that ICT investments must have a high priority relative to other investments. Where is the evidence on the relative benefits of investment in ICT infrastructure compared to education, health, roads and dams, and industrial parks? Instead, the literature presents a potpourri of anecdotes and correlations, where the criteria of inference are so elastic that correlations become causations. Area A is rich, integrated into

market relationships, and has a lot of telephones; area B is poorer, less integrated into market relationships, and has fewer telephones; therefore, a telephone rollout will make B richer and more integrated. (Wade 2002, 449–50)

Nevertheless, deployment of ICTs in Asian rural societies has to be viewed as a process marked by promises, opportunities, ironies and complexities. It is important to provide critical analyses of the impacts of communication technologies including computers, the Internet, radio, TV, mobile phones etc. based on research, teaching and outreach related to ICTs and socioeconomic development in Asian countries. One of the avowed objectives of most of the information innovation projects has been to enhance the level of income of participants. Did the introduction of ICTs create new opportunities for income generation and employment or in certain definite ways improve the existing situation? Has the expansion of ICTs contributed to the enhancement of the capabilities of the participants of the rural network society through improved access to state programmes, market initiatives of MNCs or NGO initiatives in the sectors of health and education? Did the ICT expansion contribute to enhancing productivity and creating non-farm and off-farm employment that is crucial for changing income levels? These questions have to be supplemented with questions relating to increases in capabilities and entitlements. Has the coverage and reach of poverty-alleviation programmes, literacy programmes, health care programmes etc. increased as result of enhanced use of ICTs? Strategic and technological impacts of ICT expansion are significant from the angle of information innovations as well as understanding the dynamics of rural network societies. It will also be interesting to analyse the political and ideological tensions and ironies that mark the evolutionary trajectories of technological innovation for the rural masses in the realm of ICTs.

There has been an almost overwhelming consensus among policy makers as well as governmental and nongovernmental agencies that new technologies, particularly information and communication technologies, can be put to effective use in the design, outreach and delivery of poverty-alleviation programmes. Strategic significance of ICTs in poverty-alleviation programmes is recognized by international organizations and consequently, there has been an emphasis on a few focus areas such as integration of ICTs into poverty reduction in strategies related to MDGs, leveraging of ICTs for regenerating or creating livelihood systems for the poor, developing local entrepreneurship and in the design of programmes for social inclusion. Consequently, in the last decade or so there has been a massive proliferation of ICT-based antipoverty initiatives in Asia and elsewhere. Assessing the impact of these experiments would provide some understanding of the prospects, possibilities and constraints in leveraging ICTs for poverty alleviation in Asia.

For the backdrop of this discussion, we have a set of questions with both macro- and microdimensions. As Mark Thompson observes:

> If developmental discourse is an important topic for study because of the unequal power relations it embodies, then the power relations surrounding the development and use of ICT in developmental contexts can be seen as an important element of such discourse. Approaches to the relationship between technology and peoples' behaviour vary from technologically determinist at one extreme, where ICT is seen as having the power directly to affect peoples' actions, through relativist positions, to social constructivist views at the other. (Thompson 2004, 104)

While unpacking the discourse, it is important to consider a spectrum of issues reflecting the larger concerns that have informed development debates in the past. One is the whole issue of international technology spillovers. Are they becoming less transparent and complex? Is there a re-enforcement of the patterns of global economic structures, which historically and politically hindered the development of low-income countries? Are the policies and strategies to generate scientific synergy and economic productivity through the development of information technology successful in developing countries? And finally, how successful has been the idea of innovating for the poor in the contexts of the technological possibilities thrown open by the emergence of information and communication technologies?

Scepticism on the success of such initiatives emanate from varying perspectives. Linking social development with ICTs has been identified as a difficult domain of development practice.

> The question of technology transfer versus adoption and adaptation versus ground up innovation is also quite relevant when ICTs are applied primarily to the social realm. As with applications of ICT for economic development, boilerplate initiatives to build rural telecenters or put computers in schools may not succeed if these plans are not at least modified to take account of particular local contexts. (Boas et al. 2005, 106)

Nevertheless, community activists, citizen groups and donor-dependent NGOs have initiated a bewildering variety of social experiments, which, based on ICTs, particularly the Internet, claim to enhance employment opportunities, generate income streams for alleviating poverty, empower subaltern classes/dalits/women,[7] create sustainable livelihood, strengthen neighbourhood ties, support e-governance, help overcome cultural isolation and combat exclusion and deprivation. There have also been many cross-sector engagements involving hybrid agents. The challenge has been one of negotiating the way in which existing technology could be adapted and made appropriate for the rural environment. Where appropriate technology was not available, the question of how innovations that could generate appropriate technologies for relevant projects could be promoted became a major question. Previous studies have also shown that the ICT4D approach views the questions of social inclusion and participation as fundamentally matters of choice rather than structure in the belief that the only imperative to overcome the problem is added emphasis on the role of awareness building, conscious design and incorporation of gender concerns. On the contrary, the overarching structures of social barriers appear to be far more constraining in the Asian rural setting (Sreekumar 2006; Sreekumar 2007b).

However, it is no longer breaking news that many of the ICT experiments aimed at poverty reduction are floundering. Their performance has been dismal and disappointing. They have invariably failed to deliver the promises they made. Anecdotal evidence to show the success of these projects crumbles before rational and critical scrutiny. A typical example is the story of farmers being able to access market prices of agricultural commodities, which empowers them and makes their lives a little better. Nevertheless, with some common sense, one can understand that this would only be useful for farmers who never had to pledge their future products to wholesalers or moneylenders for buying seeds, fertilizers and agricultural implements. This will only help farmers who have storing facilities. It is not without any reason that rich farmers and high castes in rural India have embraced ICTs while the rural poor remain sceptical. More generally, ICT programmes are at least partly successful in regions with higher agrarian prosperity and economic development. In the poor regions they have failed to take off even nominally. Dalit villages in India where ICT projects are implemented are facing tremendous resource constraints to sustain the projects (Sreekumar 2007b). In other regions, there has been an elite capture of the technology by upper castes and rich middlemen. In other words, ICTs in rural India are not any kind of socioeconomic equalizer (Sreekumar 2006). They are reinforcing existing divides and, more importantly, creating new social divides. The impacts of ICT expansion provide no basis for imagining an unmediated equalization of social divides. Weber and Bussell (2007, 83), pointing out that 'the implications of the digital revolution for the South are mixed', argue that the 'digital revolution is not necessarily more likely to eradicate the North-South divide than the industrial revolution did'. However, they believe that these technologies can create new spaces for debate within which developing-country actors can experiment and innovate with continued expectations of involvement in determining the shape of outcomes. Nevertheless, as Mercer (2004, 51) notes in the case of Africa, much of the debate on ICTs is concerned with finding solutions to the question of the 'digital divide' and 'most donor initiatives have been established for this very purpose', while the focus of debate rested 'squarely on the artefacts themselves, rather than on the social, political and cultural relations that shape their usage (and therefore their efficacy as "tools for democracy")'. It is further argued that 'access to ICTs among the minority has simply served to further widen the gap between Tanzania's elite urbane NGO sector which engages in the debates of international development discourse and the majority of small rural NGOs and CBOs, which do not' (Mercer 2004, 62).

ICT initiatives in Asia appeared at a time when a new set of beliefs and convictions about ICT expansion had become a powerful global discourse. A groupthink of techno-utopianism that hinges on some key assumptions about the emerging global reality of ICT expansion and the foundations of which are deeply suspect has permeated ICT4D debates in Asia (Wade 2002, 460). This new ICT discourse maintains that that digital divide is the site of a major unequalizing force in the contemporary world economy. As a corollary, it assumes that this divide could be bridged by supplying more ICTs to developing countries. This would in turn imply the fallacious position that the standard cost-benefit comparisons are irrelevant in the case of ICT projects, since ICTs form the fulcrum of a new paradigm of social and economic development. Accordingly, and with loyalty to these convictions, groupthink admits no failures as a rule; exceptions are when they could be brushed aside as a lag in rectifying training inadequacies, tackling cultural constraints or eliciting political will. In practical terms, it promotes the belief that the expansion of ICTs and increased Internet access 'will cause enormous efficiency gains in firms and public administrations with lower transaction costs to all' (Wade 2002, 460). The ways the major actors in the Asian story conceived and executed ICT-driven developmental initiatives provide us enough foundation to believe that they invariably shared this groupthink. The digital divide portrayed as a mere technological access problem is critically viewed as an instrumentally informed discourse in line with 'a modernist tendency to unreflectingly categorize and compartmentalize complex sociotechnological changes into one-dimensional social problems in a bid to resolve them through simple technological fixes' (Parayil 2005, 41).

The immediate analogy that can be drawn for the purpose of comparison is that of the impacts of Green Revolution technologies in rural Asia, particularly rural South Asia, with an appropriate focus on the Indian case. It marked the first large-scale incursion of modern technologies in the Indian countryside.

Green Revolution technologies, on the one hand, had revolutionized Indian agricultural practices and created opportunities for off-farm and nonfarm activities that changed the historical conditions of agricultural operations in the rural setting. On the other hand, it had deep impacts on the social structure. The Green Revolution attracted several scholarly studies that brought out a welter of unrevealed dimensions of the social and economic changes triggered by the new sets of agrarian technologies. There were studies on the labour absorption potential of these new technologies, studies on the changes in social and class relations, studies on the impact on capital formation, on agrarian trade unions, changes in agrarian governance, efficiency, competitiveness and the changes that it brought about in the rural market for credit, labour and capital and environmental impacts (See for example, Dahlberg 1979; Bhalla, 1981; Glaeser, 1987; Shiva 1991).[8]

However, most of the studies in ICTs social impacts unfortunately fail to go beyond anecdotal narratives of the success of major initiatives. It is surprising that against such recounted evidence as provided by these anecdotes, more substantive studies on the impact of ICTs are conspicuously absent. When the anecdotes pointed to employment creation in villages, there were no studies on the labour absorption capabilities of rural ICTs. While the anecdotes pointed to increases in productivity and efficiency of ICTs, there were no analytical studies that empirically corroborated this intuition. The anecdotes pointed to empowerment of the poor, of women and the weaker sections, but still, studies on the impacts of ICTs on caste, class or other social hierarchies in the rural areas are conspicuously absent.

ICTs and the Civil Society Argument

The moment of the ascent of ICT-oriented CSOs and QUANGOs, which are by definition state-sponsored CSOs, coincides with a general and weakly contested consensus on the need for strengthening the civil society, either against a degenerating and authoritarian state or a totalizing market. This position is often denoted as the civil society argument.[9] Even when civil society is not seen as a direct political articulation against the state and the market, it is given a predominant role in complementing these two entities in a variety of ways. Civil society, in the last two decades, has come to be identified as an ambivalent arena of social associations and activities ranging from radical social movements to lobbies for multinational corporations. The meaning of the civil society argument as it emerged in the 1980s needs to be understood in the multileveled political and theoretical contexts that gave birth to it. In the early 1980s, the concept was initially revived to explain the restricted civic associational networks that emerged under the totalitarian states of Central and East Europe and its eventual importance in rebuilding the ruptured social fabric.[10] In the industrialized world, the disenchantment with the state led to the reinvention of the civil society argument seeking to legitimize the increased role of civil society in mediating civic life where a weakening of this realm was seen as portending and precipitating the collapse of democracy and social cohesion.[11] In the developing countries, the colossal failures of the postcolonial states leading to increasing disillusionment with their effectiveness resulted in directing attention to building alternatives to the state in the realm of the civil society (Chandhoke 2003, 36). This global exaltation of the concept of civil society was celebrated by international lending agencies like the World Bank and the International Monetary Fund (IMF) along with state- and public-supported donor agencies and agents. Transnational organizations outside the domains of state and market also became more prominent actors, giving a new fillip to the funding of projects that are rooted through civil society-based organizations assumed to be working outside the realms of both state and market and in opposition to the unresponsive bureaucratic rationality of the former and profit mongering of the latter.[12] Chandhoke identifies this as the NGO turn in the civil society argument. (ibid., 78). In developed as well as developing countries this turn to CSOs forced the governments to also adopt a flexible position with regard to their development projects, and QUANGOs began to get increased legitimacy through the willingness of the state to launch its projects through this hybrid institutional setup whereby the state retained control over functional and administrative aspects of the initiatives, while technically they remained autonomous agencies, independent in the realm of civil society. Chandhoke (2003) points to the dangerous consequences of a limited understanding the concept has engendered: firstly, civil society is cleared of any other agency except voluntary agencies, in what is termed the 'third sector'; secondly, it has been stripped of its ambiguities and inner contestations and presented as an area of solidarity, self-help, and goodwill (in other words, a 'virtuous realm'); and thirdly, civil society is presented as independent of, and as an alternative to, the state (Chandhoke 2003,10) – all of which serve the agenda of the international aid industry in bypassing the 'third world' state. Chandhoke argues that civil society cannot, and must not, be decoupled from either state or market, and rejects the belief that civil society can provide an alternative to either sphere, terming such thought as 'utopian at best and dangerous at worst' (ibid.,11). Civil society is not a domain that is that easily receptive to the voices of the excluded, and hence it must be recognized as a sphere that is not only exclusive, but also exclusionary. In this study I have taken up an interesting insight from Chandhoke that the presence of structural barriers to entry means that this sphere cannot be identified with democracy per se, although I argue that it still does offer possibilities for reappropriation by social movements that can perhaps transform the discourses of civil society.

Kaviraj and Khilnani (2001) had raised interesting questions regarding the conceptual ambiguities of the term 'civil society', its goals, its composition and its realization in various contexts, pointing out at least three clearly identifiable strands in contemporary discussions about civil society: (1) in the debates about the organization of society and its relation to the state in post-Communist societies; (2) the two strands of current leftist political thought in the West that are keen to revive the idea of a civil society – the post-Communist and the associational arguments; and (3) the arguments about new social movements as the carriers of radical democratic aspirations. They not only point to the ambiguities of the term in the context of the 'Third World' or 'South' due to the variations in within that entity, but also those that arose as a result of a strange paradox in the Third World, wherein despite the differential actual political processes from the West, the language used to describe, evaluate and express the experiences of politics are more or less similar. Similarly, Chatterjee (2001, 172) while discussing the fundamental problematic of the nationalist project of modernity under colonialism defines 'civil society' as 'those characteristic institutions of modern associational life originating in Western societies that are based on equality, autonomy, freedom of entry and exit, contract, deliberative procedures of decision making, recognized rights and duties of members, and other such principles'. He believes that a normative discourse can continue to energize and shape the evolving forms of social institutions in the non-Western world. An important distinction in the study of state-civil society relations in postcolonial countries such as India is the restricted domain of civil society institutions to a fairly small section of 'citizens' (vis-à-vis the almost universal reach of the legal-bureaucratic apparatus of the state), which for Chatterjee is reflective of 'non-Western modernity as an always incomplete project of 'modernization' and of the role of an enlightened elite engaged in a pedagogical mission in relation to the rest of society' (Chatterjee 2001,172) Unlike radical theorists, he prefers to retain the older idea of civil society (even if does exclude from its scope the vast mass of the population), arguing that it helps capture some of the conflicting desires of modernity that animate contemporary political and cultural debates in countries such as India. Hence, Chatterjee describes civil society in these countries as 'those institutions of modern associational life set up by nationalist elites in the era of colonial modernity, though often as part of their anticolonial struggle. These institutions embody the desire of this elite to replicate in its own society the forms as well as the substance of Western modernity' (ibid., 174). He also makes the larger point that the practices of political society are not always consistent with the principles of association in civil society. Identifying the major instrumental form in the postcolonial period as the developmental state, he terms the major form of mobilization by which political society (party, movements, non-party political formations) tries to channel and order popular demands on the state as 'democracy' and concludes that the latest phase of globalization of capital may witness an emerging opposition between modernity and democracy, that is, between civil society and political society. Kaviraj (2001), based on the premise that political modernity in the non-Western world must be understood in relation to various strands of Western theoretical traditions, follows the evolution of three main meanings of civil society in Western social theory to understand how they might be useful to ideas of civil society in the non-Western world. For civil society discussions to be fruitful, they must at least be better informed about aspects of non-European societies: (1) specific cultural intellectual histories, (2) existing structures of practice relating to use of and opposition to power, and (3) must not confuse the normative with the empirical. Kaviraj outlines the following as failures of the state in the postcolonial era: firstly, the combination of power and utter dominance over the moral imagination of the people resulted in colonial nationalism laying hold of the state, which was not conducive for the continued growth of 'civil society' after independence. Only in exceptional cases like India, at least initially, did the elite construct the institutions of political life that adhered to liberal ideas, thereby limiting its own power. Secondly, the postcolonial state, and the elites who controlled it, therefore had unrealistic expectations about the national project, resulting in an overwhelming focus on economic development and the cultural sphere to the neglect of health and infrastructure, resulting in a gross overextension of the state. Moreover, the entrenched nature of bureaucracies, and their links with other elites resulted in the creation of an illusion of consensus and that an active 'civil society' distinct from the state was not necessary. Thirdly, in cases like India, the state has not failed in a straightforward way, but is doing things for which no precedents are found in Western history or theory, requiring new theoretical efforts to better understand these developments. Chatterjee's distinction between civil and political society is a step in this direction, and helps Kaviraj explain the curious mixture of success and failure of Indian democracy. In all these cases, the call for 'civil society' stems from the disillusionment with the state and its mode of functioning, but in each case its precise significance is quite different and specific.

Closer to my concerns in this study is Chakravartty (2008), who has looked at the nature of emerging civil society in the context of understanding labour in the information society. Examining the complex relationships between the state and the stratified categories of both workers and civil society in India's deeply uneven information society, Chakravartty (2008) argues that 'knowledge workers' occupy a privileged symbolic and economic position in the 'new' economy (referred to by a variety of terms such as the 'information economy' or 'network society'). Chakravartty examines the ways in which workers (the unorganized working class) are excluded from gaining access to formal employment in the coveted IT sector in Bangalore. These divisions are described in terms the distinction between 'political society' and 'civil society' (Chatterjee 2004), which is a useful intervention in considering the limits of an idealized model of associational life in the context of neoliberal 'development', and resonates with discussions on the ways in which middle-class NGOs have to a large extent captured the space of civil society (Chakravartty 2008 287). Building on Chatterjee's formulation that the postcolonial state is embedded in differentiated relationships with multiple publics on distinct terms, Chakravartty applies it to an emerging information society, arguing that in the current context this includes a highly differentiated minority of workers in the formal urban economy and a much larger majority of workers in the informal labour market whose formal class position is more difficult to categorize, and whom she refers to as 'subaltern publics' (ibid., 288). Her analysis of the relationship between 'knowledge workers' and civil society as well as subaltern publics who are deemed to be 'denizens' of political society, is based on the premise that aspirations to the benefits of modern society are central to political struggles in virtually all emerging 'information societies', and must take into account new modes of exclusion and new claims for citizenship based on these emerging realities (ibid., 288). In examining the labour-civil society nexus in relation to the workings of the postcolonial state, she rejects the problematic assumptions about the emancipatory potential of global civil society or the 'vertical topography of power' argument (ibid., 290).

It is hence evident that in the developing world, the ascent of the civil society argument has had tremendous consequences for the ways in which state-civil society relations got redefined. It is not surprising that radical social movements with strong ideological positions on questions of development and democracy most often find themselves in opposition to the state's policies and programmes. They resort to constitutional and sometimes more radical forms of protest leading protracted legal and political battles with the state on issues that affect the lives of the marginalized groups and communities, but where the mainstream political society has reached an uneasy consensus. The struggle against the Narmada Dam in India launched by the Naramada Bachaao Antholan (NBA) is a case in point.[13] Nevertheless, civil society comprises not only protest movements, but also other associations such as developmental NGOs, religious organizations and lobbies for different market-based actors such as chambers of commerce and social and cultural clubs. The relationship between the state and these entities is not one of constant opposition, as in the case of the resistance movements. But at the same time, it is not one of harmony and peaceful coexistence, either. In the case of developmental CSOs, the ideal situation is articulated as one of working in tandem with the state and its agencies, but in reality, this ideal is rarely achieved, if not never. As I show in my study, this may have consequences for realizing the potential of the goals and objectives of both CSOs as well as QUANGOs.

While the failures of behemoth bureaucratic states of the postcolonial world in solving the development dilemmas of their vast populations has received wide attention and recognition, the contradictions between the professed virtues and advantages of the CSOs on the one hand and their actual functioning and achievements on the other often do not get the attention they warrant. Are the CSOs able to fulfil the promises they made while stepping in the place of the state for delivering goods and services that were once the exclusive prerogative of the state? The successes and failures, for example, of the market, another entity that challenged the state on grounds of efficiency and competition, has been well recorded in terms of the actual consequences of state withdrawal. A similar systematic assessment of the promises and pitfalls of the CSOs based on their actual functioning and independent evaluations of their gains remains a marginal area of study in the context of developing countries. Most of the critiques of developmental NGOs have come from the point of view of their relations with foreign donor agencies and governments as well as international agencies such as the World Bank and International Monetary Fund (IMF). They are often dismissed as agents of imperialism (Karat 1984; Petras 1999b).[14]

As I have already noted, in the last decade there has been a proliferation of developmental CSOs in India and elsewhere that more or less share the belief that ICTs can effectively be used as a tool for bringing social and economic transformation in rural areas. In this study, an attempt is made to understand the consequences of these interventions in terms of their impact in shaping a rural network society. I look at their achievements and failures, and attempt to reassess the trajectories of human-technology interaction that unfolded in the initial phases of these projects. Instead of celebrating the virtues of civil society,[15] I take a critical look at the way in which CSOs attempt to address the question of access in the emerging rural network society. I intend to do this in terms of four major questions that have come to dominate the debate on ICT-based developmental initiatives in general and South Asia in particular – namely, by probing the working of the social enterprise model of ICT interventions initiated by CSOs, the e-governance projects launched by QUANGOs on behalf of the state, the question of social inclusion and participation in the projects initiated by both CSOs and QUANGOs and finally, the process of ICT innovations that these initiatives have triggered in the National Innovation System (NIS), creating newer forms of civil society-state-market-university interaction.

Research Questions, Contexts and Conceptual Framework

The information age, according to Castells (2000), is fast restructuring capitalist civilization and transforming institutional realities and conditions of everyday life (McGuigan 1999). Castells considers a binary relation between the 'Net' and the 'Self' as one of structural schizophrenia between structure and meaning. For him, technologies of communication are getting increasingly sophisticated, while social communication has fallen prey to widespread feelings of alienation and anxiety. At the same time, the conditions of access, capability and distribution in cyberspace (Luke 1998) have become central questions of both theoretical and practical importance as the digital ICT revolution sweeps the world, leading to the emergence of network societies. Wellman (2001, 17) argues that while complex social networks are by no means new phenomena, recent technological advances in communication 'have afforded their emergence as a dominant form of social organization' and 'technological development of computer networks and societal transformation into social networks are now in a positive feedback loop'.

The advent of ICTs spurred considerable debate on issues concerning the impact of technological changes at the local, national and global levels as well as at the level of the individual. Some of the issues are not entirely new, being debated for more than three centuries, probably beginning with the series of inventions and innovations constituting what came to be called the industrial revolution in Western Europe (Armitage 2000; Aron 1967; Tehranian 1990; Beniger 1986; Virilio 1995 and 1999). Technology has itself become a powerful mode of representation on the basis of its potential for creating opportunities for social, cultural and economic changes. A wide range of theoretical, political and philosophical positions from Luddism and various forms of technophobia to technological determinism have informed the old and new debates (Rosenberg 1976). Tehranian schematizes the contending perspectives as those of Technophiles, Technophobes, Techno-neutrals and Techno-structuralists (Tehranian 1990). The range of positions with regard to the impacts of ICTs also more or less reflects this typology.

Responses to rapid development of technology and perceptions about its concomitant repercussions and gains have at best been contradictory. The two major problems that caused considerable tension had been the radicalization of the politics of technical divide and strong scepticism about real gains of technical progress where it had happened. The emergence of ICTs has reinforced these concerns as reverberated in a welter of responses to the phenomenon. The dominant response had been to welcome the changes and understand them as the new condition of global transformation with unprecedented potential for transforming the world through enhanced productivity (UNDP 1999 and 2000; Mansell and Wehn (Eds.) 1998; United Nations 1999). Negroponte (1995, 229), in his seminal work, argued out the reasons for optimism amidst all noticeable flipsides of the ICT revolution: 'Like force of nature, the digital age cannot be denied or stopped. It has four very powerful qualities that will result in its ultimate triumph: decentralizing, globalizing, harmonizing and empowering'. ICTs represent a vast grid of virtual opportunities tunnelling through a new configuration of power, agency and structure of meaning capable of revolutionizing real-life settings (Luke 1998, 121).

Another set of responses pointed to the nihilistic ramifications of digital networking, which throws the individual into a nebulous vortex of signifiers marked by loss of identity and direction. Such perspectives stressed the enormous powers of the corporate entities to define meaning and authenticity in a deeply fragmented sociocultural and political field (Robins and Webster 1983 and 1988; Kroker and Kroker 1997; Virilio 2000). An opposite view holds that ICTs have potential for being used as artefacts for resistance against domination, as exemplified in the attempts to coordinate global opposition to totalitarian and military dictatorships as well as tyrannical economic logic practiced by multilateral financial and trade organizations like the World Bank or WTO (De Vaney et al., 2000; Lee 1997; Pickerill 2001; Smith and Smythe 2001).

Yet another set of responses were moulded by the reality of exclusion, that the ICTs with their tremendous positive potential were not inclusive, a vast section of the world population in the developed as well as developing regions being left out from the information superhighway. The phenomenon referred to in the ICT literature as digital divide with its varied racial, gender and regional dimensions has become a central issue in the political economy of ICT expansion (Haywood 1995; Schön et al. 1998; Loader 1999; Golding, 1996; Avgerou and Walsham 2000; Avgerou et al. 2004; Yates et al. 2010).

In negotiating these responses, particularly in the developing countries, the contribution of CSO and state-sponsored QUANGOs are considered remarkable. Both entities have certainly come to play an important role in facilitating ICT expansion in developing countries (Bhatnagar and Schware 2000; Richardson, et al. 2000; Sood 2001). They have become major vehicles and partners in the implementation of government programmes for governance and poverty alleviation (Ramachandraiah 2003; Karan 2006; Lin and Atkin 2007; Hudson 2006; Bagga, et al. 2005; Nalini 2007; Keniston and Kumar 2004; Arora 2010). With the expansion of ICTs, many CSOs and QUANGOs have started using ICTs on a large scale, creating new patterns of demand for them. Many CSOs use ICTs directly for developmental activities that they undertake. These ICT-CSOs focus their attention on the dissemination and use of ICTs in the rural sector, basing their programmes on a philosophy of gradual betterment of quality of life. The sustained focus of CSOs on ICT innovations among rural communities has given shape to ensembles of microlevel information societies in developing countries that can legitimately be identified as protoforms of rural network societies.

The specific ICT requirements of CSOs and QUANGOs have compelled them to adopt, adapt, procure and use new technology in community-based initiatives, creating unprecedented patterns and forms of ICT demand. This has enabled ICT-based CSOs to become partners in a new milieu of innovation where the hope of creating cost-effective ICTs for developmental activities for catering to the rural demand for these products appears to be a possibility, although the conditions under which these projects realize their cherished objectives and their actual impacts need closer scrutiny. The case of the Simputer developed in India is a typical example. There are also a host of packages and services that are created with the specific intention of making rural developmental activities more effective. The dynamism produced as a result of these activities is signalling back demand impulses for more of such technology. The process in turn becomes the hub of a new form of information-based community that differs significantly from its counterparts in developed countries. Nevertheless, the tensions and fissures that these processes have generated are important in understanding their successes and failures and how, in reality, they contribute to the formation of a rural network society.

Close case studies of ICT-based CSOs and QUANGOs can contribute to a greater understanding of the mechanisms and processes that define the contours of this integrative phenomenon, its contradictions and internal tensions. The question is how do we account for the processes involved in this phenomenon of CSO- and QUANGO-based response to technological transformation? A simple linear model of harmonious and mutually benefiting state-civil society interaction with its underlying hypothesis of social capital formation through increased participation creating rural and neighbourhood network societies facilitating social and economic change looks as problematic as it is appealing. The unique field of innovation shapes itself in a nonlinear framework of need assessment, conceptualization and appropriate technology search interlocking with state-industry-university, adoption/adaptation, volunteer training, implementation, appreciation of feedback loops and need reassessment, articulating a complex and challenging scenario of technological transformation. With its excessive dependence on an apparently residual variable of social capital that is intangible, as much as it is evasive, the simple linear model is inadequate to explain this complex process further (Putnam 1993 and 1995; Fine 2001; Montgomery and Inkeles 2000; Dekker and Uslaner (eds) 2001; Baron, Field and Schuller, (eds) 2000). All capital is profoundly social and a specific mechanism that conditions its origin and transformation into a material force is what requires interpretation.[16]

One pertinent question in the context of ICT based development intervention is how the state-civil society relationship is redefined. A second question is how real are the claims characterizing the emerging rural network society as one that transcends social hierarchies. Is it possible that instead of transcending traditions and annihilating social hierarchies, ICT projects in rural areas end up creating new edifying microtechnocracies in villages with their own logic of hierarchy, domination and subordination? It is also likely that new technocracies are co-opting existing modes of social domination rather than challenging them. The identification of civil society's interface with new technology with increased democratization and programmatic valorization of freedom in expanding capabilities through enhanced entitlements appears to suffer from representational and interpretive insufficiency due to its inadequate attention to the logic of technocratic reason. The question is whether rural network societies seek new stability and inherent virtues in ICTs or assimilate ICTs' mechanical repetitions and innovations as an e-topia,[17] where otherwise meaningless simulations are transformed in a utilitarian approach to adoption or adaptation.

Figure 1.1. Researcher with some youngsters in Veraampattinam fishing village, Pondicherry.

One of the avowed objectives of most of the information innovation projects is to enhance the level of income of the participants. Does the introduction of ICTs create new opportunities for income generation and employment or in certain definite ways improve the existing situation? Do ICTs enhance the capabilities of the participants of the network society through improved access to state programmes or CSO initiatives in the sectors of health and education? Do ICTs contribute to enhanced productivity and create nonfarm and off-farm employment that is crucial for changing income levels? These questions have to be supplemented with questions relating to increases in capabilities and entitlements. Has the coverage and reach of poverty-alleviation programmes, literacy programmes, health care programmes etc. increased as result of enhanced use of ICTs?

Strategic and technological impacts of ICT expansion are significant from the angle of information innovations as well as for understanding the dynamics of rural network societies. Our hypothesis in this regard rests on a critique of the dominant emphasis in the innovation system literature on actors such as firms (public or private), universities, research organizations and state administrations. Other social actors (in particular, CSOs) can occupy an important role in the context of developing societies. An alternative position would emphasize the role of non-state, non-market agencies. The alternative hypothesis is that civil society organizations play a pivotal role in influencing the innovation agenda through new links to other institutional variables and processes such as policy making, funding, research agenda setting, commercialization, etc. Hence, it is important to ask precisely what has been the impact of information innovations as well as ICT-based organizational innovations in rural India? I argue that it has been a crucial factor in shaping the origin and evolution of rural network societies. These protoforms of rural network societies that emerge as a result of the ICT initiatives of the CSOs and QUANGOs have to be understood in their totality as an emerging social ensemble. Some of the advantages in terms of building capabilities and entitlements are obvious. But the inner dynamics of rural network societies have not been explored to understand its implication in terms of democratization of technology.

Are both the CSOs and their beneficiaries driven by a teleological reason (Habermas 1984) where actors aim to attain their goals by choosing means that promise definite success in a given situation and applied in a suitable manner? Or do they share a normative regulated reason regarding the use of technology and sharing its impacts? In order to overcome reductionist fallacies in tackling such questions, social scientists are often urged to take contextualist or social constructivist positions with regard to the interpretation and analysis of issues relating to the field of technological transformation.[18] Human inquiry takes place within contexts and this view challenges positivism, which, in line with Enlightenment rationalist tradition, claims that reason has the ability to negotiate all problems faced by humanity.

Contextualism underscores the fact that all instances of human inquiry occur within contexts and we should acknowledge the role of contexts in shaping how we view the world. Reason invariably functions within context and cannot be divorced from context (Dembski 1994). The problem with the contextual turn, however, occurs, according to Dembski, when this moderate contextualism is transformed into a hard-core position that universalizes and absolutizes in the same way that reason was itself absolutized in the Enlightenment. Nevertheless, contextualism's moderate version offers provisional methodological artefacts for launching an enquiry into the process of social transition in rural South Asia, where CSOs are negotiating with ICTs with their emphasis on supposedly conjoining cognitive-technical rationality with the moral/practical rationality and learning that characterize postcolonial rural societies.

Broadly, placed in contextualist premises, the conceptual frameworks for understanding each of the issues taken up in this study have been discussed in the chapters dealing with them. Beginning with a critique of the social economy model that has emerged in the context of a theoretical withdrawal of grand narratives of modernization and dependency and resurgence of neoliberalism, I focus my attention on the dimensions of the interventions of ICT-oriented CSO initiatives in rural India. Critical perspectives on the approaches of governmentality and developmentalism forms the basis of the analysis of the sociotechnical processes associated with e-governance in this study. Questions of exclusion and inclusion in the context the formation of a rural network society are also analyzed subsequently, based on a review of the achievements and failures of the projects initiated by both CSOs and QUANGOs. The discussion of the ICT innovations that were expected to form the central planks of the architecture of the emerging rural network society is based on a reconceptualization of the NIS as encompassing state, industry and university as in the traditional framework, along with an attempt to place civil society in the NIS to capture the dynamics of ICT innovations that are triggered by the rural network society in varied ways and by their feedback mechanisms.

Analytical Issues for Discussion

I attempt to outline three interrelated analytical issues that emerge from the introductory discussion on the advent of the rural network society. It is important to identify the analytical questions, as they would help to consolidate the key lessons that this enquiry could offer as the analysis proceeds. Since the domain of the study is largely within the Science-Technology-Society (STS) field, the key theoretical questions as well as the major inferences drawn from the larger study would be informed by an understanding and insights gathered from the STS field. However, as a study on ICTs, particularly focusing on the dissemination of new technologies in rural areas and initiated by CSOs as well as QUANGOs, both with their rooting in civil society, the subset of analytical issues that it can raise would have a unique marking of its specific empirics while falling within the larger backdrop of reflexive critique of technology in general. Thus, the analysis relates to development theory on the one hand, seeking to explain what contributes to social and economic transformation, and political as well as sociological interpretations of an intermediate associational realm on the other, where I seek to understand how CSOs fulfill their roles.

One of the key analytical issues that attracts attention pertains to the whole understanding of civil society initiatives. Civil society initiatives have been politically, socially and culturally more appealing than state and market interventions. Civil society is identified as a domain of freedom, democracy and human rights, free from repressive apparatuses to control and monitor human life characteristic of state initiatives. It is also seen as an ethical domain free from ruthless pursuit of profit. Moreover, the idea that civil society initiatives are carried out with the non-coercive consent and participation of people at the grassroots level is also widely prevalent. As I have noted earlier, while there have been critical reflections on the domain of civil society projects, they were mostly from a conspiracy angle, viewing them with the suspicion that since they receive foreign funding, they form an instrument in the hands of imperialism for strengthening the existing world order or maintaining its status quo. They question the nature of empowerment that these projects imply, rather than analysing the localized impacts as experienced by the subjects of the projects.

My study would look at the question differently – as the primary focus is on the complex interrelationship between the agencies that initiate the projects and the local people on the one hand and the changes in the power equations within the villages as a result of the introduction of the projects – with a specific objective of delineating the working of technology initiatives in the domain of the CSOs. Most of the central questions that I address in this study are internal to the projects, irrespective of their external dependence, although I do not completely discount the impacts of external funding mechanisms in determining the evolutionary trajectory of many of the ICT-oriented CSO ventures in rural South Asia. I take a closer look at the causes and consequences of the failures of CSOs, while recognizing their importance in the context of the development history of state and market failures in developing countries. The issues that I address here are: (1) Has civil society been equipped to fulfil the grand promise of an alternative to state and market in delivering the products and services that appear crucial for the regeneration of rural economies in developing countries? (2) What were the drawbacks of these projects in terms of the structural and organizational problems they encountered while implementing the projects? (3) Has civil society been sensitive to the deep structures of inequities of class and gender in the villages where the curious ICT experiments were undertaken?

Thus, the whole set of critical issues of the gaps in theory and practice of CSOs forms an important aspect of my study. One of the questions that have prompted many of the technology initiatives in the domain of civil society was the appropriateness of the technology that was often provided to villagers by the state as well as the market. Also, as Hård and Jamison (1998) noted, the appropriate technology, in order to become truly appropriate, should be appropriated by the subjects to whom it is delivered. One of the reasons why civil society was chosen as the site of experimentation with appropriate technology is perhaps related to this need for acceptability. Civil society as a domain of voluntary initiatives remains a more agreeable site for appropriate technology validation. In the case of ICT-oriented CSO initiatives one can also delineate an implicit effort to design appropriate information technology for the poor. But there were also some key problems in trying to underscore this point. We probably cannot make an across-the-board assumption that all ICT-oriented projects were appropriate-technology initiatives. But there has been a significant effort to adapt and innovate new technologies to suit the social and economic conditions that exists in rural areas. One of the key innovations for the poor – the Simputer, for example – has been specifically designed as an appropriate technology for the rural masses living in areas with no electric connection and inadequate resources to procure equipment required to access the useful information available on the Internet. The Simputer and similar experiments with appropriate technology in the domain of civil society, however, need careful scrutiny in terms of the successes and failures and also in terms of their political and social impacts. Hence, another set of issues that find their way into our analytical discussions in the thesis pertains to questions of adaptation and innovation of new technologies in the QUANGOs as well as CSO projects. The questions that I address here will include: (1) How do we understand the nature of innovation and technology diffusion in the projects initiated by CSOs and QUANGOs as attempts to provide appropriate ICTs to the rural poor? (2) What were the major problems in the conceptualization of an innovation system when civil society, through CSOs, becomes one of the key elements of the system along with industry, university and state? (3) What were the political and ideological tensions and ironies that marked the evolutionary trajectories of technological innovation for the rural masses in the realm of ICTs?

The above two issues of problematizing civil society and technology cannot be viewed in isolation from an understanding of the role of the state. The theoretical significance of the concept of civil society in the analysis of state cannot be overlooked (Jessop 1990). Urry (1981) has argued that there are no pure classes existing outside civil society and several 'classes-in-struggle' and democratic forces other than capitalists and workers also exist within civil society. Hence, the modern democratic state operates within civil society, particularly within those domains where individual subjects challenge social relations through voluntary action and struggles. It is popular to view civil society and the ICT initiatives in it as a pure alternative to state and market under recognizable conditions of failures that mark the history of interventions for delivering products and services to the poor by these institutions. Reclaiming civil society as an agenda for political and social action largely in the contexts of these failures and hence, the urgency of imagining civil society as an alternative domain of social experiments, is in many ways, justified. Nevertheless, the role of the state in moulding the milieu of civil society innovations cannot be completely ignored. This is important not only in terms of building key infrastructure or policy environs, but also in terms of creating partnerships and collaborations. It is therefore important to understand the nature of the state-civil society relationship as it emerges in the cases of ICT-oriented initiatives in the domain of the civil society, as well as the nature of civil society participation in state-sponsored projects. Problematizing of state-civil society relationship becomes central in analysing the relative successes and failures of some of the projects. Therefore I shall address the following key issues: (1) How did state agencies influence the functioning of CSOs engaged in ICT-enabled development projects? (2) What was the nature of the relationship between state and civil society in (a) state-sponsored projects and (b) in CSO-initiated projects? (3) What were the contradictions in the approaches of both CSOs and QUANGOs that made them resistant to building a meaningful mutually beneficial alliance in addressing the issue of ICT diffusion for socioeconomic development? (4) What were the consequences of the failure of the QUANGOs to seek meaningful civil society participation, and CSOs to develop close linkages with the state and its agencies?

Methodology and Sources of Information

I have chosen widely known projects from South (Pondicherry), Central (Dhar, Madhya Pradesh) and North India (Bhatinda, Punjab) for my analysis. The relative novelty of the phenomenon of the emergence of the network society in rural South Asia had left me with a choice of using a wider set of available methods of analysis rather than limiting the analysis by traversing only any one of the conventional routes to understand similar rural phenomena. A participatory observation method was rejected because of its inherent theoretical and practical implications – namely, that although I sympathized with what some of these organizations wanted to achieve, I felt that I could not be tied to their perceived ideas of the social reality in India and the kind of solutions they mediate. The researcher was indeed not becoming part of the attempts by the CSOs or QUANGOs that mobilize people and resources to carry out their activities. There was no conscious attempt to identify with the views of these agencies on the complex set of problems that define and legitimize the interventions by these agencies or uncritically assimilate their solutions as being the ideal, given the social setting in which they operate. While the ways in which the researcher and some of these organizations look at reality differed in several respects, an a priori rejection of what they are trying to do was also not in the agenda.

Hence, the major aspect of the investigation was to make an effort to understand the activities, place them in the larger context of a sociopolitical and economic setting that underlies my perspectives on rural change in South Asia and analyse them using a reflexive approach, which is different from participation. Hence, the method of analysis is based on several types of critical engagement with a wide range of information on these projects. First, interviews with a wide section of individuals associated with the projects and those who could probably highlight some aspects of the way in which these projects negotiate their existence formed a major source for gathering information required for pursuing the study. Semi-structured interviews with individuals at various nodes of an interconnected process of formation of a rural network society; bureaucrats, technicians, village officials, representatives of CSOs, their volunteers and a wide cross-section of local village communities where these experiments were conducted became pivotal in providing an understanding of the issues involved in the trajectory of the evolution of rural ICT initiatives.

Detailed discussions with several key resource persons involved in each project was necessary to collect relevant qualitative and quantitative data required to document relevant strategies, outreach, impact, sustainability and linkages of the units under study with other institutions. It was also an essential step to identify internal and external structural factors that inhibit or promote the formation and sustainability of ICT-oriented CSOs and to delineate the synergy or lack of it in their collaboration with the state and other institutions and in creating a milieu of innovation and diffusion of ICTs for development, since this process is seen as central to the cohesion and sustenance of the rural network societies.

These interviews were designed to collect information on a range of issues pertaining to the function and organization of kiosks. They were specifically asked about their experience in working with ICT-based projects. How was the project initially conceived and how did it evolve subsequently? What were the specific initiatives that the project identified and how did they perform comparably? What were the services and products that they used to provide for the community? What were their sources of this technology and who were their collaborators in providing it? What were the learning mechanisms that they had devised and how effective were they? What were the types of management options available to them and what did they think about the practices that they were following? What were the channels through which they understood the needs and aspirations of the community and how quickly and effectively they thought the projectresponded to them? What were the major problems and limitations that that they felt were becoming important for the sustainability of the project?

Similarly, my interviews with the sample of beneficiaries addressed a set of questions relating to their perceptions on the project, actual benefits that they get from it, their initial expectations and how the project's actual implementation priorities corresponded to or deviated from them, their criticisms or comments on the management of the project, etc. Questions related to the everyday engagement of participants in the project and other players involved in the project were also included in these rather open-ended interviews to understand the conditions under which a rural network society is articulated around ICT-driven innovation initiatives.

Apart from the insights and hindsight that the interviews and discussions could provide, various genres of information from secondary sources are available for a researcher who wants to take a look at the questions related to ICT initiatives in rural areas. Nevertheless, most of the accumulating literature on these initiatives is based on an uncritical appreciation of the work carried out by these agencies and hence, needs to be used with caution. In most cases, they might have relied on the information provided by the organizations themselves or, more often than not, reports written by people involved in the projects producing results of what could be arguably presented as outputs of their own participatory action research. Moreover, critical academic studies, providing independent evaluations of these initiatives during the period, did not appear to take adequate notice of this phenomenon. Nevertheless, these reports and appraisals provide information that is relevant for analysing the activities of these organizations, although my own interpretation of the processes that they describe may vary drastically from theirs.

Media materials available on these projects are enormous and ever-accumulating. Nonetheless, as in the case of the reports and studies that got mentioned in the previous paragraph, they reflect, as a rule and with unusual exceptions occasionally, an uncritical assimilation of the information provided by the agencies themselves. Independent field enquiries leading to useful insights into the actual dynamics of the formation of these rural network societies are rare, if not nil. I have used the media materials with caution and attempted to reconstruct the narratives based on a differential understanding of the rural setting where the projects operate, as well as closely analysing the mode of articulation of these projects.

Another set of data and information on these projects is available from the agencies themselves, information that they collect as part of their own action research agenda, although it is difficult to get full access to them. However, some volunteers and resource persons sympathetic to independent research showed willingness to part with some segments of these types of information. In certain cases, some government officials were also not highly secretive about the work they plan to carry out with respect to these projects or a new initiative they would like to implement. But withholding information and denying access to official records are indeed not rare. I have also made use of the web-based materials posted by the CSOs and particularly, in the case of the Simputer, the opinions posted in their open and unmoderated web discussion forum hosted by Yahoo! Groups.[19]

Organization and Focus

Chapter 2, 'Civil Society and Cyber-libertarian Developmentalism', attempts to analyse the working of the social enterprise model of CSOs using ICTs in the hope of bringing about social and economic transformation in rural India. A preliminary scrutiny of the promises and pitfalls of the organizational models and impacts of MSSRF's Village Knowledge Centres (Pondicherry) and DA's TARAkendras (Bhatinda) is attempted to capture a wide chasm that exists between the acknowledged expectations and gains and their actual benefits. It raises some fundamental questions about the popular belief that social enterprises are invariably rooted in the resources of the local economy and their chances of reaching the levels of replicable developmental models. The chapter also probes into the state-civil society relations in ICT projects, both in the case of MSSRF's service-oriented model and the DA's market-based model. The ways in which the projects and the narrative layers they have engendered crystallize into a formative moulding of a rural network society is also explored. Chapter 3, 'Decrypting E-Governance', addresses the notion of e-governance as a critical administrative innovation facilitated by ICTs. The chapter attempts a closer study of the Gyandoot project in the Dhar district of Madhya Pradesh. A probe into the relationship between technology and governance is identified as an area that needs closer scrutiny than is often made possible by perspectives of governmentality and developmentalism in the contexts of the sociotechnological organization of these QUANGOs. The chapter questions the assumption of the neutrality of technological processes enmeshed in the notion of e-governance. Networked governance is recognized as having a potential for precipitating the creation of a network society in rural areas. Gyandoot's Intranet is identified as an example of an emerging rural network society with scattered nodes and decentralized delivery system in the contexts of contested cohesiveness. In Chapter 4, 'Cyber-Kiosks and Dilemmas of Social Inclusion', the question of actual participation by vulnerable and marginalized communities in the ICT-based developmental projects is addressed. It takes a close look at the claims of overwhelming participation of the underprivileged, including women in ICT-based projects initiated by both the CSO's and the QUANGOs. It attempts to challenge characterization of information technology as inherently a gender and caste equalizer in the context of rural South Asia and its corollary that the emerging rural network society is hence, less hierarchical and inclusive than existing social organizations in these societies. The chapter proceeds for a reality check in terms of actual participation and its implications and ramifications for the emerging rural network society. Notes based on a quick visit to the working site of an organization, Holistic Approach for People's Empowerment (HOPE) in Pondicherry, which uses ICTs in the domain of social action for human rights and combating communalism, are juxtaposed against the record of developmental CSOs and QUANGOs. Chapter 5, 'Innovating for the Rural Network Society', is an attempt to explore various dimensions of the processes of information innovations contributing to the emergence of a rural network society in India. The dynamics are analysed in terms of the fissures and contradictions that emerge in the NIS conventionally comprising the state, university and the private sector as a result of the entry of ICT-based CSOs and articulation of their demands for newer information tools and processes. The analysis hinges on a discussion on the sociotechnological domains of the backdrop of two indigenous information innovations – namely, the Simputer and the corDECT WLL. Chapter 6, 'ICTs and Development: Critical iIssues', provides some general discussion, conclusions and pointers for future research.

Chapter 2

CIVIL SOCIETY AND CYBER–LIBERTARIAN DEVELOPMENTALISM

The Cyber–Libertarian Turn

The convergence of development rhetoric and information society theories in discourses on the digital divide and informational capitalism marks a cyber-libertarian turn in development studies. While critiquing the tendency to conflate civil society and information society, Sparks (1994, 39) draws attention to the emergence of a widely held deterministic position that the increases in productivity brought about by Information and Communication Technologies (ICTs) would lead to a progressive weakening of power structures that formed the basis of social organization under industrial capitalism. Sparks particularly highlights the approach of 'new times' theorists of the now defunct magazine *Marxism Today* for advancing the argument that communication technologies can 'undermine strong power pyramids more directly' (Sparks 1994, 38). This approach largely ignores the deep contradictions of informational capitalism characterized by increasing income inequalities, reinforcing development divides, social exclusion and dependency (Parayil 2005). The new cyber-libertarian approach in development theory is characterized by two interrelated arguments on the political economy of development. On the one hand it argues that in the advanced industrial capitalist world, wider use of ICTs would provide the basis for the creation of a more equitable and democratic society, thereby obviating the old concerns of radical social transformation, while on the other hand it proceeds to show that a diffusion of ICTs to the less-developed countries and within less-developed countries to rural areas would help to bridge the development divide and create a more equitable world order. In other words, the cyber-libertarian approach regards bridging the digital divide as a precondition for emancipation from poverty through rapid economic growth.

An important practical corollary of this approach has been the emergence of the notion that ICTs provide an unprecedented socio-technological possibility in developing economies for mobilizing rural resources for community development, social support, employment creation, poverty alleviation, economic growth and increased democratic participation. This new opportunity for resource mobilization has become the basis for Civil Society Organizations (CSOs) to actively involve themselves in rural economic and social life by creating ICT-based social enterprises to pursue these ends. Consequently, community activists, citizen groups and donor-dependent CSOs have initiated a rich variety of social experiments, which, based on the use and diffusion of ICTs, particularly the Internet, claim to enhance employment opportunities, generate income streams for alleviating poverty, empower Dalits and women, create sustainable livelihood, strengthen neighbourhood ties, support e-governance, help overcome cultural isolation, and combat exclusion and deprivation. These ICT-CSOs began to focus their attention on the dissemination and deployment of ICTs in the rural sector, capitalizing on the lead role taken by donor agencies or 'social venture capital'.[1]

It appears that the rhetoric on the potential of these organizations was, more often than not, highly pitched and imbalanced. I would argue that there existed a wide chasm between the expectations and actual benefits of CSO initiatives in rural India. While recognizing the fact that the incremental values created by these experiments were important in the contexts of relative deprivation and social degeneration, it may also be noted that they did not constitute a case for adopting techno-determinist models of social and economic development. Further, the model of ICT initiatives that evolved in the contexts of direct state interventions showed a strong reluctance to accept the role of civil society in these enterprises in any meaningful manner. Interestingly, the attempts by CSOs to negotiate with the state for joint action in their own initiatives were also becoming increasingly problematic. Moreover, CSOs' claims of the social benefits of the projects they undertake more often than not hinged on unsubstantiated narratives of success and achievement. These narratives served the purpose of eulogizing ICTs in developing countries and rationalized the diversion of scarce rural resources for sustaining ICT programmes, often disregarding the cost-benefit calculus.

The dominant model of these social experiments in the rural setting had been the establishment of multipurpose kiosks catering to local specific, clientele-based packaging and delivery of information.[2] This chapter draws upon the experience of two major projects in India – namely, the M. S. Swaminathan Foundation's (MSSRF) Information Village Research Project (IVRP) in Pondicherry, Southern India, and Development Alternatives' (DA) TARAkendras in Bhatinda, Punjab, Northern India. The analysis uses the insights from recent research in community informatics to inform its framework.[3] The primary information was collected through interviews with project officials, beneficiaries, volunteers and bureaucrats through fieldwork during January through August 2002.

This chapter is organized as follows: An attempt is made in the next section to understand the new prominence of the gradualist neo liberal paradigm in development thinking, and its implications for the ICT- oriented social enterprise model as a prelude to the empirical discussions on the organizational dynamics of these initiatives. Two subsequent sections are devoted to understanding the formation of a network society based on the dominance of the rural kiosk as a complex social process involving several layers of tensions and contradictions, often overlooked in the analysis of community informatics of social change in South Asia. The following section would provide an analysis of the expectations and outcomes of the projects, their relations with the state and its agencies, and a critical assessment of the narratives of successes which that superficially glorify the achievements of these initiatives, lending further credence to the cyber-libertarian paradigm of development. In the final section, the chapter concludes with a discussion of the larger political economy implications of the deployment of ICTs for rural development.

ICTs and Neo-Liberal Developmentalism: The Rise of the Social Enterprise Model

As suggested earlier, this discussion is placed against the backdrop of the emerging scenario of the seemingly unstoppable ICT fetish reinforced in the wake of glorifying narratives of information capitalism and cyber-libertarian developmental thinking that has gained uncritical acceptance among policy makers and politicians, particularly in the developing world. A vacuum has been created by the gradual but palpable dissolution of the grand narratives that defined the terms of debates in development theory and practice such as modernization, modes of production and dependency theories in the last three decades of the twentieth century. This has been filled by fragmented (intentionally) but powerful discourses of participation, empowerment, microenterprise, self-help, good governance and a host of other ambiguous interventions and concepts defined and practiced by an emerging nexus of bureaucrats and CSO professionals across the third world.[4] The issue of underdevelopment, initially viewed in terms of its geopolitical dimensions are at best seen as national/subregional or local level problems that can be overcome by 'strengthening the local people', 'enhancing people's participation', 'promoting good governance' or facilitating microcredit availability, all of which are now expected to receive a new impetus from innovative use and diffusion of ICTs. The shifting of the terms of the debate from economic power of the multinationals to 'empowerment of the marginalized', from political struggles for freedom and democracy to participation and self-help action and from international debt crises of poor nations to microcredit (one form of self-help) for the rural poor, reflects the replacement of the grand narratives by a set of vaguely defined and fragmented frameworks, concepts and practices.

It might be asked how the new fragmented narratives are less clear than the older paradigms. The 'grand narratives' such as Dependency Theory or Modernization Theory had an idea of social transformation that was more messianic than implied by the new concepts of empowerment or governance. Modernization Theory, for example, argued that technology spillover, or merely technical advances, would lead to the catapulting of developing nations into the take-off stage of economic growth and consequently to the level of development achieved by advanced capitalist countries.[5] It was a path all economies were destined to traverse no matter how they tried to achieve it, through domestic market expansion or internationalization. Salvation was assured for the nation either way. Dependency Theory claimed that underdevelopment was the result of internationalization and integration of these economies into the world capitalist system and that a delinking effected through socialist revolution can reorient these economies into the path of development.

The new project, however, makes no such grand claims of macrosocial transformation. But this does not mean that it is devoid of any political agenda. On the contrary, it is a political intervention that, with its rhetoric, conceals its politics and economics. The hidden agenda becomes explicit only when we look at the varied modes through which the project becomes operative. The important fact about it is its fragmented character. In one region or in one locality, the emphasis might be on microcredit. In another place and time, literacy might be posited as the major concern. In yet another place, emphasis may be on poverty alleviation or the empowerment of women. Yet, these seemingly disparate activities are part of a common practice of development action across the third world. But at the same time, they are thoroughly desegregated, propelled by different CSOs, and funded by diverse aid agencies. The target of these operations, unlike in the case of the grand narratives, is not clearly specified. There is neither a timeline for development nor a specified path. Nevertheless, that it is elusive and vague in its motives and motivation does not provide it any immunity from criticism. Neither does the fact that no metatheory illuminates its fragmented rhetoric.[6]

Pieterse (2000) points out two major strands of development thinking from the 1980s onwards: neoliberalism and human development. The pattern of hegemony and theoretical explanation underlying those strands are apparently different. While the hegemonic context of neoliberalism is the continuing prominence of finance and corporate capital, that of development is placed within the economic milieu of the performance of the Newly Industrializing

Economies (NIEs) and the emergence of new, big markets in the Asia-Pacific Region. The explanatory narrative in the case of the former is neoclassical economics and monetarism, while the latter is explained in terms of such concepts as capability, entitlements, and the developmental state. Interestingly, the UN publication series *Human Development Reports* (HDR), have curiously tried to bridge the gap between these two strands and provide a basis for making them mutually supplementary. The HDRs do not argue against the neo-liberal agenda. On the contrary, they argue for strengthening it. Discussing globalization, HDR 1999 states:

> 'The challenge of globalization in the new century is *not to stop expansion of global markets*. The challenge is to find the rules and institutions for stronger governance-local, national, regional and global – *to preserve the advantages of global markets and competition*, but also to provide enough space to ensure that globalization works for people-not just for profits' (UNDP 1999, 2–3; emphasis added).

HDR 1999 envisaged a globalization that underscores ethics, equity, inclusion, human security, sustainability and development. While commenting on the marginalization of poor countries in the emerging international economic regime, the report argues that 'this risk of marginalizing' does not have to be a reason for despair. Instead, it calls for action to increase connectivity, community orientation, and creativity to adapt to local needs, collaboration, and finding innovative ways to fund the knowledge society. The international arrangements envisaged by the report emphasize the continued role of the World Trade Organization (WTO), the International Monetary Fund (IMF), the World Bank, and aid networks in strengthening global governance.

The new discourse on globalization points to the convergence of two strands of development thinking that replaced the grand narratives of development of the 1960s and 1970s. The growth of the knowledge society has created a new field of discourse where development is decentred and moved to the margins of the debate. It appears from thick layers of absurd reasoning that mystifies this new discursive field that 'human development' means making life a little better at the local level with the help of CSO professionalism and 'Development'. The emphasis, with a capital D, is intended to showcase the unbridled expansion of markets, which supposedly propels economic growth. In other words, globalization, as it is understood in relation to this new development thinking, is economic globalization manifested in the reinforcement of market forces.[7]

Economic globalization is thus an integral part of the expansion of the knowledge society across the world. The United Nations (1999, 138) defines economic globalization as growing economic interdependence of countries worldwide, marked by increases in the international division of labour consequent on the phenomenal growth in international foreign direct investment (FDI) flows. As a result of this, it is envisaged that there would be a massive increase in the volume and variety of cross-border transactions in goods and services, capital mobility, international migration and a more rapid diffusion of new technology. Knowledge is identified as the key resource, representing a fourth factor of production along with land, labour and capital.

The increasing visibility of the information economy is primarily manifested in the proliferation of technopoles, the majority of which are situated in the United States, England, continental Europe, and NIEs in South East Asia and Japan. Castells and Hall (1994) argue that technopoles exemplify the reality that cities and regions are increasingly being structurally reconfigured. They are also conditioned in their growth dynamics by the interaction of major global historical processes. These include a technological revolution based on information technologies (including genetic engineering), the formation of a global economy that works as a unit in a worldwide space built for capital, management, labour, technology, information or markets, and the emergence of new forms of economic production and management, where horizontal networks substitute vertical bureaucracies and flexible specialization replaces standardized mass production (Castells and Hall, 1994).[8]

The United Nations (1999) also argues that rapid advances in information and communication technology promote growth by increasing efficiency, integrating markets and supporting growth in services. Nevertheless, it is also true that the spread of the benefits of globalization is highly uneven across nations. There is a widespread belief that international technology spillovers are becoming increasingly transparent and smoother with the new phase of globalization and liberalization of domestic economies in the developing countries. But in reality, when the process of globalization has set off a race to claim new knowledge, the global gap between haves and have-nots has, in fact, widened (UNDP 1999, 57). This could be due to a reinforcement of the patterns of global economic processes, which historically and politically hindered the development of low-income countries. Also, the more deeply rooted structural problems of domestic economies interacting with the rapidly changing business climate in the international finance and technology markets have exacerbated the situation. The strategic significance of these aspects is underscored by the differential progress made by low-income countries in reaping the benefits of the global information economy expansion.

The strong push made by many regions to become the 'next Silicon Valley' has mostly failed. Castells and Hall (1994) argue that the magic formula often worked out by opportunistic consultants is a small dose of venture capital, a university or technology institute, and fiscal and institutional incentives to attract high technology firms. The magic formula, often wrapped in a glossy brochure and futuristic name, do not help build a new 'technopolis'. According to them, 'the world is now littered with the ruins of all too many such dreams that have failed or have yielded meager results at far too high costs' (Castells and Hall 1994, 8).

If the technopolis model has failed to deliver in the developing countries, except in a few places such as Bangalore,[9] in many countries, particularly countries of South Asia, new 'social venture capitalists' are now establishing organizations and launching projects that claim to generate scientific synergy and promote rural economic regeneration through the application of information technology in rural and semi-urban localities. These programmes and projects have been internationally acclaimed as making a tremendous contribution toward bridging the digital divide, as well as providing enormous opportunities for reorganizing the rural economy by generating income streams for the poor by creating rural employment.[10]

The cases discussed in this chapter are widely acclaimed examples of organizations that claim to have delivered these promises based on the social enterprise models that they developed and practiced. Development Alternatives, a CSO in Bundelkhand, has come up with TARAhaat.com, a portal designed especially for rural communities, and TARAkendras, multipurpose kiosks with a thrust on e-education. Its major objectives included attempts to use ICTs for creating jobs, promoting sustainable livelihoods, and altering rural marketing systems. It believed in social engineering. James Martin & Co., an international management consultancy, HUGHES Escorts Communications, KLG Systel and Excelsior Ventures Management LLC (Khanna 2001, 1) were its partners. Hindustan Lever, a monopoly industrial house, had also backed the portal. The World Bank entered the scene with a research grant under the Global Development Gateway project. Angel Investors in New York were considering collaboration with this CSO at the time of my visit to Bhatinda. In this study only the centres in Bhatinda are considered.

The Village Knowledge Centres, the second case run by the MSSRF in Pondicherry aimed to undertake activities for enskilling rural farmers and fisherfolk in using ICTs by providing 'useful' information.[11] The project uses CB radios for data analogue voice transmissions between a nodal centre and its satellites. In Pondicherry, the Foundation's IVRP selected 12 villages to provide information and knowledge to the rural needy.[12] It provided, for example, thermal wave maps to fishermen to 'help' them to snare bigger catches. They also provided weather information, accessed from the US Navy website, to fishermen in a fishing village in Pondicherry. The goals and achievements of these two organizations and their influence in bridging the digital divide as well as the development divide in rural India will be scrutinized below. Further, the issue of whether the newly emerging rural network society is more equitable and democratic is also examined.

Information Village Research Project (IVRP)

The IVRP centres, initiated in 1998, aimed to provide sustainable food security to rural areas in Pondicherry, a union territory in the Indian Union. The International Development Research Centre (IDRC), Canada, supported the project.[13] The concept was based on the idea of catering to the information needs of farmers for promoting sustainable agricultural practices, credit and marketing of produce. The IVRP centres were originally designed to provide information and technical assistance to farmers through packages prepared locally, making use of both indigenous knowledge and modern science. The project identified value addition made to generic information to render it locale-specific as the key step in the use of ICTs. Nevertheless, the project eventually set for itself a wider range of objectives. The first step was to set up village information kiosks that enable rural families to access a basket of modern information and communication technologies. Second, these kiosks were also to be used to train educated youths, especially women, in rural areas to operate the information centres. Training is aimed to empower the youths in the organization and maintenance of a system that generates locally relevant information from generic information. Third, the project aimed to undertake maintenance, updating and dissemination of information on entitlements to rural families by providing access to various governmental schemes and programmes from departmental websites and other governmental sources. The fourth objective is related to the action research priorities of the project such as conducting impact assessment based on organization of surveys, participatory rural appraisal and so on. Finally, the project also aimed at demonstrating that it serves as a replicable and sustainable model of information dissemination and exchange in rural areas by means of advanced ICTs. Central aspects of the evolution and sustainability of the project will be discussed later.

The project was launched after conducting a detailed village-level survey to assess the picture of communication habits and channels in the rural areas, especially among the poorer households. It was claimed that due attention was given at the time of the inception of the project to develop it as pro-poor, gender-sensitive, and environment-friendly programme.

The formation of information centres was a complex social process encompassing a wide spectrum of activities and more often than not, spanning several months. As mentioned above, a survey was initially conducted to understand the 'mindset' of the people. As pointed out by a middle-level functionary of the project, 'We wanted to see if the community is willing to take the responsibility for providing space, voluntary service and electricity.'[14] The technical personnel of the project were aware of the usual scepticism of the rural people towards programmes initiated by CSOs. This happened when the kiosks were initiated, despite the fact that MSSRF had been working in Pondicherry since 1995, promoting their BIO-Village Project, which is claimed to be a comprehensive attempt to integrate all aspects of village life, including its environment, in formulating microlevel planning. This project covers 19 villages in Pondicherry.[15] After the first survey, several meetings were held with the villagers using Rural Participatory Appraisal Techniques (Balaji et al. 2001). Organizing the meeting in itself is a difficult task, given the local political conditions. According to a respondent, 'There is an added difficulty in Pondicherry due to the virtual absence of any formalized Panchayati Raj Institutions. The local Government is called *Nattaimai*,[16] which is the rule of the traditional village Headman. Unless everything is channelled through them, no project can take off.'[17]

It was with the permission of the Nattaimai that they could liaise with youth associations, women's associations and the Village Development Councils to create a friendly environment for holding the meetings to communicate to the villagers the benefits of establishing an information centre in their locality. In most places, the Nattaimai had been extremely cooperative. Resistance, wherever it occurred, was not due to any inherent opposition to the project's modernization plank. As Kankeyan, Head of the Nattaimai puts it:

'Feeble but serious initial resistance to the project was based on two major interrelated problems. First was the demand for free resources such as space, volunteer services and electricity by MSSRF. This problem was actually an offshoot of another problem i.e., neither the MSSRF staff nor their local supporters were able to tell anything concrete about the benefits that the projects can bring'.[18]

This was corroborated by the retrospective reflections of the project staff themselves. They remember that during the initial period before the first centre was ever set up, the going has been extremely tough.

It is claimed that the content of the programme evolved through a process of continued dialogue with the community. The villagers themselves identified volunteers in most cases. MSSRF had stipulated that the basic qualification of the volunteer should be from the fifth through the eleventh standard of schooling. But overwhelmingly, the volunteers were technically qualified youth, except in places like *Embalam*, where they have refused to work without remuneration.[19]

Local Elites and Management of Kiosks

It is important to understand that the process of launching the kiosks and their subsequent management was deeply enmeshed in the social realities enveloping the implementation of such initiatives in rural India. The participation of the local civil society was marginal or notional, while village elites and temple trustees gained the upper hand in the day-to-day administration of the kiosks. Temple trustees in Indian villages are mostly upper-caste elites, and Dalits, in many places, are often not allowed to interact with them on an equal footing, even though practicing untouchability and unseeabilty are illegal. Even today, Dalits are prevented from drawing water from public wells and ponds in certain rural areas in India, and atrocities against Dalits and Adivasis (aborigines) are reported frequently in the media. It appears that Pondicherry is no exception. This is evident from the fact that MSSRF itself was forced to close down some of its kiosks where Dalits were not allowed to enter. A sympathetic report on the project (Krishnakumar 2001) confirms this reality. Since the MSSRF could not change the social setting, they shut down the kiosk when Dalits were not allowed to use the facilities. According to the report, the MSSRF closed two centres for this reason.

The very fact that two kiosks had to be shut down in a small and relatively more developed state (Union Territory) like Pondicherry because

Figure 2.1. Protected by the caste Hindu Pantheon – The Embalam kiosk.

Table 2.1. Management of MSSRF kiosks.

Location	Management
Kizhur	Village Development Council and Volunteer's Family
Embalam	Temple Trust and Women's Self-Help Groups (SHGs)
Veerampattinam	Grampanchayat (Local Body) and Temple Trust
Poornonkuppam	Temple Trust and Grampanchayat
Pillaiyarkuppam	Bio-centre – (Training and Demonstration of biovillage) owned by MSSRF
Thirukanchipet	Village Public TV/Radio centre
Villianur	Hub Centre (owned by MSSRF and operated by project staff)
Kalitheerthalkuppam	Gramapanchayat and Milk Cooperative Union
Nallavadu	Grampanchayat
Ariyur	Housed in a public building under the public water tank run by volunteers.

Source: Based on field visits and www.mssrf.org

of the practice of untouchability is significant in understanding the local power dynamics of rural India. The village headmen and temple trustees have the upper hand in the management of the kiosks (See Table 2.1). Even though some of them are not explicitly practicing untouchability, the impact of this influence on participation from and acceptability by Dalits and non-Hindus could be problematic, given the deep divisions along caste and religious lines that still exist in rural areas at a time when secular institutions in India are increasingly penetrated by caste forces hostile to non-Hindus and Dalits.

The analysis of the complex nature of the formation of information kiosks in Pondicherry points to the role of social and economic factors in shaping access as well as the sustainability of the project. Most important, it is worth noting that the consent of the local elite, the availability of unpaid labour by educated youth and free access to scarce resources of space and electricity provided by the community, either through the income of the temples controlled by upper castes or revenue of local bodies controlled by the political elite, were some of the critical inputs required to launch the centres.

Technology

The technical personnel in the IVRP distinguished between two types of information that they disseminate – namely, static information and dynamic information. The former was not required to be updated at frequent intervals.

But the latter, like weather information or market prices, had to be updated every day. Information on prices was collected from the three regulated markets in Pondicherry. These markets, on an everyday basis, decide the prices of farm produce according to local demand. IVRP had an arrangement with the paid staff of the Pondicherry Marketing Committee of the Department of Agriculture who collected the price data and passed it to the Vilanur station of IVRP through mobile phones. The station translated the information into Tamil and transmitted across its kiosks.

The Village Knowledge Centres accessed the Internet through a hybrid of two-way VHF radio Motorola) and the wired public telephone network. As one of the project's self-assessment reports points out,

> This approach provided an integrated voice and data communication capability. The data transmission was restricted to a maximum speed of 14.4 KBPS on the wireless, where Email (SMTP) or fax protocols were used. Through a PBX (office intercom-style), every village center could be connected to this hybrid network. To overcome power outages, a hybrid system of solar photovoltaic panels and grid power, interfaced by a commercially available digital circuit, was used as source of power. (MSSRF n.d., 3)

From the beginning, MSSRF has been using Motorola VHF business radios for instantaneous communication and data transmission between the villages and the hub (Senthilkumaran and Arunachalam, 2002, 80). The technology using Motorola became insufficient when the number of centres increased. The central kiosk in Vilanur was connected through a full duplex wireless link, using Motorola's technology. The centre also functioned as the Local Area Network (LAN) hub, providing data and voice transmission to the other kiosks of the area. Each kiosk was considered a node that functions on VHF radio (full duplex). It was maintained that this saved the expense of laying expensive communication infrastructure like copper wires and/or fiberoptic cable. The local language, Tamil, was used for all information exchange over a wide array of media. Another ICT-CSO called C-DAC, Pune, developed the necessary I-Leap Tamil fonts and keyboard layout for the project. Trained volunteers skilled in using data-cum voice network operated the village centres. The project staff had designed and developed several locally useful data sets that are frequently updated (in some cases twice daily). The main responsibility of the volunteers was to carry out activities such as information dissemination, data provision and feedback collection. The technological assemblage, ostensibly, pointed to the complex nature of the techno-social relations that underlie the projects evolutionary trajectory.

TARAkendras

TARAhaat, an Internet portal supporting a network of franchised computer Kiosks, launched TARAkendras in Bundelkhand (Uttar Pradesh) and Bhatinda (Punjab). It aims to deliver a wide spectrum of services through ICTs and expects to earn revenues by pricing these services, as well as levying membership fees and commissions. One of the striking features of TARAhaat is that it was not conceived as a voluntary venture from the very beginning, although its sponsoring agency, DA, is a CSO operating in Bundelkhand. TARA (the acronym for Technology and Action for Rural Advancement) is the marketing wing of DA. The concept of TARAhaat took shape in 1998 although it became functional only in 2000, indicating the formidable challenges in the execution of ICT-based projects by civil society organizations. The first few kiosks were established in Bundelkhand, a region where DA has been active for several years.

Development Alternatives was founded in 1983 with the objective of developing models for sustainable livelihood. The formulation as well as the implementation of the concept of TARAkendra materialized as a result of a group of young professionals committed to the cause of social development who have come together in the region.[20] It is a for-profit venture, and pays taxes.[21] Nevertheless, the progenitors and functionaries of the organization did not attach much significance to its profit orientation other than for demonstrating that such market-based ventures from civil society foundations are commercially viable and sustainable. It was a business model with a relatively stronger emphasis on social economy.

> DA is the R&D brain of the organization, developing innovative products and technologies for rural markets, such as cost-effective building materials, handmade recycled paper, energy-efficient wood stoves, clean drinking water and sanitation facilities, and energy systems. TARA then commercializes these products, and when possible, transforms them into sustainable livelihoods for rural people. DA and TARA created TARAhaat with the belief that, by harnessing the power of Internet, TARAhaat will enable the entire DA Group to more effectively bring sustainable jobs, useful information, and economic opportunities to rural Indian populations. (Peterson et al. 2001, 4)

Moreover, they hope that:

> TARAhaat's NGO roots and an ownership structure that allocates a 51% share to the nonprofit Sustainable Livelihoods Foundation will ensure that social objectives are not overlooked. (Peterson et al. 2001, 4)[22]

TARAhaat followed a 'business model' different in some respects from the MSSRF model, which depended on voluntary unpaid labour and free access to scarce rural resources. Nevertheless, the process of setting up a TARAkendra was quite similar to the processes and patterns that underlie the launching of kiosks by nonprofit initiatives. Identifying *mandis* (small towns or villages) in Bhatinda where TARAkendras could be set up was initially undertaken with the collaboration of District Rural Development Agencies (DRDA). But this alliance ran into problems following the transfer of a bureaucrat sympathetic to the concept of rural kiosks. TARAhaat moved out of the 'focal points' identified earlier, to expand its operations. However, the process is quite complicated and requires constant interaction with a wide spectrum of individuals and institutions in the small towns or villages. TARAhaat sends its business managers to tackle the initial problems related to the setting up of a kiosk. Within the organization, this activity is identified as business promotion.[23] The work would involve winning the confidence of the local elites and then finding an entrepreneur willing to collaborate with TARAhaat on its terms of franchising. The process is well summarized by a TARAhaat functionary as follows:

> When I go to a *mandi* I first try to meet the *aarthyas*[24] who are the most reputed people in many villages. Talking to them and winning their confidence is essential to broach the concept of TARAhaat with [the] local community. I also talk to the teachers and other professionals in the village. Sometimes it is also necessary to talk to people in the neighboring villages also. It takes time for them to understand the concept and respond positively. Several visits are required to put across the idea.[25]

The process thus involved an initial contact with the village elites identified by the business promoters and subsequent discussions with them as well as other villagers. An entrepreneur with minimum investment capacity also had to be identified and given training in the mode of operation of the organization as well as in running a kiosk. The paid staff of the kiosk, generally computer-educated youth, also had to be trained. The TARA Academy was set up with the objective of serving this requirement. Once the centres were established, TARAhaat attempted to consolidate the operations by providing a range of community activities and programmes including seminars and group meetings through carefully structured institutional means.

Technology

Confronted with the problem of low quality of lines inadequate to transmit data that were serving remote villages, TARAhaat opted for the alternative of using VSAT (Very Small Aperture Terminal) technology. VSAT technology, a communication network set up through a series of receiver/transceiver terminals ranging from 0.6 to 3.8 metres in diameter and connected by a central hub through a Satellite, would enable Internet, data, LAN and voice/fax communications. Development Alternatives adopted it, since this offered to connect geographically dispersed areas where there was no adequate infrastructure. The adoption of the technology was facilitated by a partnership with Hughes Escorts Communications Ltd. They provided six Extended C-Band VSAT units worth INR 550,000 each for the pilot phase.[26] Hughes expected the project to expand as projected by TARAhaat and wanted to become the exclusive VSAT supplier during the expansion stage of the project. This intervention supported TARAhaat in their attempt to connect ten computers in six villages to the Internet with practically zero financial input, since under the agreement TARAhaat was responsible to pay only for bandwidth use and a special fee to the Department of Telecommunications for use of the VSAT units (San Miguel 2001). At the time of my visit, Bhatinda was still not brought under this technology arrangement. The server in Gurgaon, on the outskirts of Delhi, was serving as a 'hub' from which the VSAT units in the Bundelkhand (UP) connected with communications satellites. Sharing Hughes's bandwidth of about 60 KB, which had only slightly reduced the overall connection speed, TARAhaat could provide Internet access to villages previously unable to receive a telephone call. It is also noted that the VSAT units are highly sensitive to changes in voltage and hence they had to be properly earthed to protect the equipment from overloading and lightning strikes. A copper plate had to be placed in a deep pit and connected to the unit via copper wiring in order to provide protection ((San Miguel 2001)). Digging the pit, finding skilled electricians and keeping the copper plate moist in the semi-arid climate had been tremendously difficult tasks for the organization to cope with (ibid.). Nevertheless, Peterson et al. (2001, 14) considered VSAT as a higher reliability, high bandwidth solution and hence capable of providing competitive advantage to TARAkendras that would opt to install it.

'Typical cost of a Satellite dish, currently subsidized by Hughes-Escorts, ranges from INR 150,000 to INR 200,000. Annual bandwidth costs range from INR 100,000/KBps to 6000,00/KBps but are expected to drop by 80–85 per cent over the next two years' (ibid.).

IVRP and TARAkendras: A Comparison

Both IVRP and TARAkendras are organizational innovations in initiating ICT-based projects for social and economic transformation. The objectives, both long term and short term, as set by these organizations, reveal a high level of sensitivity towards the contexts of rural deprivation, economic degeneration and need for sustainable models for development. I will concentrate on three major aspects of their performance as social enterprises, and seek to study the dynamics of success and failures as they arise in different social settings. The first set of issues that are being addressed relates to the expectations and actual achievements of these initiatives. Although they are widely separated in space, these initiatives have a set of objectives with common tangents in that they bear similarities, in terms of their larger social content, that make a comparison possible and relevant. The second set of issues I address in this section pertains to the contested nature of state-civil society relationships emerging from the developmental trajectories of both IVRP and TARAkendras. Reference to the state is essential in conceptualizing the social economy, even though the extent of dependence upon the state and the nature of conflicts and cooperation between CSOs and the state vary widely. Finally, I will look at the sustainability question, along with a discussion of the narratives of success that are often disseminated through media as indicators of the growing demand for IT-enabled services in rural India, reflecting the viability and sustainability of the projects and legitimating an implied cyber-libertarian development paradigm.

Expectations and Outcomes

While the benefits of the spread of ICTs into the rural areas have considerable social and economic impacts, the projects cannot deliver the range of outputs that were initially envisaged due to a multitude of factors such as limited local participation, lack of availability of local resources, fractured relationship with the state agencies, limited integration with other local CSOs and the exogenous social and economic environments that these enterprises are unable to control. These factors are often overlooked when projecting the promises of the projects. This approach has consistently led to the overestimation of expected outcomes while underplaying the pitfalls.

In the case of MSSRF, it can be seen that it relies heavily on local resources in terms of space, non-paid labour and electricity. In the case of facilities, the centres are highly uneven because most communities, which are poor and socially backward, are unable to acquire the infrastructure required for setting up the kiosks as well as maintaining them (see Table 2.2). The volunteers invariably pointed to either indifference or inability of the local body for lack of comparable facilities in their respective kiosks. The Poornankuppam and Thirukanchipet kiosks are good examples of the ways in which limitations of resources and low demand for ICT-enabled services

Table 2.2. Unevenness in basic infrastructure facilities in selected IVRP centres.

Centre / Item	Veerampattinam	Embalam	Poornamkuppam	Thirukanchipet
Connectivity	Phone Connection	Phone Connection	Not connected	Not connected
Internet	Available	Available	Not accessible	Not accessible
Web camera	Available	Available	Not Available	Not available
No. of PCs	8	3	3	3
Speaker system	Available	Not installed	Not installed	Not installed
Allowance for Volunteers	INR 500 paid by panchayat*	No allowance	No allowance	No allowance
Spread spectrum	Installed	Installed	Not installed	Not installed
Solar Panel	Not installed	Installed	Not installed	Not installed
Siren	Not installed	Installed	Not installed	Not installed
Wireless Phone	Connected	Connected	Connected	Connected

Source: Based on authors visits to centres.

* Allowance was being paid to only one of the volunteers and the payment had become irregular at the time of my investigation.

could stand in the way of the dreamy projections of the successes of such initiatives in rural India.

The Poornankuppam Centre: An Evaluation

A visitor to the centre can instantly note the presence of an active band of self-help groups in the village by looking at the display board placed at the main junction listing the names of several women's self-help groups in the village, such as Mahatma Gandhi, Jhansi Rani, SEVA, and Sarojini. But none of these organizations are involved in the management of the kiosk. One of the four volunteers in charge is a 23-year-old male volunteer who has completed his PGD (postgraduate diploma) in Computer Applications. He joined as a volunteer in August 2001 when the centre was on the verge of being closed down for want of personnel to manage it. He remembers:

> I first came here as a user and met the staff of MSSRF. After my graduation I volunteered along with three of my friends when the centre had been closed for more than two months during June–July 2001 for lack of volunteers to run the centre. I went to the Vilanur office and offered my services with other three friends.[27]

One of the reasons, perhaps, for the reluctance of the local youth to associate with the centre is its relative lack of infrastructure. He maintains:

> In this centre there is no Internet or phone. We have only the wireless phone facility offered by MSSRF and the computer fax. The calls can be made only on weekdays. We charge INR 2 for a call irrespective of the duration.[28]

The temple offers the space and electricity for the centre free of charge. The relationship with the temple trust is relatively tension-free except for the festival season, when they ask the centre to vacate the space for opening the reception committee office for the festival. But through lobbying of the panchayat (local body) members who were sympathetic to the centre, the volunteers succeed in revoking this decision by the temple trust. However, the relationship of the centre with the panchayat appears to be very weak, with the panchayat offering no help, support or assistance to the project. It appears that the kiosk cannot afford to pay the monthly rental charges of the phone, a paltry sum of INR 250. According to my informant, there were very few foreign visitors and little media exposure to this centre, unlike the one in Veerampattinam.

The fax message from the Vilanur centre used to reach the centre on weekdays around 10:30 a.m. and included: (1) price list, (2) weather report, and (3) daily news. This is immediately placed on the notice board. On an average, a maximum of six to ten farmers would visit the centre to make use of this information. The volunteer was worried that their numbers would be still less if the centre decided to charge for the information in the future to make it a business model. The user fees that centre received from the services were just notional. According to my informant:

> We have just three computers and with that we offer training courses in MS Office to youth and children. But the enrolment rate is very low. We collect a monthly fee of INR 50 for training. For the games children play, we charge INR 5 per hour. The locality is relatively poor. So many children cannot afford to pay the amount for games. So there is no huge demand for it either.[29]

It is in the month of May, during school vacation, that the maximum numbers of students enrol for the computer course. The register for May 2002 showed that, on the average, seven or eight students visited the centre for the purpose of learning to operate a computer. It appeared that the centre attracts 10 to 15 students to its computer courses, each paying INR 50 per month as user fees. A number of people also used the centre as a telephone booth, since it provided the availability of wireless local calls for INR 2. Nevertheless, the revenue from the centre could not be considered as breaking even, if subsidies were withdrawn.

The Thirukanchipet Centre

This centre was a classic illustration of how resource-poor, lower-caste Dalit villages struggled to maintain knowledge centres in the absence of subsidies. The panchayat was providing space and electricity to the centre by default, since the centre operated in the small room where the panchayat television is kept for villagers to watch programmes aired by government channels. Before the arrival of the television, this room was used for listening to the radio. While one could see a gradual progress of the village public centre from radio to television and eventually to a computer, the inability of the panchayat to provide additional resources for running the kiosk had left volunteers dependent solely on the subsidy provided by the MSSRF. Although there was a temple in the village, the centre did not get any assistance from its management. One of the volunteers of the centre explained:

> There is a temple nearby. The temple management is not able to offer us any help, because being a Dalit temple they themselves have very little resources. The panchayat has not agreed to pay the phone bill if we

take Internet connection. Since the people are Dalits and poor the local
panchayat is also not rich. So we have no Internet, no phone connection,
no spectrum, no siren and no speaker system.[30]

But he hoped that the panchayat would soon find a solution to the problem
of a phone connection and would somehow find means to pay for the utility.
The user fees that the centre could generate appeared to be negligible. They
charged the children playing the computer games at INR 4 per hour. But
not many parents in the village could afford this cost. Some school children,
however, used to get an opportunity to learn some of the basic computer
skills at the low user fee. According to the informant, farmers were not very
enthused about the centre:

> We campaign and canvass people to use the facilities in the centre. I would
> say that students and the youth of the locality mainly use the centre.
> MSSRF has said that they will withdraw all subsidies in 2004. By then we
> are supposed to stand on our own. Their logic is that external funding will
> not continue. They have to use the money to start new centres elsewhere.
> Now if there is a technical problem or [a] need to repair the machine we
> have to wait for the technician of MSSRF from Chennai. But even though
> we have to wait, we prefer it since it is free of cost. But now we are told that
> such free support will not be forthcoming after 2004. Now we get even the
> stationery free. In [the] future we would have to pay for them.[31]

The experience of these two MSSRF kiosks points to the resource constraints
that stifle the diffusion of knowledge centres. Consequently, the kiosks were
established only in a few villages, and even in the case of centres with more
facilities, they were mostly visited by children to play computer games and
nearby youths for their academic projects. In the case of some centres, the
value addition to generic information and its dissemination appeared to be
useful for farmers and fishermen. But in what ways this information sounded
crucial in everyday life depended on specific contexts and it was difficult, if not
impossible, to assess how they contributed to productivity improvements.

In the case of TARAkendras, the success of each enterprise depended upon
the market size in the *mandis* where they operated. TARAkendras were expected
to expand and take root at a faster pace than what actually materialized. An
early projection of the possible proliferation of TARAkendras estimated
phenomenal growth in the number of kiosks as well as users for TARAkendras
by the year 2005. Khanna (2001, 8) projected a growth of TARAhaat kiosks
from 11 to 22,725; users from less than a thousand to 20,022,000 and PCs
from a few hundreds to 1,016,054 by 2005–2006 (See Table 2.3). In reality,

Table 2.3. Projections for TARAkendras 2002–2006.

TARAkendra	Year 1	Year 2	Year 3	Year 4
	2002–2003	2003–2004	2004–2005	2005–2006
Total Kiosks	328	4165	13525	22725
Total Users	161820	2811480	10266500	20022000
Total PCs	1055	15463	54247	1016054
Students per computer	11	12	12	13

Source: Khanna (2001, 8).

the progression had stagnated, and TARAhaat had reportedly closed down its operation in Bundelkhand. The euphoric expectations were being completely unrealized. As discussed earlier, the real difficulties in setting up a centre were formidable, and it was unrealistic to make overly optimistic projections on the possibilities of growth.[32] TARAkendras were hoping to get 10–12 or more students per computer. Envisaging a commercial model of computer education broadly offering different kinds of content delivery, it was hoped that they would 'get about 12 registered students per computer at any time in a TARAkendra' (Prakash 2001, 5).

The performance of different centres, as in the case of IVRP kiosks, depended heavily on local-specific factors. The education model, however, had failed to be appealing, as the experiences of several TARAkendras illustrated. Massive job creation and poverty alleviation were lofty goals, but turned out to be extremely difficult to pursue, with an overemphasis on the potential of new technologies. This was evident from the fact that some of the TARAkendras with a longer history had either been closed down or disenfranchised. Moreover, the older centres were performing badly in terms of student enrolment and user turnout, making them economically unviable. The stories of two TARAkendras in Gonniana and Lehra Mohabbat would illustrate this point better.

The Gonniana TARAKendra

This centre was established in April 2002 with an initial investment of INR 200,000. The franchisee of this centre learned about TARAhaat from a relative and applied for a franchise based on his experience owning and running a similar centre in Bhatinda. He holds a PGD in Management from the United Kingdom and a Business Administration Diploma from Hyderabad, India. He opted for TARAhaat franchise because of two reasons, viz., the belief that the public will value TARAhaat certificate in computer

education since Development Alternatives is recognized by the Ministry
of Science and Technology, New Delhi and the promise that TARAhaat
will make the curriculum in the local language. He also felt that the fee
structure was competitive. According to him, four months into operations
these expectations had not been met. He offered the BASIC IT course of
TARAgyan (the education service through TARAkendras), which had a
duration of four months, for a monthly fee of INR 500. Special courses,
such as TALLY, were charged slightly higher, but students were willing to
join. Some private-sector outfits in the locality attempted to compete by
lowering their fees, but could not sustain the price war. He had purchased
a generator to offset frequent power failures during the day. Including debt
servicing, rent and other payments, he incurred a monthly expenditure of
INR 10,000 to run the centre. This was inclusive of the salary he paid to
the trainers. He had 26 students and earned between INR 12,000–15,000
per month. He considered this breaking even and expected that the centre
would become viable when the number of students increased. He had taken
a keen interest in the community-based activities of TARAhaat and had
taken steps to launch an innovative programme for women and children
called TARAbaathcheeth in his centre. He believed that the community-
based approach of TARAhaat would help his centre to attract more students
as well as clients for the services that he could offer through TARAhaat.com.
He also offered the new Practical English Course designed by TARAgyan,
for which he found an enthusiastic response from students.

The Lehra Mohabbat TARAkendra

Unlike the kiosk in Gonniana, the Lehra Mohabbat centre, established in
March 2001, was one of the older kiosks of TARAhaat. The franchisee pooled
the initial loan investment of about INR 280,000 by pledging one acre of
land, and pays INR 5,000 per month for debt servicing. He incurs a monthly
expenditure of INR 3,000 in telephone and electricity charges and pays a rent
of INR 4,500 per month. A salary of INR 2,500 had to be paid to the trainer.
His total monthly earning from TARAgyan courses was a meager INR 6,000,
and an additional income from printing and Internet services is INR 1,000–
15,000. Inevitably, he ran a deficit of INR 6,500–7,000 per month, which is
offset by family income from other sources. The student enrolment has come
down from 40 in the first year to 12 in the second year, causing a marked drop
in his earnings. The Practical English Course, about which functionaries in
the TARA Academy in Bhatinda would be eloquent, was first launched in
Lehra Mohabbat in November 2001, but has since been wound up as it failed
to attract a sufficient number of students.

The experience of both IVRP and TARAhaat suggested that the success of their social enterprises depended heavily on several factors, which are contextual as well as structural. The CSOs were excessively credited with an overwhelming record of creating jobs, enhancing capabilities, generating income streams for the poor, developing locally relevant services and making markets work for the underprivileged through ICTs. The jury of the Stockholm Challenge Award, for example, is as follows:

> Today, thanks to Information Village Research, ten villages near (sic) Pondicherry, India, are linked with computers, providing information on such aspects as health, crops, weather and fishing conditions. These new technology tools are bridging the economic and social divide between the haves and have-nots. They are empowering everyone with knowledge and opportunity by an inclusive use of local languages and a multimedia format that allows all to participate. (MSSRF 2002)

TARAhaat.com was initially seen as

> (A)n impressive blueprint for transforming the poverty-riddled country side into a vibrant economy. It hopes to catapult villages still mired in the 19th century directly into the digital era, create jobs, promote sustainable livelihoods and transform rural marketing systems-things that will lead to a quantum jump in the pace of rural development. (Jishnu et al. 2001, 30)

While such tall claims are a far cry from the reality, the projects have been marginally successful in addressing the question of the prospects of introducing ICTs in the rural setting. Understanding the pitfalls and demystifying the projects are essential for creating a balanced perspective on the incremental benefits of harnessing ICTs for improvising developmental strategies in rural India. This is particularly important, since the possibility of mobilizing additional resources required for sustaining these projects if the sponsor CSO withdraws subsidies is highly doubtful, in contrast to the overly optimistic beliefs held by some CSO functionaries. Comparing later developments with an early statement on MSSRF's project is illustrative. In 2001, *Businessworld* reported that 'For Pondicherry, the test of viability is close at hand. In the next six months, the foundation will be withdrawing its staff and support to the project' (Jishnu et al. 2001, 33). They quote Arunachalam, who heads the project, 'We have already trained local volunteers. *There is nothing left for us to do*' (italics added). But even after three years, no viable alternative had emerged. One year later, during my visits, the volunteer training was still continuing, and many volunteers expressed the fear that the project would have to be discontinued if alternative sources for stationery, equipment and maintenance services are not identified. They felt that it was impossible to pool the required funds from the local economy.

State–CSO Relations: Emerging Contradictions

Interventions in the social economy by ICT-oriented CSOs are highly dependent upon continued support from the state and its agencies, since most of the services that these enterprises offer in the villages have historically been the responsibility of the government and the major chunk of information demanded by the villagers is on government services and welfare schemes. Nevertheless, the relationship between CSOs and state agencies in this sector is highly precarious and uneven.[33] In its initial efforts to anchor in Pondicherry, the MSSRF had sought immense logistical support from government departments, particularly the Department of Agriculture.[34] However, the rapport did not extend to the creation of a joint platform.[35] On the contrary, their efforts began to diverge, culminating in the emergence of a parallel concept of Uzhavar Uthavi Agam (UUA, literally Farmers' Support Kiosks) initiated by the department (GOP, 2002). The major objectives of the UUA were strikingly similar to the MSSRF goals. The department was planning to set up UUAs by updating the already existing Farm Clinics that provided technical support to farmers and were run by the department. The department intended to connect, through a server, the Farm Clinics (rechristened as UUAs) and the divisional offices with Central Directorate. The department did not want any formal or informal link with the MSSRF. However, the MSSRF functionaries were still optimistic about linking up with the government agencies.

The MSSRF continued to maintain links with the Department of Science and Technology in New Delhi. But even the functionaries of MSSRF would consider this a notional tie. The nature of relations was limited to the provision of one-third of the INR 250,000 required for setting up a new kiosk. Another wing of the government, which has some ties with MSSRF, was the Department of Rural Development. This department had suggested that out of the 500 microfinance units run by women under DRDA, they were willing to identify a few 'best' units to run information kiosks. The required amount of INR 250,000 was to be provided by the department as a loan with a 30 per cent subsidy. The role of MSSRF was limited to developing local content. This proposal was not seriously considered by MSSRF for various reasons, including problems of trust and confidence. The MSSRF's attempts to link with Farm Clinics to train the staff to run UUAs had not been successful. The department had rejected this informal proposal and was not planning to get any assistance from the MSSRF for staff training.[36] The absence of strong

Figure 2.2. The Thirukanchi kiosk notice board displaying local news and names of sponsoring agencies.

linkages with the government agencies severely limited MSSRF's ability to provide e-governance services to its clientele.

TARAkendras also faced a similar problem, though the situation was somewhat different from the MSSRF's experience. The failure of TARAhaat to deliver on its promises of e-governance had dented its credibility with the franchisees and customers (Kaushik and Singh 2002). This happened partly because of the discontinuity in TARAhaat's strategy of expansion. Initially, it could link more effectively with DRDA and the prospects of delivering e-governance-related services looked relatively bright. The breakup with DRDA incapacitated TARAhaat from accessing governmental information and providing e-governance-related services. However, the progenitors of the TARAhaat concept attempted to underplay the impact of this failure. Ranjit Khosla, for example, argued, 'We have nothing to do with the Government. TARAkendras are based on a sound business model'.[37] Satish Jha considered TARAhaat's failures on the e-governance front as a consequence of projecting it as an omnibus concept in the beginning.[38]

The experiences of both the MSSRF and TARAhaat showed that social economy initiatives did not always receive the state's support and patronage. The relationship was more often than not fractured and precarious. One of the reasons for the state's indifference to CSOs was based on the premise that experiments sponsored by the state and implemented by its bureaucrats would work better and deliver more efficiently than CSOs. Further, such entities, often called QUANGOs (Quasi-Autonomous Non-Governmental Organizations) can be more systematically controlled and channelled by state agencies.[39] The twofold strategy of the state appeared to be to keep its involvement in CSO activities to the minimum and limit the representation of CSOs and other civil society actors in its own initiatives, including the functioning of QUANGOs. Further, the possibility of establishing easy legitimacy for QUANGO-based developmental work with international donor agencies has led the state to pursue its own strategies, sidelining CSOs almost completely. The newfound success of state initiatives with ICT-based developmental initiatives was, consequently, redefining and reorienting state-civil society relationships in the realm of social mediation.

Narratives of Success and the Sustainability Puzzle

Despite the problems, there were several successes credited to these projects. These successes were, more often than not, communicated by the organizations as anecdotes and stories that primarily narrated individual or group gains as a result of the introduction of the project. A closer look at these stories, however, provides a rather different picture of the nature of the rural network society that these projects aim to create. Illustratively, some stories about the MSSRF project can be scrutinized to analyse the conditions for the real success of ICT-based social enterprises by juxtaposing the narratives against grounded realities. Surprisingly, even the evaluations of the performance of the centres were sometimes carried out on the basis of these stories, as admitted in a report by the PANAsia Telecenter Learning & Evaluation Group of IDRC, which conducted its evaluation of FOOD (Foundation of Occupational Development) and the MSSRF kiosks. According to this report:

> Prior to the mission, it was decided that the group would focus on stories from telecenter users and operators. Stories whilst anecdotal, offer a rich picture of the impact of ICT interventions in local, complex and dynamic social settings. They are accessible and verifiable during short visits and they acknowledge the often indirect influence that development interventions have on their beneficiaries. (PANTLEG 1999, 1)

A frequently told story is about an old woman and her cow. This story has at least two versions. In one of the versions, it is Bubrayan Panjali, 'a round faced illiterate woman' from Kizhur village in Pondicherry, who was able to get a veterinary doctor to attend her cow, her 'only source of income', in labour; the cow would have died without the information from the MSSRF e-kiosk.

A report says that 'for *five* days the cow moaned while in labour' (Dugger 2001, italics added). The report continues:

> Word of Mrs. Panjali's woebegone cow soon spread to Govindaswami, a public-spirited farmer who uses one name. The village computer, obtained through the Swaminathan Foundation, is in the anteroom of his home. The computer is operated full time and for no pay by his 23-year-old, college-educated daughter, Azhalarasi, who *used it to call up* a list of area veterinarians. One doctor arrived that night and…then dragged the calf into the world. (ibid., italics added)

In the second version of the story, it was Panchavarnam's pregnant cow that had been in pain for *four* days but could not deliver her calf. For Panchavarnam, the cow's survival was crucial, as it was her 'only source of income' since her husband's death. News of the cow's plight spread, and G. Ezhilarasi, a college student who operates the computer from an anteroom in her house, *surfed the Internet* for veterinarians and contacted several of them in the area. On the fourth day, one doctor responded to the message. He came to the village and assisted in the delivery (Krishnakumar 2001, italics added).

Setting aside the discrepancies in the stories and the details that change with iteration (such as the number of days the cow suffered, the name of the old woman, the means by which the veterinary doctor was contacted, and so on), it is still evident that the story had been blown out of proportion to show that the impacts of ICTs were enormous. During my fieldwork, I found that it is true that there were no veterinary doctors or hospitals in Kizhur. Nonetheless, the nearest one was only just three to four kilometres away, in the village of Sivarandhagam. The hospital worked on all weekdays as well as on Saturdays and Sundays with working hours from 8:45 a.m. to 1:00 p.m. and 2:00 p.m. to 5:00 p.m. On Saturdays and Sundays the working hours were from 8:45 a.m. to 12:30 p.m. The hospital had been functioning since 10 June 1998 and its phone numbers are available from the local telephone directory. If no one turned up to help the old woman for four or five days, it shows the breakdown of the neighbourhood offline support systems that the kiosk cannot replace. And more interestingly, none of the versions of the story claimed that the old woman approached the e-kiosk for help. The story was thus a typical example of crafty narration transforming ordinary everyday events as parables to show rural change through computers and the Internet.

Much has been reported about the weather information provided to the fisherfolk in Pondicherry through information kiosks. Actually, this facility was available only in one kiosk in Veerampattinam and curiously, fishing

Figure 2.3. Sivanandapuram village veterinary hospital (It is located only 3–4 kilometres from Kizhoor).

communities in other parts of coastal Pondicherry did not appear to be enthusiastic about setting up similar facilities for themselves. It was claimed that weather information about storms and so on, downloaded from the public website of the US Navy and conveyed to the fisherfolk in Pondicherry, helped them to save their lives (Kapoor 2001). Thermal wave maps provided by the kiosks supposedly enabled the fishermen to snare bigger catches (Jishnu et al. 2001). It is reported that '(F)ishermen in Pondicherry do not go out to sea without first looking up the thermal wave charts and weather bulletins provided by a local network' (ibid., 30). Interaction with local fisherfolk revealed that the weather information provided to them was not that crucial.

There are two aspects to this observation: The fishermen's traditional methods of weather prediction based on cloud formations and wind directions are more or less accurate, according to local people. The reason why some fishermen still venture out to sea in rough weather is because of their acute poverty. When asked about the importance of weather information, one of the fishermen in Veerampattinam said, 'We know what will happen. Still we go because we don't want our children to starve.' Probably caught between 'tradition' and 'modernity', the village head, however, was apologetic. He said, 'The weather information provided by the centre is more credible.' The question of local knowledge versus modern science discussed in a growing literature on postdevelopment appears to be relevant in this context.[40]

These stories fall apart as credible indicators of the social and economic benefits of the projects as we probe further into the contexts and backdrops of their origin and trace them through the layers of iteration that turns them into new folklores of the rural network society in the making. The question of sustainability, hence, has to be analysed on the basis of more solid criteria than what these stories could teach, even in cases where there is a grain of truth in them. The potential for sustainability of the rural kiosks depends heavily on local contexts, which the projects are often unable to control. Keeping costs low can be practiced to a satisfactory level when the cost of the most important items such as computers and Internet access have their prices falling in the international market. However, the degree of affordability of replacement requires that the project becomes self-sustainable. The Information Technologies Group (ITG) of the Centre for International Development at Harvard has mapped a matrix of the factors that could influence rural Internet sustainability (quoted in Best and Maclay 2002, 77). It is argued that there are at least six broad categories that must be considered for economic sustainability of the Internet kiosks, viz., costs, revenue, networks, business models, policy and capacity (ibid.). Table 2.4 illustrates this idea as developed by the ITG.

For the MSSRF, the equipment was provided by the CSO from donor money. For TARAkendras, the cost was borne by local entrepreneurs who hoped to generate sufficient income and gain profit. Recurrent costs of computer stationery, electricity, maintenance and repair, telephone charges and salaries, if any, had to be met from the revenues and any subsidy received. The revenue source for these projects was the user fees they hoped to receive from poor rural users. It is sometimes hoped that:

> Given that the technology components and public access business model is essentially a platform capable of facilitating a wide range of activities, more applications and content will allow revenue generation from a greater variety of sources and effectively lower the level of income necessary for the sustainability of each unique application. (Best and Maclay 2002, 79)

As Best and Maclay (2002, 77) note, such user fees are difficult to generate. They believe that there could be three main classes of revenue generation of rural Internet services: The first set consists of a fee for services such as core communications, education, commerce, government applications, entertainment, training, etc. The second source consists of a wide set of remote services and back-office activities that could also become sources. The

Table 2.4. Sustainability matrix of rural Internet kiosks.

FACTORS	Costs	Revenues	Networks	Business Models	Policy
Capacity	LOW: Unless access to computer maintenance is limited	HIGH: Business, IT and outreach skills key for new industry	MEDIUM: More users ease awareness raising and training	MEDIUM/HIGH: Capacity suggests limits of model	MEDIUM/HIGH: Education, training opportunities
Policy	HIGH: Competition, taxes and tariffs, requirements for entry, spectrum, interconnection.	HIGH: VoIP alone is significant	MEDIUM; Policy broadly affects readiness, users become political constituency	HIGH: Decides potential for RSP and franchisees, public sector as network client	
Business Models	MEDIUM: Appropriates models reduce costs	LOW: Location guides clientele and applications	LOW: Little direct connection		
Networks	HIGH: Metcalfe effect costly to leverage (or else it would be done), scale economies grow with network size	HIGH: Size and scope drive content, utility of medium			
Revenue	LOW: Except specialized services requiring extra investment assuming always on connection				

Source: Slightly modified from Best and Maclay (2002, 77).

third source, they argue, could come from the aggregation of services and user opportunities for revenue through the Metcalfe effect (ibid.). The Metcalfe law states that the value of any complete network such as the Internet would tend to grow with the square of the number of users, as opposed to a simple linear growth. In other words, the law states that the value realization from networks is critically affected if the network is quite small. Our analysis of the MSSRF's IVRP kiosks and DA's TARAkendras shows that the potential for enhancing the network was severely limited, and these projects had stumbled upon the challenges of expansion due to a variety of factors. In Pondicherry, for example, the progenitor of the project had hoped that the government would come forward to facilitate kiosk proliferation that would help reap economies of scale and increased networking. However, in most projects the relationship between the state and its agencies had already been too fractured or ambivalent to benefit from partnerships. The cyber-libertarian approach of gradualist development mediated through ICTs grossly ignored these limitations faced by the projects in achieving expansion as well as inclusiveness.

Lessons and Non-Lessons

Cyber-libertarian development thinking has pervaded contemporary development discussions. The intervention of ICT-oriented CSOs in development initiatives is often eulogized and receives undue thrust in the media as well as international development discourse. However, it may also be noted that the question of cyber-libertarianism has to be located in the larger theoretical and historical backdrop of India's development trajectory. As Kaviraj (2001) has pointed out, colonial sovereignty (that arose as a close local/regional equivalent to absolutism) gave rise to some early ideas of civil society, including that part of social life free of their direct control, creating an inchoate, early 'civil society'. With the stirrings of nationalist ambitions, political groups began to claim certain aspects of social life as the arena for decision making by the indigenous people, rather than the foreign state authority. The author points to the extreme diversity in regimes produced by European colonialism, and highlights India as an interesting case, as it comprised high levels of political 'civility' that were relatively rare in the generally violent history of colonial empires, as well as the generally orderly transfer of power (ibid., 310). Nonetheless, even in India, this civil society's tacit acceptance of liberal individualist premises of social existence were partial and limited, as was the restricted nature of the colonial civil society, which has long-term implications for postcolonial politics in two ways: Firstly, associational life was 'a strange complex of the opposite principles of universality of access and a particularity of membership'; and secondly, was the much larger problem of the exclusion of the large masses of the peasantry and country-dwellers from these activities due to their lack of an English education (Kaviraj and Khilani 2001, 311)? By the 1970s, however, democratic practices had communicated themselves to this segment of the populace, resulting in the merging of *gemeinschaftlich* behaviour into the democratic arena, altering the meanings and consequences of all democratic procedures, and occasionally creating tension between the individualistic premises of the legal-constitutional structure and the predominantly community-oriented self-understandings of large electoral groups (ibid., 312)

The interest of the public sphere in the working of the CSOs in general and ICT-based CSOs in particular has resulted in the creation of a set of impressions about their practices, promises and potential. First and foremost amongst them is the view that they are rooted in the resources of the local economy, and even if this is not so in the beginning, they have the prospects of evolving into a structural mould capable of drawing on local community resources for their sustenance (see also Amin, Cameron and Hudson 2002, ix). The second impression is related to their ability to contribute to local economic regeneration and thereby contribute significantly to the national economy through creation of jobs, developing local services and markets and providing training for enskillment and entrepreneurship, and building social capital. Poverty alleviation through creation of entitlements and capabilities has, hence, become a sloganeered objective of ICT-CSOs. Finally, it is also believed that they form replicable models that would deliver universally, provided similar conditions are reproduced through the involvement of state and non-state agencies, both nationally and locally, in a continuum of mutual sharing of resources and experience.

This chapter explored the contemporary practice of many civil society agencies or CSOs to use ICTs as an instrument of social and economic change in rural India. A scrutiny of the performance of two such CSOs, the MSSRF Village Knowledge Centres (Pondicherry) and Development Alternatives' TARAkendras (Bhatinda) shows that a wide chasm exists between the expectations and actual benefits of CSO initiatives in rural India. Contrary to popular belief, these social enterprises are not rooted in the resources of the local economy. Moreover, their prospects of evolving into developmental models capable of drawing on local community resources for their sustenance appear to be bleak. Their ability to contribute to local economic regeneration through such claims as job creation, developing local services and markets, enhancing local skills to inculcate entrepreneurship and building social capital is yet to materialize.

CSOs are not universally replicable models for configuring social enterprise projects based on ICTs. The incremental values created by these experiments in India's rural setting are, nevertheless, important, given the extreme deprivation and social degeneration in rural areas. Nonetheless, they do not constitute a case for adopting techno-determinist models of social development. It could also be noted that both models, e-service oriented and market-based, have systematically overstated their achievements, leading to a glorification of the potential of ICT-based initiatives.

State-civil society relations in ICT projects are marred by tensions and contradictions. State-led projects have tacitly followed a model of limiting the role of civil society, while the social enterprise models of CSOs have varying degrees of failures in making the state respond to their signals. The 'quangocratic' organizational models adopted by the state and the gross failures of the social enterprise models to work with the state and its agencies reflect a growing fissure in state and civil society relations in India and elsewhere.

There are, indeed, larger lessons to be learned from the brief history of the Internet in rural India. The social enterprise models depend heavily on direct and indirect subsidies and are effectively controlled by the local elites. The Aarthyas, Nattaimai and upper-caste temple trustees have been more enthusiastic in collaborating with CSOs in facilitating the implementation of the projects, pointing to an elitist capture of these projects. This would tend to reinforce the existing social divides in the villages rather than bridging them. The economic sustainability of the projects, on the other hand, rests on the potential for enhancing the rural network society to reap the benefits of economies of scale and the Metcalfe law. Limitations of resources as well as low demand for IT-enabled services have affected the option of expanding operations negatively.

Concluding his remarkable study of the invention and diffusion of telegraph and the discourses it generated in the nineteenth century, Standage made a perceptive observation:

> The similarities between the telegraph and the Internet – both in their technical underpinnings and their social impact – are striking…The optimistic claims now being made about the Internet are merely the most recent examples in a tradition of technological utopianism that goes back to the first transatlantic telegraph cables, 150 years ago. (Standage 1998, 210–11)

It is evident that the deployment of ICTs in resource-poor regions and nations cannot be based on the overhyped narratives of rural e-topia now pervading the discourses on new technologies and their potential. The CSOs initiating such programmes and projects have to understand the importance of assessing the complexities of the realm of their social action. As Castells (2000,76) puts it, 'the complex matrix of interaction between the technological forces unleashed by our species is a matter of inquiry rather than of fate.'

Chapter 3

DECRYPTING E-GOVERNANCE

Technology and Governance

The notion of 'e-governance', along with such other 'epithetized phenomena' as e-learning, e-banking, e-marketing etc. played a major role in shaping the futuristic e-topias of the global information society discourse. Woolgar (2002, 3) points out that 'epithetizing' various existing activities and social institutions with notions such as 'virtual', 'digital', 'electronic' (or simply 'e'), 'cyber', 'tele' etc. helps to 'conjure up a future consequent upon the effects of electronic technologies'. Given the backdrop of the increased involvement of new media technologies in delivering e-governance, it is important to understand the social and historical specificities of the emerging technological systems that facilitate the construction of the notion.[1] It is also pertinent to take a closer look at the relativity of technical design and absorption into the culture and strategies of actors (Feenberg 1999) in order to discuss e-governance from a nonessentialist perspective. Social constructivism provides some provisional but meaningful theoretical foundations to look at e-governance in nonessentialist terms. One of the important conceptual endeavours to understand e-governance initiatives from a constructivist perspective would be to disaggregate the question of technology from the differential perspective of the dominant and subordinate subject positions of the actors involved. Arguably, e-governance projects are rationally planned and implemented by technocrats in an effort to exercise a far more effective control over resources and social organization. Nevertheless, common people encounter these technologies of systematization as part of their life world and appropriate, reject or force revisions in the designs as well as systems. As Feenberg argues:

> (T)he invariant elements of the constitution of the technical subject and object are modified by socially specific contextualizing variables in the course of the realization of concrete technical actors, devices and systems. Thus technologies are not merely efficient devices or efficiency oriented practices, but include their contexts as these are embodied in design and social insertion. (Feenberg 1999, xiii)

In the case of ICT-based networked governance, the possibility of the formation of a rural network society, imminent and, in its protoforms, with deep crevices and conflicting layers of incorporation of different actors, had appeared in the contexts of many e-governance projects where the C2G (icitizen-to-government) interface and to a limited extent, person-to-person relations, are reaffirmed by the technology of the Intranet. In this chapter, an attempt is made to understand the social dynamics that underlie the initial practices of e-governance in India on the basis of an analysis of the Gyandoot Intranet, a massive e-governance project launched in India in the state of Madhya Pradesh. The relatively weak, but undeniable structuration of the rural network society was manifested in the narratives of networking facilitated by the design of the project, with scattered nodes connected to a centralized service monitoring centre. Nonetheless, the rural network society was emerging as a complex social domain of opposing interest groups, and a space where some of the political and ideological conflicts in the larger society manifested in newer forms (Sreekumar 2007c). The fact that the technology itself got enmeshed in the relatively autonomous logic of the network society partly explains the inertia that halted the predicted progress envisaged in the visions moulded by concepts and paradigms of rapid social change consequent on the implementation of e-governance projects.

This chapter, organized as described here, is an attempt in that direction. Following these introductory remarks, I provide an outline of the recent developments that point to the complex trajectory of e-governance in India. The technological organization of the Gyandoot project, and the dimensions of the social dynamics of the Gyandoot kiosks that provide access to the Intranet will be discussed in the subsequent sections. Further, a closer look at the meaning of the seemingly hyped anecdotes and narratives of success, along with an exposition of a realistic narrative that explains the interplay of technology and power enmeshed in the local dynamics of absorption and appropriation of Gyandoot's Intranet technology will also be discussed. Finally, I attempt to outline the contours of the emerging model of e-governance and its implications.

The Beginnings of E-Governance in India

The Indian state began to design and execute rural development programmes with a relatively visible ICT content in the 1970s, while international attention on the potential of harnessing ICTs for developmental activities can be considered a relatively later phenomenon. The early attempts were to use ICTs for improvising development planning – a key area of state action in the import-substitution era. Early examples of attempts to use computer applications for cost optimization and decision making are the deployment of ICTs in the Dharampur Sub-District Infrastructure Planning for Development (1977) and in the The Karwar Rural Development Information System (1984). The latter initiative was designed with a focus on reducing delay and curbing corruption – key concerns of the matured model of e-governance in developing countries – through a monitoring programme based on computer applications (Kaul et al.1989 (quoted in Bhatnagar 1990,7)). The trajectory of attempts for computer installations in the early phase of ICT development in India shows that the efforts were mostly concentrated in the public sector (see Table 3.1) pointing to vigorous state involvement in the diffusion of ICTs at the early stage of development of computer application-driven initiatives in India.[2]

Given the policy of import substitution and heavy reliance on public sector-driven development of technology during this phase of the evolution of the Indian economy, we can safely presume, that most of the computers installed in the R & D sector were also procured by the state for use in state-owned laboratories.[3] Thus the figures in Table 3.1 clearly show that state investment

Table 3.1. Sector-wise installation of computers in India 1965–1980.

Year	R & D	Public Sector	Private Sector	Total
1960	1	0	0	1
1961	1	1	0	2
1962	1	2	0	3
1963	4	2	0	6
1964	10	6	0	16
1965	14	9	5	28
1966	16	14	12	42
1967	22	22	21	65
1968	24	35	29	88
1969	28	42	37	107
1970	30	49	42	121
1971	38	59	58	155
1972	39	71	76	186
1973	44	78	81	203
1974	49	93	89	231
1975	63	126	92	281
1976	75	143	94	312
1977	86	168	100	354
1978	109	194	111	414
1979	127	213	113	453
1980	138	225	119	482
Year Unknown	16	34	14	64
Total	154	259	133	546

Source: Calculated from Gupta (1981, 63).

in computers by way of R & D or for production in the public sector, far outweighed private investment throughout the 1960 and 1970s.

By the late 1980s India had developed networks such as NICNET connecting government users, EDUNET for education institutions and INDONET for the benefit of industrial users in major cities (Bhatnagar 1990, 10). These efforts coincided with the early phase of economic liberalization and administrative reforms in India. Computerization of major institutions such as nationalized banks and state-owned enterprises also began during this period. Organizational restructuring and enhancement of fees called rationalization of rates and tariffs of public utilities and retrenchment of workers in the public sector enterprises, was conceived against a backdrop of the large-scale use of computers in these organizations. While computerization was seen as a panacea for major economic ills such as productivity decline and low growth rate, it also served to legitimize large-scale retrenchments and cutting down of employment within the public sector as well as government departments. In other words, the governmentality dimensions of technology use were apparent in the applications of ICTs as implemented by the Indian State in the 1980s, a decade that witnessed the first phase of liberalization strategies and structural adjustment policies taking a firm root in India's economic agenda

The use of ICTs for restructuring and redeployment of key resources as well as retrenchment was met with severe opposition from trade unions in the public sector, while the employees' unions resisted computerization of government departments. However, the invention of the slogan of ICTs as a tool of development administration had some ideological effects on the perceptions of the role of the new technologies. It helped to alter people's perception of computers from a machine causing unemployment to a potential job creator and source for future economic growth. The opposition to computerization projects on the grounds that it eliminates jobs and exacerbates educated unemployment, built up by both trade unions and students and youth organizations, gradually began to disappear.

'Electronic governance' became a buzzword in the Indian state's efforts to revamp its administrative system in late 1990s, based on the principles of 'good governance' as part of the structural adjustment strategies dictated by the World Bank and other international agencies:[1]

In the second phase, the implementation of the national IT Task Force and State Government IT policies symbolized a paradigm shift in e-governance policies towards using IT for a wider range of sectoral applications reaching out to a large number of people in rural as well as urban areas. Moreover, there has been a movement towards a greater input of NGOs and private sector organizations in providing services to the public. These projects have been influenced by the increasing focus of international agencies such as DFID, G-8, the UNDP and the World Bank under the banner of 'E-Governance for Development. (Madon 2008, 269)

The Ministry of Information Technology was constituted and the Central Government initiated some tentative projects aimed at testing the potential of e-governance. Besides the Central Government, many state governments also responded, seeking the possibility of improving administrative functions by introducing e-governance at different levels of the bureaucracy. Specialized agencies have also been instituted within government to initiate innovative experiments. In 1999, a national conference was organized in Bangalore, attended by 75 senior bureaucrats including IT secretaries of 32 states and union territories in India.[5] The conference affirmed a resolve to create 'one-stop, non-stop, efficient, effective, responsive, transparent citizen governance through the use of information technology' (Katakam 1999, 78). The conference came up with a declaration on the intent and content of e-governance programmes in India, although it was criticized as being bereft of specificity and the plans lacking time frames (ibid.). The declaration emphasized the need for shifting the focus of governance from government-centric to citizen-centric in the wake of the opportunities opened by information technology for large-scale delivery of quality services. The use of IT was expected to facilitate efficient delivery of government services to citizens and business, 'to anyone, anytime, anywhere through a variety of channels at a reasonable cost' (quoted in Katakam 1999, 79). The declaration recognized the need for reengineering the process of government to achieve synergy with technology. A critical factor identified in the declaration was the centrality of upgrading skills of the existing workforce, while also underscoring the necessity of industry-community-state partnerships in e-delivery of services. A sound communication infrastructure for ubiquitous access, a conscious effort to harmonize IT with regional requirements and innovative use of IT to prevent possible social exclusion were considered essential components of the future e-governance strategy. The role of the central government in supporting capacity-building efforts of state governments was also emphasized.

Many projects were announced at the conference, although many of them were eventually abandoned for various reasons.[6] However, since 1999, the proliferation of e-governance projects in India has been phenomenal. Surging numbers of what is identified as e-governance projects indicate that most of the state governments and union territories in India claim to have accepted the need for undertaking e-governance initiatives.

Although the initial efforts on the part of the Indian state to link ICTs with development projects have been limited to localized projects and district-level planning, we can also observe that it soon advanced to centralized projects for connectivity and regulation (Chakravarty 2004; Bagga et. al. 2005; Roy 2005). There are clear signs of a realization that ICTs, while providing a potential for reassuring the state's commitments to the developmental agenda, opens a gateway for strengthening the arms of governance. Nevertheless, most of the e-governance initiatives have focused on the development of infrastructure, capacity building and policy changes as well as the participation of the private sector, while showing a growing reluctance towards integrating civil society into its fold (Sreekumar 2002).

This is true of relatively successful initiatives such as Gyandoot. The Gyandoot Project has emerged as a benchmark for innovation in e-governance and in e-commerce according to several commentators (Sood 2001). Local bodies in collaboration with government officials have started ICT kiosks operated by unemployed youth that were selected and trained by the Gyandoot Samiti to run these kiosks. It aimed to cater to the everyday needs of a wide section of rural consumers. The project, which sets its objective as social engineering and development through ICTs, has marked a paradigm shift in the way government functionaries relate themselves to the needs of the poor. This major ICT project was first launched in a region that is largely tribal and impoverished. Nevertheless, it remains an administered programme with little relationship with civil society. No major social organization has been partnered with in its implementation.[7]

Gyandoot: Organization and Technology

Gyandoot, an Intranet-based Government-to-Citizen (G2C) service delivery portal in Dhar district of Madhya Pradesh was commissioned in January 2000 with the objective of creating a cost-effective, replicable, economically sustainable and financially viable model for e-governance. Rajesh Rajora, one of the main architects of the project and district collector of Dhar when the project was implemented, has claimed that it was envisaged to enhance participation by citizens/government in community affairs through creative uses of ICT and to also ensure equal access to emerging technologies for the oppressed and exploited segments of society (Rajora 2002,66–67). Gyandoot, managed by a society called 'Gyandoot Samiti', was registered under the Madhya Pradesh Societies Registration Act with the district collector as president. The CEO of the district panchayat functioned as secretary and various departmental heads were members of the Samiti. The Gyandoot operated with a team consisting of a project manager, an assistant project officer, a technical head and a few computer operators. The promised services offered by Gyandoot encompassed a wide range of government departments. These services could be accessed from any Gyandoot information kiosk, called *soochanalaya*, on payment of a nominal fee. There were about 40 kiosks located in different parts of the district run by local managers called *soochaks* during at the time of my visit to Dhar.

These soochanalays would be equipped with a PC, printer and Uninterruptible Power Supply (UPS), as well as facilities to provide e-governance services, commercial Internet, and voice connectivity in rural areas. A host of government information and application forms were available on the net, and villagers could access these and submit applications to the government departments on the net. Inter-village communication was possible, and relevant software was being being developed and ported. The soochak was, in a sense, a rural entrepreneur earning a living primarily from the income that the kiosk could generate. Soochaks were trained to run the kiosks by the Gyandoot Samiti. The Dhar Intranet project was one of the largest rural Internet/Intranet projects in India. It was chosen for the Stockholm Challenge Award in 2000.[8]

Initially, the kiosks were provided intranet communication using the telephone lines supplied by the government-owned Bharat Sanchar Nigam Ltd (BSNL). At that time, communication on telephone lines being poor and unreliable, and the dial-up connection charges relatively expensive, the project faced serious limitations of coverage. Later, corDECT WLL (Wireless Local Loop), developed by IIT Chennai and Midas Communications, providing a wireless access solution for expanding telecommunication networks, integrating voice and Internet services, was adopted with reasonable success (see Chapter 5 for detailed discussion). n-Logue Communications also offered a business model to enable rural connectivity using corDECT Wireless terminal, a telephone instrument, a 100 MHz Pentium PC (with color monitor, local language word processor, browsing and e-mail software) with a 16-hour power backup for telephone and 44hour backup for PC.[9] Backbone Internet connectivity was supplied by Satyam Infoway. In the first phase, villages within 25 kilometers around Dhar town, the district headquarters, were covered. An access centre was set up in the District panchayat computer room in the civil station office premises.

The kiosks were offering a wide range of facilities and services, including the gathering and disseminating of agricultural prices, online registration of applications, online public grievance redressal, rural email, village auction sites, online matrimonial sites, information regarding governmental programmes, career counselling for students, technical advice channels between experts and villagers, online application formats, village newspaper, etc. If they were fully functional, the centres had the potential to be of very high utility to the villagers.[10]

Nevertheless, setting up a kiosk in a village does not necessarily mean that these services are provided or that they are availed by people. More importantly, the question of who avails themselves of these services and who are excluded – either intentionally or involuntarily – remains a significant poser in the social context within which the project is implemented. In order to understand this, we may need to go deeper into the actual practices of these kiosks in the rural setting.

E-Governance and the Kiosks: The Social Dynamics

In this section, an attempt is made to identify some of the key features of the soochanalays and take a closer look at their everyday practices. The analysis is based on the information collected from the five Gyandoot centres that were visited during fieldwork, as well as my visit to the Gyandoot Samiti headquarters housed in the Dhar civil station. The overarching narrative of e-governance initiatives as inherently good is a major assumption in the literature on e-governance. The basic problem with this macroperspective is not only the hype, or even the 'sweeping grandiloquence' of its rhetoric, as some writers would call it (Woolgar 2001,5), but more importantly, the disregard of what really happens on the ground. These technologies are actually used and experienced in everyday practice quite differently from the way their potential uses and benefits are configured for public consumption by their progenitors as well as techno-determinist commentators.

The locale-specific dynamics of the operation of Gyandoot kiosks provided a key to the understanding of e-governance initiatives with a social content and significantly based on a G2C (government to citizen) interface. In the following subsections, I discuss four major issues that provide a reasonable assessment of the actual and potential abilities of the kiosks and the model of ICT diffusion it stands for. The issues I map out below are (1) entrepreneurship and employment, (2) local infrastructure, (3) user perceptions and (4) sustainability. I also look into the major tensions and contradictions that envelop the project from a microlevel perspective.

Entrepreneurship and Employment

The entrepreneurship model of launching soochanalays was at the centre of the strategy of Gyandoot Samiti, the QUANGO (Quasi Autonomous Non-Governmental Organization) sponsored by the district administration of Dhar.[11] The soochaks who managed the kiosks were chosen from the educated youth of the village who were willing to explore the potential of self-employment by launching a soochanalay in their own village. The minimum qualification requirement of a soochak suggested by Gyandoot Samiti was education up to the 12th standard. A soochak should have also been capable of self-financing the basic infrastructure for running the kiosk either through a bank loan or by using his own resources.

The user fees from the G2C services offered by Gyandoot and additional services using the same infrastructure that the soochak could provide formed the basis of the earning portfolios of the entrepreneurs. The actual earnings, however, depended on a variety of factors. This included the relative prosperity of the village, which will determine the demand for both the Gyandoot and non-Gyandoot services that the kiosk could offer, the demand for computer training from students and the number of students willing to undertake the training for a payment of a monthly fee. Tiwari and Sharmistha (2008), comparing the impacts of Gyandoot and Drishtee (Bihar, India), argues that although Gyandoot is a state-led initiative of the government of Madhya Pradesh and the other project is run by a 'not-for-profit' organization, both projects deploy a similar operational strategy of kiosk-based networks run by independent rural entrepreneurs (Sreekumar and Rivera-Sanchez 2008, 169). In the case of Gyandoot, the authors found evidence of market imperfections through sluggish demand-side factors and information asymmetries, impeding the uptake of the majority of services offered by the project.[12]

The employment potential of the kiosks was, in fact, very limited. The income from a kiosk could not, in most cases, provide for the subsistence wages of more than one manager. The services, belonging either to the G2C or G2B (government-to-business) categories, could not be identified as providing employment opportunities in the villages. The soochaks supplemented the services from Gyandoot Samiti with other activities – an effort that the Samiti also encouraged. Various other activities, such as data entry operations, small DTP jobs, screen printing, photocopying, computer training, horoscopes and match making etc. are the most prominent supplementary activities that the soochaks undertake using the facilities available in the kiosk.[13]

One interesting aspect that deserves mention was the social meaning of being a soochak. The advantages of a being a soochak were obviously greater than being just another small entrepreneur in the village. This followed from the nature of the services offered by the kiosks, which required the soochaks to be in regular contact with government officials. Many soochaks understood that this has an empowering element ingrained in it. As one soochak placed it:

I am happy that I can mediate between people and government officers. The close contact that I can enjoy with senior officers is really very important. Similarly, fellow villagers also understand the fact that I have contacts with officers. This is definitely some kind of recognition.[14]

Figure 3.1. Gyandoot's promotional material showing how kiosks provide matrimonial assistance.

(Soochak says: 'Just with the touch of the button you are able to get the groom and all his particulars for your daughter. You can register the particulars of your marriageable boy/girl in the village information centre. You need not search for the groom/bride in different villages; the information centre helps in making this search easier.')

However, the complex layers of social power that characterized the village society limited the empowerment of the soochaks. Political parties and caste elites had a major role to play in the everyday life of the communities. The caste and social status of the soochaks became enormously important in defining their domain of influence. The untold story of the three Gyandoot centres of Badnaver is an illustration of this important aspect of village life in rural India.[15]

Majority of the soochaks belonged to the 'educated-but-unemployed' category of the village population. Although they had been given reasonable technical training in operating the kiosks, they had never been exposed to any substantive training on entrepreneurship or management of small enterprises. Surprisingly, this aspect was largely ignored when the model was conceived and eventually implemented. It is certainly the fact that some of the soochaks showed innate talent as successful entrepreneurs by trying to supplement the earnings from Gyandoot services with numerous other small-scale activities that earned them moderate additional income, although the market for such services in the vicinity of the centre determined the potential of such efforts.

But in many cases, a shrinking stream of earnings from the Gyandoot services remained the major component of the gross earnings of the soochaks.

Moreover, the possibility for increasing the number of kiosks, and thereby enhancing the chances of educated youth becoming small entrepreneurs in places where Gyandoot kiosks did not exist, was also limited by social as well as technical and infrastructure-related problems. Apart from the uncertainties of inadequate demand for these services, unstable supply of electricity in rural India poses a major challenge for the operation of the kiosks. The soochaks invariably reported that the availability of electricity to the kiosks averaged only to four to five hours a day, which strictly curtailed operating hours. As one soochak pointed out:

> How can I run the kiosk with power supply limited to four to five hours only in a day? Even this is not steady. I don't think the problem will be solved soon. We have to live with this. Working with low voltage is also a serious problem. The villagers understand these problems but when I can't deliver, the credibility is affected.[16]

Tapping nonconventional sources of energy appeared to be a remote alternative to the power supply problem encountered by the entrepreneurs. There has been an attempt to deploy solar panels, harnessing solar energy for running the kiosks. It has been established on an experimental basis in one of the three Gyandoot kiosks in Badnaver. The soochak of the kiosk was not able to comment on its utility, as it was yet to become operational at the time of my visit.[17]

Local Infrastructure

Apparently, huge disparity in terms of the kiosk-wise infrastructure facilities did not exist. Most kiosks had a minimum set of facilities that helped them connect with the Intranet services that Gyandoot offered as well as supplementary equipment such as photocopier, printer, and UPS. While some soochaks had procured scanners in the kiosks with their own resources, it was unaffordable for many smaller operators, unless they availed credit facilities. This was not considered a viable option by entrepreneurs in rural kiosks who were doubtful as to whether the demand for the scanner services would be sufficient to cover the repayment costs. A solar panel is set up in one of the kiosks in Badnaver, as we noted in the previous section, after paying a safety deposit of INR 9,000. Surprisingly, the pool of equipment in some of the kiosks did not include a printer as was seen in the case of the Amjera Kiosk. Of the five centres I visited, only one, Nagda, did not have a phone connection and Internet facility. Nonetheless, the intranet of Gyandoot was operational at the Nagda kiosk through a WLL.

User Perceptions

Each soochanalaya was presumably catering to 20 to 30 villages, although in practice, visits from people beyond a five-kilometre radius of the kiosk were the exception rather than the rule, according to some soochaks and local informants.[18] These villages varied drastically in terms of population, ranging from tiny hamlets with less than 500 inhabitants to large villages with nearly 8,000 inhabitants. The actual coverage of each centre was very limited. The experience of many kiosk managers was that the services of the Kiosk were mainly availed by a small group of people residing in the villages surrounding the kiosk. Disregarding this geographical aspect of the kiosk utilization, reports often equated the total population in the villages with people who avail the services of the kiosks. For example, many case studies on Gyandoot point out that the kiosks in a particular locality may be serving thousands of people in nearby villages. The statement from an earlier case study on Gyandoot is typical in this regard: 'Twenty kiosks ("soochanalays") were initially set up in various rural centres, with each kiosk typically serving a population of 20,000 to 30,000 villagers' (Sanjay and Gupta, 2003.). A similar uncritical observation can be seen in Prahalad and Hammond (2002, 52): 'The company has a network of 39 Internet-enabled kiosks that provide local entrepreneurs with Internet and telecommunications access, as well as with governmental, educational and other services. Each kiosk serves 25 to 30 surrounding villages; the entire network reaches more than 600 villages and over half a million people.'

Not surprisingly, people belonging to different social groups had different perceptions about Gyandoot, although as a rule, the villagers tended to see positive elements of the project as outweighing the failures. However, many of the regular customers were dissatisfied with the range of services offered by Gyandoot and believed that it could do much better, even though many of them would not attempt to articulate in clear terms how it could be improved. The common complaints about the operation of kiosks can be classified into five groups: (1) connectivity-related problems, (2) failure to adhere to the stipulated timeframes for redress of grievances as well delivery of routine services, (3) huge disparity between the range of promised and actual services, (4) failures in delivering G2B services, and (5) attitudinal factors as well as poor performance of the soochaks. The connectivity problem, as we pointed out in the previous section, has been a primary factor in creating an environment of apathy among villagers.

Table 3.2. Infrastructure, ownership, earnings and expenses: A comparative picture of selected Gyandoot centres.

Centre/Facilities	Tirla	Amjera	Nagda	Badnaver 1	Badnaver 2
Number of PCs	2	1	2	2	1
PC purchase	Own resources	Own resources (Bank Credit)	Own resources + Panchayat	Own resources (PMRY)	Own Resources
Phone	Yes	Yes	WLL	Yes	Yes
Internet	Yes	Yes	No	Yes	Yes
Printer	Yes	No	Yes	Yes	Yes
Ownership of the centre	Community	Self	Panchayat	Self	Self
Photocopier	1 (PMRY)	No	No	No	No
Education of soochak	BA (Political Sciences) & DTP	12th	12th, DCOA, DTP	12th, DTP, AutoCAD	BE (Electronics)
Solar Panel	No	No	No	Yes	No
UPS	Yes	Yes	Yes	Yes (Nos.2)	Yes
Scanner	No	No	No	Yes	Yes
Generator	No	No	No	Yes (Hire)	Yes
Average No. of visitors/day	10–15	5–10	5–10	2–5	2–5
Computer Training for students	Yes	No	No	No	Yes
Gross Income	6,500–7,000[1]	2,800–3,200	3,000–3,500	2,500–3,000[2]	8,000–10,000[3]
Income from Gyandoot services	1,200–1,500	1,500–2,000	1,500–2,000	500–700	1,500–2,000
Centre Expenses					
Rent	Nil	Nil	Nil	Nil	Nil
Phone	300	300	Nil	300	400
Electricity	300	400	300	300	500
Loan Repayment	2,500	1,400	Nil	1,550	Nil
Stationary & Misc.	200	200	300	300	400
Total	3,300	2,300	600	2,750	1,300
Net Income	3,200–3,700	500–900	2,400–2,900	≥300	6,700–8,700

Notes: 1. Figures for income and expenses are in Indian Rupee (INR). 2. The soochak could earn INR 3,000 or more every month from photocopying. There was a high demand for copying, the centre being closer to the block office. [19] The soochak reported that he may not renew his Gyandoot franchise. 3. The high income was from the education programmes conducted in the centre comprising 25 to 30 students. [20] The soochak in this centre was an engineering graduate and his brother was a franchisee of AISECE, which was explained as 'All India Society for Electronics and Computer Education'.

Although many centres had already been connected with fiberoptic cables, the instability in power connectivity remained a major cause of user dissatisfaction with the kiosks. It was also widely felt that the departments responsible for delivering the services did not adhere to timeframes set by the Gyandoot Samiti, although the officials at the Gyandoot headquarters informed me that these timelines have been fixed after discussions with the departments concerned.[21]

Media reports on the delays in delivering services had also pointed to the lethargy and unresponsiveness of government employees as a major reason for declining credibility of the Gyandoot project. *The Hindustan Times*, for example, reported that:

> The entire plan can get stuck if the downslide in its back-end operation continues. Largely attributed to the lethargic and ignorant government employees, the project has been witnessing snags of late. 'Against the promised reply within a week of a complaint being lodged through Gyandoot, delay has become the order of the day,' says an official of the District Rural Development Authority (DRDA), the Government agency handling the nitty-gritty of its operations.[22]

Another report puts the scenario as follows: "The operator at the information centre in Nalcha Block in Dhar has no clients. He has no electricity for hours and his information kiosks are deserted... It would appear as though Gyandoot has not been able to provide all the 44 services it was set up to deliver."[23] While some farmers complained that timely updating of market rates are exceptions rather than the rule, concerned officials would point out the slow process of computerization of government departments as a possible reason for the delays. The mainstream media had been critical of Gyandoot on this front as well:

> The mandi-rates, supposed to be updated daily, are not changed for two-three days on end. As the rates can change many times in a day, the facility is more or less useless. Moreover, a farmer has a cheaper option of a telephone call at 80 paisa (INR 0.80) to Dhar mandi to ask for rates instead of paying INR 5 user charge at the cyber centre. Land records of only three out of seven tehsils (village administrative unit) in the district are available on the network. There has also been duplication of work. The Land Records Bureau was doing the job for the last many years while it was undertaken simultaneously by the district administration, only to abandon it later.[24]

Several case studies have pointed to complaints from users that the kiosks remained closed during office hours. Soochaks invariably tried to deny this and said that such occasions were rare and occurred as a result of prolonged failures in power supply.[25] An exploratory study conducted by the Centre for Electronic Governance (CEG), the Indian Institute of Management, Ahmedabad, India (IIMA) came to the conclusion that centres closer to the district headquarters attracted more visitors, and that these visitors were generally the elite of middle-level farmers:

> Generally, awareness of Gyandoot exists among the literate and middle-income group families. The poor laborer or landless farmer is not aware or even interested, as he (sic) sees no value addition, in it, for him (sic). All the 16 daily wage labourers interviewed felt this way about G2C services. (CEG-IIMA 2002, 10)

The report further noted that:

> There seems to be varied understanding, among the people, of what services are available through Gyandoot. At the remote soochanalays (and away from the central hub of Dhar), confusion is more widespread and awareness levels are very low or nil. Even where a board enumerating the services exists, people are unsure of the nature of services and how to avail of them from the soochanalay. (ibid.)

It is also widely felt that the big farms and merchants mostly availed the services. Poorer farmers and landless agricultural labourers failed to see any benefits. Children from richer families were also able to avail of the facilities in the kiosks at a subsidized rate compared to market rates for similar services. There had not been any antipathy to the new technology from the rural elites. On the other hand, they welcomed it, and in a certain sense, exercised absolute control over its diffusion.

Sustainability

The question of sustainability has to be addressed on two counts: at both the macro and micro levels. The macro question is related to the issue of sustaining the Gyandoot Samiti as a QUANGO with the revenue from the kiosks. The entrepreneurs have to pay a lump sum of INR 5,000 every year as a license fee to the Gyandoot Samiti to renew their franchise. However, this was a paltry sum, given the fact there are only 30 to 35 kiosks operational at a time and that the proliferation of new kiosks in Dhar appeared to have been halted. The District Council, an elected local body at the district level that funded the initial investments for launching Gyandoot Samiti, would have to continue channelling resources for the everyday operation of the Gyandoot infrastructure.[26]

The sustainability of the soochanalays depended on its net earnings. We can see from Table 3.2 that of the five cases I have examined, three were break-even, whereas the other two seemed to be earning much less than a respectable monthly income for an initial investment of about INR 7,5000.[27] The Gyandoot Samiti had a modest expectation of a net income of INR 36,000 per annum for each kiosk manager.[28] It can be seen from Table 3.2 that three out of the five centres did not fulfil this expectation. In the case of the Nagda centre, the kiosk was owned by the panchayat (the elected village local body) and it paid the electricity bill.

In the case of the kiosks that appeared to be financially viable, the major source of income was from non-Gyandoot services. Many of the soochaks believed that the income from Gyandoot services was shrinking and that in order to survive they needed to expand their operations. The prospect of introducing additional services depended on the local demand for such services. In Dhar District, where 60 per cent of its population lived below the poverty line, the chances of an immediate surge in demand for information-related services to the scale of bridging the income gap for the kiosks seemed doubtful.

One of the most important questions regarding the operational dynamics of the kiosks was the linkages that it had with the local economy. In many cases, the panchayat was financing the infrastructure of the kiosks, which involved channelling local resources towards the establishment costs on a monthly basis. As the resources of the panchayat were drawn from the tax pool as well as from funds allotted to them by the state government, the opportunity costs of financing the everyday working of the kiosks without palpable and effective benefits for the community could be very high.

E-Governance and the Network Society: Deciphering the Narratives of Success

The most interesting aspect of the ICT-based development initiatives was the accent on narratives from the field that find their way into the media and public at large. They highlighted the achievements of the projects in ways that differed drastically from the narratives of successes of other developmental programmes, which depend primarily on statistical data (whether engineered or real) on their performance and achievements. Stories about the multitude of ways in which the absorption and use of ICTs by the rural folk were being facilitated by the initiatives became instrumental in constructing the idea of a rural network society as it was emerging in developing regions. However, in this section, based on stories told and untold, I argue that the contested nature of the emerging network society and its limitations can be fully understood only when these success stories are deconstructed in their own local contexts and further, by telling the concealed stories of conflicts and tension that mar the implementation and evolution of these initiatives. This, in effect, would also open a new pathway to understanding the social and political structure of the nascent rural network society. In this section I make a provisional attempt to demystify the discourse on individual achievements that seek to glorify the relevance and role of the Gyandoot project. Further, I also examine the entrenched social factors that overdetermine the delivery mechanisms institutionalized by Gyandoot. The stories that were already showcased, and a story I gathered during my visit, narrated by a local political activist of ShivSena, (a Hindu fundamentalist outfit) are exemplary cases of the way in which technology–society interaction could be interpreted in a deterministic paradigm, while the social-shaping aspect is relegated to the background or completely ignored. The case summaries reported in Table 3.3 invariably point to the emergence of a rural network society. Nevertheless, the problematic nature of the network society is also brought to light with the aid of hindsight and locale-specific information on social factors that should underlie any interpretation of these narratives generally considered as examples of the project's success and good performance. The anecdotes analysed in Table 3.3 have some common threads: they invariably point to layers of hyped narratives that envelope the descriptions of the achievements of the project. As the first five cases in Table 3.3 indicate, the strategy in discourses on project benefits had been to identify isolated cases of successful use of the project, instead of using standard indices of success and achievements in terms of the overall changes it had brought to the area covered under the project. A close look at the anecdotes, however, reveals that these narratives fail to account for any meaningful qualitative change in the life of the people concerned, and instead attempt a superficial glorification of the project's benefits in particular and of ICTs in general. These hyped narratives fail to impress when they are juxtaposed against the hidden social and economic backdrop of rural realities in India. In Table 3.3 I have made an attempt to show that most of the inferences drawn from the anecdotes with regard to the benefits of the projects are either misplaced or exaggerated.

In Case 1, for example, an email is presented as a superior medium of communication vis-à-vis direct or voice contact. It glorifies the fact that a bureaucrat responded to an email complaint; in reality, however, other

Figure 3.2. Gyandoot's promotional material on how kiosks solve rural credit problems.

(Answer for all problems: the villager wonders what kind of loans he can avail; who will give; who will fill up the form; who will file the application; who will pass the application and who will save him from middleman? The soochak in the kiosk answers: 'I will'.)

channels of communication are either more effective, such as communicating over a phone, or cheaper than sending an email, which costs INR 10. The way the anecdote is narrated amounts to admitting that the technology involved in communication is more important than the content of the communication for eliciting responses. In the second anecdote, the whole set of issues relating to the economic realities and market interlinkages that characterize rural transactions are squarely ignored in order to glorify isolated incidents of a profitable transaction facilitated by the technology, without explaining if the same 'knowledge' could have come from sources other than the internet. In the case of anecdotes 3 and 4, we also could see careless assumptions, such as the Internet having emerged as the only medium of information for facilitating rural transactions. The narratives lack credibility if the points that they try to drive home are placed in the contexts of the socioeconomic realities of rural areas in India. The case of the email-led vaccination of the milch animals that the anecdote described in Bhatnagar and Vyas (2001) is also not dissimilar. In the course of my fieldwork, I queried several informants for such stories and rarely did they have any important incident worth mentioning in relation to their use of the Internet. However, one such case of using the Intranet for a social purpose, narrated to me, is given as Case 6 in Table 3.3. Here the anonymity of the sender played a crucial role. The cases point to the social embedment of technology that is neglected while glorifying them as 'success' stories. The value of information that the new technology could generate depends heavily on contexts and it does not flow from any inherent virtues of the technology itself. A detailed case study that helps examine these issues is provided in the following subsection, highlighting the entrenched social factors that determine trajectories of technological innovations in Indian rural settings, challenging the futuristic e-topia of the narratives of success.

A Tale of Three Kiosks

A visitor to Badnaver will be surprised to see three Gyandoot kiosks functioning just within a 3-kilometre radius of the block headquarters if s/he knows that the stated position of Gyandoot Samiti was to encourage not more than one kiosk in one locality, because of the low number of villages actually covered by Gyandoot in the district.[29] Nevertheless, it could be too early to conclude that Gyandoot's popularity and utilization could be high enough in Badnaver to warrant the operation of three kiosks.

The first kiosk was operating within the premises of the block office. It was not open when I made my initial visit. A villager volunteered to find the soochak, but after nearly one hour, he returned to announce that the soochak was untraceable. Some villagers complained that it was not unusual for the kiosk to remain closed during office hours. When asked if they had any business with the kiosk, they said they had none. They had just come to see the administrative staff of the office for local development called the Block Development Office. Randomly quizzing a few villagers in the vicinity, it was found that none of them had used the soochanalay for any of their requirements. An employee of one of the government offices housed in that campus tipped that the other two soochanalyas were quite nearby. He was right, and it was only a five-minute walk from the first soochanalaya to the next (Badnaver 1 (B1) in Table 3.2). The soochak of B1, which started at a relatively recent period sounded extremely resentful about Gyandoot Samiti. He said that the income from Gyandoot services was practically inconsequential and that he was running the kiosk on a loss.

> I cannot even recover my license fee of INR 5,000 that I have already deposited with the Gyandoot Samiti. I survive because I earn moderately from this computer centre which I started before the Gyandoot franchise was taken and from a parallel screen printing service.[30]

One of the major complaints he had was regarding the unstable connectivity of the Gyandoot Intranet, which he said was different from the usual

Table 3.3. Narratives in contexts: Understanding the tales from Gyandoot villages.

The story	Source	Thrust	Remarks/Questions
1. An email complaint for INR 10 brought drinking water to a tribal hamlet of 39 households. The villagers' previous complaint to local authorities had not yielded results for six months. The complaint filed through the kiosk brought a handpump mechanic to the hamlet within two days, and he repaired the handpump within three hours.	Bhatnagar and Vyas (2001); Jafri et. al (2002)	Efficiency and reliability	Is technology capable of changing the mindset of government employees? Why did the mechanic fail to respond when the complaint was registered through conventional channels? Is there a fear or reverence for technology when email is used as a medium of communication that prompts people to act differently?
2. Farmers in Bagadi village were quoted a rate of INR 300 per quintal from local traders for their potato crop. The kiosk was used to get the prevailing market rate in a town 100 miles away, which paid INR 100 more. Consequently, their potato produce was sold in the distant town. The prices paid to farmers have increased approximately 3–5%, keeping about INR 200 million from the pockets of middlemen and traders*	Ibid.	E-business, liberation from middlemen	Why do middlemen get an upper hand in their dealings with farmers? In most cases, it is not because of the lack of awareness of the farmer about the market price. On the other hand, there exist deep interlinkages between the credit and product markets in rural India that force the farmer to sell his produce to the middlemen and traders from whom they have taken credit for cultivation. Moreover, the perishable nature of some of the agricultural products and lack of warehousing facilities compel framers to sell at a price lower than the market rates. Only the big farmers actually benefit from the information in this particular case.

Example	Source	Theme	Commentary
3. 'I asked for the price of apples at the Dhar wholesale market. The coordinator pressed some buttons, and there it was on the screen. I cannot read, but he told me it was 50 rupees cheaper per crate than the rate in the village market. Next morning, I travelled to Dhar to buy fruits.'	Chatterjee (2000)	Consumer freedom	It would be a surprise if a local retailer or consumer does not know that the wholesale prices are lower in urban areas than in rural areas where incremental transportation costs might lead to a certain percentage of markup. If everyone travels to Dhar from this village to buy apples, or any other commodity they require as the price would be invariably lower there, the retail business in the village would come to a standstill!
4. Kalsingh, a milk farmer, wanted to sell his cow. He registered with the auction facility of Gyandoot (which enables trading of commodities like milch animals, cultivable land, tractors, agricultural tools, etc.). He received four trade enquiries and finally sold his cow to the highest bidder for INR 3,000	Bhatnagar and Vyas (2001); Jaffri et. al (2002)	Rural e-business	Farmers will not hesitate to use the Intranet services of Gyandoot for selling agricultural implements and livestock if the coverage and usage of kiosks for this purpose is high. But the limitations far more outweigh the potential in this respect.
5. 256 milch animals vaccinated in one day: Upon receiving an e-mail from a kiosk that an epidemic had broken out amongst the milch cattle of the village Kot Bhidota, a veterinary rescue team was dispatched the same day. The disease *hemorrhage septicemia* was detected; the team promptly started curative treatment and vaccinated the remaining animals against the disease. They also conducted a search in neighbouring villages for signs of the disease and carried out preventive vaccinations. No deaths were reported.	Bhatnagar and Vyas (2001)	Efficiency and reliability	The superiority of emailing technology in speeding up the government machinery is not clear in this example also. The alternative of dialing the office could have worked just as well, if not better than, e-mail.

(Continued)

Table 3.3. Continued.

The story	Source	Thrust	Remarks/Questions
6. Closing an illicit liquor shop: In Nagda, some miscreants ran an illicit liquor shop near the panchayat office. The devotees of a temple and children attending the girls school in its vicinity faced bullying by liquor shop patrons. Since everyone feared a nexus between the police and the mafia running the shop, no one dared to complain. An activist of the local unit of Shiv Sena, a Hindu fundamentalist outfit, used the email facility of the Gyandoot centre to send an anonymous petition to the District Collector. Three days later the shop was raided and the perpetrators arrested.	Interview with Mohan Jat, Nagda on 14 August 2002	Anonymity, efficiency	Anonymity was important in reporting the matter and a self-styled local custodian of values (Shiv Sena is an organization that protests celebration of 'Valentine's Day and similar symbols of 'Western culture' in India) could make use of the facility and avoid direct confrontation with the mafia. Shiv Sena, incidentally, had 186 volunteers in the village and they mainly work to stop the selling of cows and oxen for slaughtering. Mohan Jat is the manager of a goshaala (a place to keep cows rescued from being slaughtered). The person who sent the anonymous mail keeps the soochak in good humour because if he fiddles it out to the mafia, his life will be in danger.

Source: Various sources including fieldwork.
* There are different versions of this story; see, for example, http://www.sustainableicts.org/Gyandoot%20F.pdf

troubled connectivity that soochaks in other kiosks were also pointing out. He said that the Internet failed to connect when the 8th,10th and12th standard public examination results and marks lists were made available through the Gyandoot Intranet for INR 10 per copy. This was regarded as the most lucrative of the services demanded by the public. When the Public Examination Board publishes the results, Gyandoot would immediately access it and send it to kiosks. Students visit the centre with their respective roll numbers to get the results.

> I don't even have a problem during load shedding. I hire a generator. But I can't connect when the results are published. I complained to the Collector. He said 'I will take care'. But nothing happened. I still cannot access the results. On the other hand, another soochanalaya here has no problem with the connectivity. I have a problem and the one housed in the panchayat office campus also has problems. I suspect corruption. The project manager is a very honest man. But I can't say the same about operators at the Gyandoot office.

He said that people, in fact, demanded no other Gyandoot service. 'The mandi (market) is in Badnaver itself. So why should they visit the kiosk for price list? All offices are housed here. What service can we offer?[31]' This was getting nowhere. So I asked him a pertinent question: In that case, when there were already two soochanalys in Badnaver, why did he apply for a third one?

> The Blockwala never opens. The other one is little interior [sic[32]]. When I first approached the Collector he refused. He wanted me to open the kiosk in another village where no soochanalaya had been opened. But I was not interested. I wanted to take the franchise since I had already had the computer centre here. In another village I would have had to rent in a new room. But when the CEO of the District Council visited the block I met him and later he recommended that as youngster I deserve encouragement and the kiosk was allotted to me.[33]

We can see the familiar stories of corruption, favouritism and arbitrariness in decision making emerging as the rural network society was taking shape. Is the technology that promised transparency and responsiveness itself getting entangled in the labyrinths of corruption and nepotism? The narratives and counter-narratives pointed to the social tensions created by the high-profile technology-driven project in rural Dhar. It was with these allegations of manipulation at the back of my mind that I visited the third soochanalaya in Badnaver (Badnaver 2 (B2) in Table 3.2).

Badnaver 2 was run by an upper-caste engineering graduate from a relatively wealthy family. Before taking the Gyandoot franchise, the family had already launched an Internet centre under the Bharat Sanchar Nigam Ltd (BSNL, the government-owned telecommunication company) scheme of one Internet dabha (shop) per block along with an e-education programme under the AISECE license. The BSNL scheme envisaged giving 25 percent commission to the licensee with a free telephone on which only Internet could be accessed. Further, he had also acquired contracts for computerizing land records in a few village patwaris, the lowest level offices of the Revenue Administration. His response was cautious when asked about his motivation to take the Gyandoot franchise when there was another soochanalaya operating within walking distance of his centre:

> Gyandoot soochanalaya was opened in 2000 in the block office premises. But the soochak was not a trained computer operator. He got the franchise due to political connections. I met the collector and the CEO of the District council when they visited the Block during the inauguration of the soochanalaya. I personally felicitated the Collector, presented him a memento and invited him for dinner. During dinner, he asked me to oversee the working of the kiosks since the operator was not properly trained. Removing him was not possible due to his political connection. Further, it could have led to some bad publicity. We were advised to send in a proposal to the Janpath panchayat requesting them to remove him. But I thought it was unfair. I said: 'I get my Dhal Roti (Food). Why should I prevent him from getting his?' The Collector was impressed by my answer. So he himself took the initiative to give me Gyandoot franchise. Thus, this is the first private Gyandoot centre in Dhar.

He was soon nominated to the Gyandoot Samiti as one of the two representatives of the soochaks in the QUANGO. He said computers are being installed everywhere – in schools, offices and the hospital in Badnaver – and that he had played a major role in the installation of the machines in all these places. I asked him if he experienced any problems in connectivity. I told him that the soochak in Badnaver 1 had complained about connectivity problems when public examination results are published. His response was quite characteristic:

> I have no connectivity problem. Others have problems because they don't know how to operate. They are not skilled enough. They have no proper training. When private people are given Gyandoot franchise it should be ensured that they have adequate experience in handling the

machine. [B1] was started after I took Gyandoot franchise. It came up because the CEO of the Janpath Panchayat, who was the tenant of the soochak, recommended it. In fact, I was consulted before it was given. I tried to stop it. But the project manager told me that whoever gives INR 5000 can start a Gyandoot kiosk, and anybody who is efficient can make money from it.

The narratives differed, but the story was a familiar one of bureaucratic muddle, political interference and mutual distrust. The local elite had been effectively controlling the new technology facilitated by the interplay of cross-linked forces such as political power, influence in bureaucratic circles and caste structure. The narratives of poor farmers and agricultural labourers benefiting from the technology are often exaggerated and misplaced in the contexts where such experiments are made possible.

QUANGOs, Civil Society and the Private Sector

This leads us to the larger question of civil society participation in e-governance projects initiated by the state governments. As indicated in the beginning of the chapter, civil society organizations appear to be kept out of the institutional structures of e-governance. Even in cases where such participation is sought, the linkages are either weak or notional. While the state-led projects in e-governance showed a relative reluctance to work with civil society organizations, they had attempted to follow the QUANGO model wherever relevant and possible. QUANGOs, like Gyandoot Samiti, form the backbone of the projects launched by several state governments. QUANGOs are defined as organizations that essentially undertake the responsibility of implementing state-sponsored programmes or public policies, funded by the state but operating at arm's length of the executive without an immediate hierarchical relation with it (van Thiel 2001,5). The formation of QUANGOs is part of the general strategy adopted by states, informed by the logic of civil society mediation. As pointed out in the *Pliatzky Report*, QUANGOs are created since:

> [T]he work is more effectively carried out by a single purpose organization rather than by a government department with a wide range of functions; in order to involve people from outside of government in the direction of the organization; in order to place the performance of a function outside the party political arena. (*Pliatzky Report* (quoted in Flinders 1999, 29))

Nevertheless, QUANGOs are not real substitutes for CSOs and most often degenerate into behemoth bureaucratic entities. Further, this leads to the incorporation of individuals and organizations, not accountable to any constituency – even notionally – into the governing structures of developmental and e-governance programmes. The conceptual model of the emerging e-governance programmes being carried out in India is a complex institutional model,[34] where sustainability issues are embedded in the policy prerogatives that mould the state's interest in the programme.

While the civil society involvement in e-governance projects is either notional or limited, private sector participation was seen as essential to the successful implementation as well as sustainability of the project. My visit to Gyandoot kiosks also led to a chance meeting with a representative of Hindustan Lever Ltd (HLL), the Indian subsidiary of Unilever who was interested in learning more about Gyandoot kiosks.[35] A presentation by Naveen Prakash, Project Manager, was aimed at exploring the possibilities of future partnership with HLL. The district collector was hoping that the private sector involvement would help overcome the project's financial crunch and make it viable in the long run.[36] Gyandoot's offers to HLL can be listed as follows:[37]

1. HLL can test the success of its new products in rural areas through Gyandoot
2. Gyandoot kiosks can be used for collecting feedback from HLL customers.
3. HLL can profile rural consumers using information available at the kiosks. Moreover, the soochaks could be used as surveyors for HLL, for a fixed remuneration.
4. HLL could use the Gyandoot portal for marketing and advertising its products.
5. Soochaks could display HLL posters, banners etc. in the soochanalayas.
6. Since many of the soochanalyas are located at bus stands, haat bazaars and block headquarters, etc., HLL can use the kiosks for selling its products. The brand identity of Gyandoot as a provider of quality services would be useful for HLL in selling their products. The kiosks managers would be paid the normal commission HLL pays to its retailers.

Although private-sector participation in paid technical services was visible in the case of most projects, strategic partnerships as envisaged by Gyandoot were not forthcoming for a variety of reasons. Private companies were more interested in exploring the possibility of setting up their own kiosks instead of using the Gyandoot soochanalays.[38] HLL, for example, was looking for avenues to establish information kiosks of its own with the involvement of women's Self Help Groups (SHGs) to 'sell the products at the consumer's doorsteps'.[39] The e-Choupal set up by the ITC has been considered a massive success in kiosk-centred rural marketing and business initiatives.[40]

Beyond Technocratic Definitions

The central themes addressed in this chapter relate to the critique of the notion of e-governance as an essentially administrative innovation facilitated by ICTs, and recognition of e-governance as a social process, which involves not only attitudinal change and transformation of traditional forms of governmentality, but as a contested arena of social forces shaping the trajectory of the evolution of this technocratic innovation. Governmentality represents continuity in terms of rule of self, household and the state, whose ruptures will cause and precipitate crises in governance (Baddeley 1997, 64). Hence ICTs and government are thoroughly intertwined (Frissen 1997, 111). Frissen argues that

> The dominant technology of our age affects the heart of government. The impact of ICT on government and public administration therefore is revolutionary. Public administration uses ICT as an instrument of its internal organization, for its operations, for transactions, for the development and implementation of policies, for monitoring and disciplinary ends, for the provision of information to politicians, citizens and societal groups and organizations. Public administration also addresses ICT as an object of regulation and policy making. (Frissen 1997.)

ICT-based e-governance initiatives thus entail a reinvention of government in terms of the relocation of artefacts for provision of utilities and services to the point of direct contact with citizens and lateral integration of official records, making them available for users. It also involves redesign of governmental institutions (Bellamy and Taylor 1994 (quoted in (Frissen 1997, 68)).

E-governance delivered simply as an improvement in the pragmatics of governance, exemplified in the efforts to make service delivery quicker or more accessible, probably ended up in reproducing technological practices that hinged for existence on the crucial technology component rather than its social dimensions, and helped the consolidation and centralization of power in the hands of those who, directly or by proxy, own, control or manipulate the technology. One of the central issues that emerge in the context of exploring the interrelationship between technology and governance is the need to challenge the assumption of the neutrality of technological processes enmeshed in the notion of e-governance. Technical processes defining the contours of e-governance are embedded in the structures of power that reinforce the power relations that e-governance, according to the developmental perspective, is expected to eliminate. This is particularly obvious when we closely scrutinize the consequences of the introduction of ICT-based administrative projects in villages where the local magnates play a key role in the implementation of projects and evidently benefit from this public good. It can be seen that the projects were often implemented with the active support and participation of the village elites, and that their collaboration was a major aspect of the survival of the project.

It can also be seen that automation, on the one hand, and projects with a social content on the other, form the key strategy of defining the pace of development of e-governance as identified by the state. The Indian state had shown an early interest in automation during the 1970s and 1980s and took a lead role in the implementation of innovative e-governance projects in the late 1990s. In this chapter I argue that it is important to understand the e-governance projects in the social contexts in which they are embedded, taking exception to the implied essentialism of technocratic perspectives. The computerization of government departments and the launching of projects with a social content emerged as a near universal pattern for e-governance processes in India at the state level as well as the national level. Even states with relatively poor performance in terms of social and economic indicators surged ahead with innovative projects in e-governance. Nevertheless, many of these projects are floundering and have been unable to break the initial inertia. Even when the programmes were able to make modest successes in terms of expansion and sustainability, the conflicts generated in the domain of technology-society interaction in these projects were enormous and deserved closer attention than the developmental perspective could offer. The invention of e-governance as a ICT-driven project for development administration had some ideological effects as well. It helped to reduce the resistance to computerization, which was mostly opposed by trade unions and students and youth organizations on the grounds that computers eliminate job opportunities. It turned people's perception of computers from a machine causing unemployment to a potential job creator and source for future economic growth.

One of the crucial aspects of networked governance was its potential for creating a network society in rural areas. Gyandoot's Intranet is an example of an emerging rural network society, with its scattered nodes and decentralized delivery system. However, the sociological aspects, such as power relations, and technological aspects, such as connectivity, are important in defining its contours of effectiveness and success. The rural network society that developed as an offshoot of networked governance could at best be considered as akin to a technosocial network, with the potential to increase both citizen-to-government and person-to-person communication in a specific geographical unit. However, if we consider the contemporary history of projects such as Gyandoot as evolving techno-social networks, their potential for reproducing traditional lines of social inequalities and reinforcing rural power hierarchies, rather than eliminating them, cannot be overlooked. The idea that ICT is inherently a liberating technology and hence, e-governance is a new way of transcending inept and inefficient bureaucratic systems that empowers 'end users' appears to be completely inaccurate in the rural societal setting. Moreover, despite the claims of active networking of people in rural Dhar made on behalf of Gyandoot, its ability to connect to multiple social and economic domains was found to be extremely limited and, ostensibly, mediated by the social power equations that enveloped its institutional setting.

Chapter 4

CYBER-KIOSKS AND DILEMMAS OF SOCIAL INCLUSION

ICTs and Social Change

The idea that ICTs are a unique technological intervention capable of challenging traditional barriers for social change and economic development continues to be the central pillar of ICT-based civil society initiatives in rural South Asia. Contrary to this widely held belief, the actual experience of many acclaimed developmental ICT projects provides grounds for reassessing the strategies and options of ICT deployment in rural spaces, given the fact that the application of information technology has not in itself led to any profound transformation of the social and economic milieu of marginalized communities. While major ICT-based projects, initiated by either the state or CSOs, are floundering due to the existence of formidable social and economic obstacles that they are unable to overcome, several new ICT-based projects are proliferating in rural South Asia. The attempt to usher in economic changes through providing access to net-based services and information has not had a significant impact on the rural economy in India. Besides, the potential for the organizational as well as technical innovations that lay at the base of these interventions, remoulding microlevel practices for generating sustained growth in incomes and jobs, appears to be rather limited and conditioned by the historically given the socioeconomic milieu in which they operate.

In India, one of the major claims made on behalf of these projects, besides their ability to redefine the economic contours of Indian villages, is their potential in engaging in social transformative action at the village level (Dugger 2000; Arunachalam 2002; Rajora 2002). It is widely recognized that caste and gender inequalities in rural Indian society have shown extraordinary resilience. Despite decades of social and political struggles, rural, and to a great extent urban, social life in India is marked by caste-based social divisions and feudal gender values biased against women. ICT-based developmental initiatives in India have apparently taken note of the issue of unjust social structures, arguing that deployment of new technologies into rural areas would enhance participation of marginalized communities and vulnerable groups such as women and the aged in developmental and political processes. The question was often identified as one of increasing the level of skills and providing organizational support (Goyal 2003). An attempt to increase participation by women and Dalits (lower castes) thus become a major objective outlined by these projects in their mission statements and publicity materials.

Nevertheless, the existing literature mostly understands the question of inclusion as a matter of choice rather than structure. In these analyses, social exclusion is a matter of lack of awareness and inappropriate project design, although mention is occasionally made of societal contexts; incorporation of gender concerns 'from the very beginning of the project design' is a more or less universal solution for enhancing participation (Hafkin 2002; Gajjala 2002; Ramilo and Cinco 2005). While participation could to a certain extent be a matter of choice – either of the project implementers or 'beneficiaries' – the overarching structures of social barriers appeared to be more inhibiting than was often appreciated. It was in this regard that some of these projects began to make claims about the social transformative potential of new technologies and defined their own role as one of mediating social change through deployment of ICTs.

This chapter takes a closer look at this position and argues that the question of inclusion cannot be satisfactorily addressed within the paradigm of understanding failure as a matter of design and choice. The failure is deeply embedded in the social and institutional processes through which projects necessarily become part of the rural social setting. Further, it is argued that the potential for transcending these constraints by taking the role of social movements is limited due to the inability of these organizations to challenge the existing institutional agencies and social forces that assist them in their project implementation. I first focus on the question of women's participation in ICT-based community projects in India in the initial phase. I then look at the claims of selected initiatives regarding their social transformative capabilities to act as a caste equalizer in the rural social structure and examine the huge gap between reality and rhetoric that provides useful insights into the dynamics of human-ICT interaction in the emerging rural network society in South Asia.

Gender and Information Technology

The research in the area of ICTs and women, mostly conducted in US and European contexts, has highlighted the recurrence of some of the traditional gender issues relating to technology, such as its impacts on housework, labour market and leisure and perhaps, also the much familiar questions of stereotyping women in the contexts of their relations with computers and

Internet (Turkle 1995; Wolmark 2000; Green and Adam 2001; Shade 2002; Adam 2005; Kendall 2002; Bury 2005; Harcourt 1999; Flanagan and Booth 2006). The research in this area has also opened up a whole new set of issues relating to sexuality, such as its positive and negative consequences and the perceived gradual erosion of women's agency in the everyday practices of the net despite their growing visibility on the web as well as in the lab (Spender 1995; Balsamo 1996; Cherny and Weise 1996; Barak 2005; Eriksson-Zetterquist 2007; Finn and Banach 2000; Kendall 2002; Magnet 2007; Morahan-Martin 2000; Ray 2007). One important drawback of the research on ICTs and gender is that it has not satisfactorily addressed the question of exclusion, preferring, rather, to look closely at the processes and practices of gendering as it unfolds among participants of the net, although gender divide has been understood as a major from of digital divide (Young 2002). However, there has been a growing uneasiness and concern regarding the question of net access for women, particularly in the context of increasing digitization of traditional governmental functions and services both in the developed and developing countries. As Scott and Page point out:

(W)ith ongoing government promotion of informatics and the new communication technologies, there are growing pressures on the community sector to change its working practices – and thus to keep with the changing social economic and political context in which the sector is operating. This has particular implications for women's organizations... which have always been particularly poorly resourced, and for which there are specific issues concerning access of ICTs. (Scott and Page 2001, 149)

The issue of access is significant, given the impressions about ICTs as increasingly women-friendly transformation noted in some more recent research. Green, for example, observes that

In the past, Internet techno-culture has been constructed as a hostile environment for women, although that is likely to change in some areas as female participation rate continue to climb. Examples of harassment are particularly evident from early to mid 1990s, however, when the Internet was growing exponentially but was still grossly distorted towards masculine users. Current research into Internet is likely to indicate masculine and feminine areas ...but the Internet itself is a much less threatening environment for women than it was. (Green 2002, 191)

While the new technologies are, arguably, becoming more women-friendly, the question of women's net access becomes an interesting research question in itself in the emerging context of increasing universalizing of ICTs in everyday practices of governance and commerce. Quoting Moore (1998), Holloway and Valentine (2003, 21) point out that ICTs are often tied to political visions of social inclusion and cohesiveness and seen as potentially facilitating higher participation levels producing democracy that is more informed. According to them,

> At the scale of the individual, ICT are promoted as empowering or liberating, particularly for disadvantaged groups. This is because of the freedom that they offer users to access information and communicate with whom they want, forced from the material and social constraints of their bodies, identities, communities and geographies. (Holloway and Valentine 2003, 21)

Nevertheless, it is evidently clear that such an overhyped view of new technology might not be true when tested against the grounded realities of digital divide. There are two central issues of crucial significance in this context: One is regarding the gender divide in terms of differential stream of social cultural emotional and economic gains that women are able to accrue from participation. This also includes the questions of harassment and a feeling of vulnerability to cyber violence. The second is the question of absolute exclusion:

> (M)ore comprehensive formulation which refers to the dynamic process of being shut out, fully or partially, from any of the social economic political or cultural systems which determine the social integration of a person in society. Social exclusion may be seen as a denial (or non realization) of the civil, political and social rights of citizenship (Walker and Walker 1997 (quoted in Holloway and Valentine 2003, 39)).

Green (2002), addressing the issue of women's exclusion from the Internet, points out that both the online technocultural environment and the physical spaces like laboratory or computer barns may themselves be hostile to women as a result of male superpresence. The absence of women, which according to her has been decreasing, has tremendous sociopolitical consequences. Spender (1995), in an earlier study, pointed to the historical exclusion of women from power, using their illiteracy as a social instrument following the invention of print. To quote Green,

> The structural disadvantage of illiteracy has deliberately been compounded by socio political systems. In most western nations, men had the vote for decades before women, and they justified the exclusion

of women on the ground of their lower educational standard, and their inability to read and write. A competent electorate, ran the argument, is an educated one-but for many years only one of the genders was educated. Spender's concern in the 1990s was that the Internet was shaping up to replicate this privilege/discrimination dynamic. (Green 2002, 188)

In rural South Asia, also, it can be seen that the ICT projects initiated by both state and civil society made unsubstantiated claims about social inclusion, while the gap between this rhetoric and grounded reality appeared to widen. The ICT projects in rural India had assumed lack of access to ICTs as the main hindrance to empowerment of women. Huyer and Sikoska (2003) identified lower levels of literacy and education, including training in languages that are predominantly used in ICT platforms and the Internet, time constraints due to women's triple role of domestic, productive and community management responsibilities leading to a much longer workday than men's, less access to financial resources to cover the cost of equipment and access, and unfavorable geographical location of ICT kiosks that makes travel to ICT centres is more difficult due to cost, time and cultural reasons, and so on, as reasons for lower women's participation in ICT initiatives. An interesting study by Wajcman and Pham Lobb (2007, 2) on gender segregation in the Vitenamese software industry, notes that while there is a substantial literature on gender issues in information technology in the United States and Europe, the situation in developing countries has not received adequate attention. Nevertheless, the growth of the IT industry in India. Nevertheless, the growth of the IT industry in India has drawn scholarly attention on the IT workforce in general and consequently, there has also been critical studies that look at the gender dimensions of the labour process in the industry (Arun and Arun 2002; Antony and Vasudevan 2008; D'Mello 2006; Radhakrishnan 2007; Fuller and Narasimhan 2008 and Remesh 2008). Issues of gender equality at work, self and identity, sexual segregation and work force participation have been rigorously examined in the current literature on information technology. At the same time, critical appraisals of the wider claims about ICTs' role as a potential leveller of gender inequalities and participatory and inclusive nature of ICT initiatives have been fewer, if not completely absent. In the next section, I focus on the evidence regarding social inclusion of the marginalized, particularly rural women in the some of the major ICT projects in rural India.

Women and ICTs: Rhetoric and Reality of Participation

Given the backdrop of a euphoric ideology of social levelling attributed to ICTs, it was not surprising that the major ICT-based projects launched in South Asia had gender sensitivity as their flagship. Even when none of these projects were initially aimed exclusively for women's empowerment, most organizations and projects soon began to project the potential as well as actually women's empowerment as their major contribution. In posters, pamphlets, and standard publicity materials as well as those newly appearing as either sponsored or as voluntary media exposure, these organizations projected pictures of rural women flocking around computers in large numbers in cyber kiosks. Videos and similar publicity material emphasized the benefits of the initiatives to rural women who are marginalized or excluded from social and political processes due to illiteracy, traditions, patriarchal values and general state apathy. For example, the video 'Reaching the Unreached: Village Knowledge Centres in Pondicherry for Sustainable Food Security' by MSSRF Foundation, Chennai, begins with a statement by a woman named Indira Gandhi identified as a user from Embalam village, Pondicherry on the e-kiosk run by the organization (MSSRF 2000). She says:

> During rainy season, cattle and sheep are more prone to diseases. We don't know the type of all diseases and are often unaware of them. We approach the local information centre, collect the address of veterinary doctors and phone them up for immediate attention. We take care of our animals better this way. (MSSRF 2000)

Hence, ICTs, ever since they began to become popular with bureaucrats and policy makers, have thus been characterized as an emancipating technology particularly for disadvantaged and marginalized women (Sharma 2003; Ng and Mitter 2005). The notion that ICTs in the rural Asian setting can be liberating, particularly for women, has been one that has received continued favourable attention and appreciation.[1] Moreover, the nature of political, social, psychological, educational and economic benefits that ICTs can bring to women and minority groups has remained a main concern in the literature that looks at ICT expansion and adoption (Gurumurthy and Sarkar 2003; Arun et al., 2004; Gurumurthy and Singh 2006; Ghosh 2006; Mukhopadhyay and Kamble 2006; Mukhopadhyay and Nandi 2007; Best and Maier 2007; Bhushan 2008; Khan and Ghadially 2010). The question of digital divide in terms of gender is mostly identified in the literature as a barrier to be overcome with increased use of ICTs in rural areas, ostensibly strengthening the rural network society. Nevertheless, it is important that we consider digital divide as a social phenomenon better addressed as a question of structure rather than as one of choice. More ICTs does not necessarily bring more equality. On the contrary, the patterns of ICT deployment and control in the rural setting could reinforce existing social divides and, in certain cases, create new divisions.

Gyandoot: Tribal Women at Large

The Gyandoot kiosks offered a wide set of facilities and services, such as gathering and disseminating agricultural prices, online registration of applications, online public grievance redressal, rural email, village auction sites, online matrimonial site, information regarding governmental programmes, career counselling for students, and a facility to receive feedback on queries from experts, technical advice channels between experts and villagers, online application formats, village newspaper, and so on. It can be imagined that if functioning properly, the centres can be of very high utility to the villagers. It becomes apparent that if such services are offered, and any particular sections in the community are excluded from accessing them, then that would lead to the emergence of new social divides or reinforce existing divisions within the village community.

One of the most important aspects of the Gyandoot project has been its location. Dhar is a tribal district and the notion that a relatively underdeveloped tribal district can be the site of an enormous experiment involving the application of ICTs in governance is an inspiring one. Nevertheless, the decision to implement the project in a tribal district was not part of any larger

Figure 4.1. Gyandoot's promotional material offering small monetary rewards for reporting illegal activities to the Kiosk.

('The place to Report All Major Social Evils. If you come across the major four problems inflicting in the village – Child Labour, Bonded Labour, Child Marriage and Caste Discrimination – Report it at the Kiosk and get a reward of INR 50'.)

scheme of wiring economically poor regions in the state of Madhya Pradesh. On the other hand, it was contingent upon the fact that the senior government official who masterminded the project was the chief administrative official – the district collector of the Dhar, a relatively backward tribal region.

When the project was conceived it was believed that it would provide equal opportunities for men and women, as well as people belonging to weaker sections such as Dalits. The aims and objectives set out by the innovator revolved around the idea of equal participation. Hence, the first two major goals of the project as outlined by Rajora (2002, 66) were 'enhanced participation in community affairs through the creative use of information technology and ensuring equal access to emerging technologies for oppressed and exploited segments of the society'.

Nonetheless, the project has not been able to achieve a critically significant degree of participation of women and Dalits to ensure that these objectives are met. The problem of inadequate participation by women means further marginalization of women in Dhar because of a variety of reasons. The first and foremost factor that deserves attention in this context is the fact that Dhar is a tribal district and tribal women are one of the most marginalized groups in India. When most of the government services are made available through Gyandoot, the insufficient participation of women would imply that these services eventually fall outside the reach of tribal women. Besides, it would also imply that instead of bridging the gender divide characteristic of rural India, the new technology is reinforcing the existing divide or even widening it.

Hence, it turns out that one of the important and most visible divides that was reinforced in the context of the emergence of Gyandoot kiosks was the gender divide. While the number of people accessing the utilities provided by the kiosk was abysmally low in relation to the total population of the villages, it is all the more clear that female users of Gyandoot were much fewer than male users (see Table 4.1). The data shows that three years into the project, women were still not in a position to make use of the facilities made available through Gyandoot kiosks. Further, it can be seen from the table that children and youth were the major users of the Gyandoot kiosks, revealing the exclusion of the aged as another important social problem that had arisen in the context of e-governance services provided by the ICT-based projects. What is notable in the table is the pattern of female participation, besides the most glaring fact that female participation was relatively low. In the age groups below 18 years and above 60 years, we can see relatively high usage of the kiosks. In itself, this is an encouraging and positive development. It means that schoolgoing girls and aged women have a greater potential for being the clients of the project. However, when we try to unravel the deeper implications of this phenomenon, the picture that emerges is not a promising one. What the pattern tells us is that young women and middle-aged women have been staying away from the kiosks, and this group includes young mothers and workers. It is striking that the lowest level of participation is from women belonging to the age groups 18–30 and 30–40 and, perhaps, this points to the whole set of issues pertaining to the question of gender divide in rural India, and the inability of the project to address the question that I bring out below.

The fact that schoolgoing girls and destitute women form the majority of the women visitors to the Gyandoot Kiosks is corroborated by observations made by the soochaks. In the Nagda kiosk, for example, the soochak mentioned that less than 10 per cent of the users are women. Many soochaks have pointed out that for long intervals, no women ever visit the centre. As one of the soochaks would put it:

> Mostly, men visit my centre. However, occasionally some women who have no male members in their family would come for help. They mainly come for the welfare schemes. Sometimes they visit the kiosks seeking help for resolving land disputes when others using their might, encroach their land. Land disputes can go violent at times. Children come here to play computer games when I allow them once in a week. Some of the children are girls.[2]

The officials and the soochaks were, in fact, aware of the relative nonpresence of women as users and offer a variety of reasons for the relative nonparticipation of women in the activities of the project. Even among the soochaks, not many were women. At the time of our visits, only one kiosk was managed and operated by a female soochak. Moreover, at the executive level also there is an absence of females. Even though one of the sloganeered objectives of

Table 4.1. Users of Gyandoot by gender and age during 2000–2002.

Age group	Male	Female	Total	Percentage of women users (Age category)	Percentage of women users (Cumulative)
Below 18	770	422	1192	35.40	38.00
18–30	406	6	412	1.46	0.54
30–40	2,092	211	2,303	9.16	19.00
40–60	1,014	234	1,248	18.75	21.14
Above 60	376	234	610	38.36	21.14
Total	4,658	1,107	5,765	19.20	100.00

Source: Adapted from CEG-IIMA (2002, 17).

the project was to bring more women into the net and make it a weapon for their liberation, in the formation of its organizational structure, the basic requirement in achieving this goal has been overlooked – the Gyandoot programme did not have a single woman coordinator.

The oft-cited reasons for nonparticipation of women by male coordinators as well as soochaks of Gyandoot were illiteracy, family ties and tribal customs and traditions that are prohibitive for women.[3] While these are all facts relating to the social realities of rural India, particularly in tribal areas, the account stands as a testimony to the failure of the belief that information technology is inherently capable of resolving existing social divides. Problems like illiteracy and tribal customs that prohibit women from participating in the project are not isolated issues that one or even a set of development initiatives can properly address. They are deeply embedded in the ensemble of power relations of both caste-based and patriarchal hierarchy of social organization in rural India.

It is noteworthy that some of the attempts by Gyandoot officials to launch awareness campaigns to attract more women to the centres also did not produce the desired results. An apparently innovative programme that Gyandoot officials conceived was to organize competitions for children in the villages on behalf of the kiosks, expecting that this would result in increased understanding of the working of the kiosk for their mothers who bring them to these contests. In order to break the inertia in female participation, for example, the Samithi conducted a 'healthiest child' competition at the village/kiosk level. Nevertheless, according to the accounts of the officials themselves, it did not succeed in attracting women customers.[4]

TARAkendras: Accepting Gender Divisions

Challenging gender divisions and providing greater access to women and disadvantaged groups is the most publicized benefits of ICT-based developmental projects, including TARAhaat. While conceiving TARAhaat in response to the fact that illiteracy is especially high among vulnerable groups such as women and Dalits, they were recognized as 'part of the core audience for the TARAhaat website', a reason why developing a non-text-based medium was believed to be an imperative for the success of the project (San Miguel 2001).[5] In one of the presentations made to an international audience, where TARAhaat portrayed itself as an Internet-based organization with social objectives, commercial strategies and multilayered partnerships, it outlined an implementation plan to achieve nationwide deployment of TARAkendras by March 2002, an expectation that remained unfulfilled even in 2004. The unique means of outreach was expected to employ associations of government pensioners, mahila mandals (women's groups) and soldier–sailor boards for popularizing the kendras.[6] The belief that the model has been performing well in India has led many to believe that it is replicable. Ironically, in the post-US invasion of Afghanistan, attempts to use ICTs for developmental action, admittedly, attempted to emulate TARAkendras', with its 'success' as a source of inspiration. The image of the project as a major initiative drawing village women into the dawn of the information revolution, sidestepping conventional disadvantages of illiteracy and inadequate education, was deeply ingrained in the narratives of the project:

> Education programs for illiterate women allow women to skip over their first two prerequisites – literacy in their own language and in English – and jump immediately into learning how to use a computer to access information. TARAhaat.com in India is an ideal example of a source of information that is made to suit the needs of women at the village level. In this website, pictures are used to represent things that are important to women in Indian villages, such as clinics or schools. The women click on the object and access information such as why it is important to educate their daughters. (Abirafeh 2003)

Sponsored studies also have attempted to highlight the issues of women as a major agenda of the project in the discussion of the social components that the project would address:

> TARAhaat's overarching social objective is the creation of sustainable rural livelihoods and the enrichment of the rural Indian economy through improved information flows, education, and direct job creation. In addition, TARAhaat will address a number of social issues including women's health and education, governance, and resource conservation, primarily by providing relevant and easily accessible information on its Web site. (Peterson et al. 2001, 4)

However, the reality has been far from the ideal that these discourses attempt to portray. Interestingly, the promoters of the TARAkendras visited the villages and held discussions with the village elites as well as others before entrepreneurs were identified to set up the kiosk. Once the centres were established, TARAhaat attempted to consolidate the centres by offering a spectrum of community activities and programmes such as seminars, group meetings, workshops, and so on, in order to draw the attention of villagers to the centre and its benefits. The staff and the entrepreneurs connected with the project were aware that female participation in the activities of the telecentres was relatively low.

The TARAkendras had a flexible organizational structure, so that informal initiatives by entrepreneurs often played a major strategic role in launching awareness campaigns. In Raman Mandi, for example, the kiosk manager arranged an entertainment programme for children every Saturday.[7] The TARAhaat team welcomed these initiatives, since they hope that its info-tech centres could be transformed into village or peri-urban community centres. However, initially considered as a good marketing strategy,[8] these independent initiatives did not result in any increased participation of women in TARAkendra's activities, despite a good number of female students being enrolled for their e-education programmes. It may be noted that female students were not sent to these centres to attend courses when mixed classes were proposed. Realizing this problem, some centres began to offer separate sessions for girls, and employed women tutors.[9] Reports highly sympathetic to the organization also noted that the reluctance of parents to send their daughters to TARAkendras had been a major problem:

> In Bathinda, the *Pacca Kalan* franchisee found villagers hesitant to send their daughters to the TARAkendra because they thought that the girls might be harassed there, especially by boys from surrounding villages. The franchise owner offered personally to guarantee the girls' well-being during visits with their parents (Peterson et al. 2001, 14)

The operative model of the TARAhaat kiosks was based on the computer educational services it provided to students. The enrolment of girls in these programmes was lower than that of boys. Traditionally, girls and boys are not allowed to sit together in the classroom, and hence separate hours had to be scheduled for them. However, this strategy also did not result in any substantial increase in girls' participation. It was also noted that women franchisees were singled out for ostracism or vandalism in Bathinda.

> A franchisee in the Bathinda region, for example, suffered early vandalism and threats because the villagers felt that her TARAkendra would disrupt their peaceful existence. They argue that an intervention by the district authorities to quell the threats and later stage campaign by the franchisee herself eventually helped to allay their fears. (Peterson et al. 2001, 14)

While these local initiatives were either floundering or registering moderate successes, the TARAhaat team conceived a comprehensive strategy to increase local participation in general and female participation in particular.

TARAhaat experimented with a new organizational arrangement called 'TARAbaathcheet' to attract women. Originally envisaged as an interactive forum for people, particularly women, to raise their problems and grievances and find solutions, TARAbaathcheet was conceived with the aim of evolving as a forum to provide exposure to the activities of the kiosks to rural women. Separate 'baathcheets' were visualized for different groups of people, such as elderly men, women, youth, and children. However, the coverage of the programme was limited to a few centres and it was barely successful in most of the kiosks where it was implemented. After realizing that female turnout for common meetings was practically negligible, exclusive meetings for women, moderated by a female resource person, was also attempted in some centres. A female medical practitioner from Chandigarh was appointed as consultant for these meetings. Another 'successful' case of inclusion sheds more light on the social complexities that envelop such projects in rural India:

> The three girls who own and operate the Punavali Kalan franchise near Jhansi belong to one of India's higher social classes. Some villagers were reluctant to visit the TARAkendra because they considered it just one more way to increase the power vested in the higher class. The franchisees have managed to overcome this initial resistance through door-to-door visits with the villagers. Several people showed up when personally invited to visit the TARAkendra and see the 'new type of TV' for themselves. (Peterson et al. 2001, 14)

It becomes clear from these narratives that in the process of formation of the kiosks, there was an over dependence on the support of the rural elite in its evolution. These elites control the social milieu of the domain of activities often offered by the kiosks and in order for the telecentres to function in this milieu, they had to invariably accept the traditional social divides, including the gender divide, instead of striving to transform them. Hence it is highly unlikely that the technology in itself will have any emancipatory effects as far women and the underprivileged are concerned.

Knowledge Centres and Women's Participation

As in the case of the other projects, non-participation of women and the elderly stands out as a major drawback of the project, although the rhetoric on the participation of the marginalized and underprivileged was at a very high pitch in the publicity materials produced in support of this project. Nonetheless, the grounded reality in most cases stood in sharp contrast to this orchestrated overhype. The all-women centre in Embalam was perhaps typical of this contrast of rhetoric and reality.

In Embalam, a group of eight female volunteers were managing the MSSRF kiosk. In the publicity materials and information literature supplied by the organization, it was often noted that 50 percent of the volunteers were women. The IVRP had a total of 26 to 28 volunteers spanning 11 centres during the period of my visit. There was a surprisingly high concentration of women volunteers in Embalam, which partly explained the high percentage of women volunteers for the IVRP as a whole. Also notably, this was the centre with the maximum number of volunteers to manage a single kiosk. In other centres, one could normally expect two to four volunteers with a chance of one of them being a woman in a few places. One of the most striking aspects about the volunteers in Embalam was that their educational background was 10th standard or below, whereas in other kiosks a good majority of them had attended college or even acquired technical education before joining IVRP.

The Embalam kiosk was set up as a result of the initiative by the office holders of the project who interacted with the key personnel of the Mangalam Society, an organization with local roots in Pondicherry, working with the objective of social advancement of disadvantaged women. It regularly conducted training camps for women and followed this up with additional activities to refresh their knowledge on topics such as personality development, time management, various schemes, interpersonal relationships, family harmony, consumer awareness, and so on.[10] It appears that the project failed to elicit the interest of the educated and skilled youths in the locality, who refused to offer unpaid labour to manage the kiosk. As one volunteer at Embalam notes:

> You can see only women volunteers here. But it is not because there are no young men who can run this. The fact is that they asked for a salary. They said they need at least 2000 rupees per month. It is reasonable but the project does not pay [a] salary.[11]

The women volunteers said they take shifts in batches of four. If one is surprised by the relatively large number of volunteers to manage the kiosk in Embalam, the reason is to be found in the social milieu, which remains unchanged in spite of the intrusion of technology:

> We are all housewives and we have children to look after. Since we are not paid for this work, we have to take up casual work for our livelihood. We have to sit here in groups because it is not probably safe to be alone as we are women. So four of us sit here in the morning and the other group would manage in the evening.[12]

The volunteers recollected that the kiosk was set up as a result of contacts established with the IVRP staff through a Chennai-based, high-level functionary of the Mangalam Society called Anjali Dayanand. Usha Rani, a local organizer of the society, had attended a training programme led by Anjali Dayanand. She instructed Usha Rani to take other members of the local group to a meeting organized by Rajashekhar Reddy of IVRP to seek the possibility of setting up an IVRP centre in the locality. The meeting was held not in Embalam, but in Ariyoor.

What is remarkable about the centre is that the kiosk is being run by relatively lesser-educated women. They seem to be at ease to be with the machine as well as with the procedures for running the kiosk. However, the fact that it was run entirely run by women had not, according to their own assessment, led to any enhanced participation of women in the project. They explained that this may be due to the fact that the information available from the kiosk, such as market prices, was demanded more by men than women. In this sense, the Embalam kiosk did not have any striking differences with other IVRP kiosks. The clientele were children and youth who visited the centre to play computer games, CDs and DVDs.

The data provided in the annual report of the MSSRF is also revealing, although it is a bit misleading. Table 4.2 gives the compiled user profile of probably a cumulative distribution for the years 1999 through 2001. While nonparticipation of women, lower castes, aged and the underprivileged has been a glaring feature of the project since its inception, the attempt has always been to underplay this fact.

In the following section, we try to compare the user register for two randomly selected months in 1999, the year in which the project was launched, and in 2002. I have chosen the most celebrated of the MSSRF

Table 4.2. Categories of users of knowledge centres in Pondicherry.

Village	Total no. of users	Men	Women	Children (Below 14 years)	Dalits	Below Poverty Line	Illiterates
Veerampattinam	5,823	4,842	813	168	29	2,552	117
Kizhoor	7,425	5,226	862	1,337	100	2,694	179
Embalam	12,601	6,681	2,401	3,519	336	3,278	238
Pooranangkuppam	1,344	983	94	267	—	373	49
Thirukanchipet	1,693	1,379	102	212	1,455	1,400	58
Kalitheerthalkuppam	961	767	97	97	16	128	146
Ariyur	140	71	30	39	12	51	1
Pillayarkuppam	620	300	260	60	—	—	—

Source: MSSRF (c. 2001, 133).

Table 4.3. Users by gender at the Veerampatinam kiosk in March 1999.

Group	Male	Female	Total
Adult	75	7	82
Child	13	0	13
Total	88	7	95

Source: Users Register, Veerampattinam Kiosk.

Table 4.4. Users by gender and age at the Veerampatinam kiosk in June 2002.

Gender / Age Group	Male	Female	Total
Below 15	58	0	58
16–25	106	6	112
26–35	48	1	49
36–45	5	0	0
46–55	0	0	0
Above 55	0	0	0
Total	192	7	199

Source: Users Register, Veerampattinam Kiosk.

kiosks – Veerampatinam – for this comparative exercise. Due to differences in the manner in which data are recorded at the centre in the past and at the time of the fieldwork, we do not get strictly comparable age-wise information of users. However, since a separate category of student users is kept, even in the earliest registers, this limitation is not overly constraining.

The noticeable absence of women in the user list of Veerampatinam kiosk in the year of its inception has not been a temporary phenomenon, as evidenced by the user statistics for June 2002 (Tables 4.3 and 4.4). If in 1999 seven visits out of a total of 95 were made by women after 3 years while the total number of visits has almost doubled, the number of visits by women remains unchanged. This clearly shows that female participation in the project is low, and declining as a share of total visits, while propaganda had maintained just the opposite.

Social Enterprises as Social Movements

It is also necessary to reassess the promises of the ICT-based CSOs regarding their social transformative role as crusaders of social equity and gender equality. We need to address this question against the backdrop of the claims made

Table 4.5. Telecentres and their activities.

Activity / Project	TARAkendra (DA)	IVRP (MSSRF)	Gyandoot
E-governance and civic information	Nil	Limited	Major thrust
Horizontal exchange of information by participants	Nil	Nil	Limited
Access to online networking	Limited	Limited and subject to availability of necessary facilities in the kiosks.	Limited

by the supporters and functionaries of these organizations. While it is widely accepted that ICTs are increasingly being used as a vehicle for channelling social protests and mobilizing resources for social struggles (Castells 2001), the ability of the ICT-CSOs to take up this task appeared to be limited. Participation in the projects by the marginalized and vulnerable communities was more often than not dictated by the facilities as well as the social dynamics that defined their existence.

Castells (2001) identifies three major characteristics that are shared by community telecentres as they become operational in urban settings. First, he regards these centres as providing information from local authorities and various civic associations, acting as a 'technologically updated bulletin of city life'. The ITC initiatives in rural India have not yet been able to deliver on this count, as the network society is technologically as well as financially limited by constraints of resources. IVRP, probably recognizing this limitation, was publishing a printed newspaper called *Namma Ooru Sheyvi*, meaning 'Our Local News', which was not available online or in any electronic format!

In the case of TARAkendras, there was practically no information on governance that could be communicated to participants and not surprisingly, many of the TARAkendra managers had not even heard about e-governance. However, probably since Gyandoot had been tailor-made to provide e-governance information, most of its activities involved C2G (i.e., citizen to government) interface.

The second factor that Castells identifies is the ability of these centres to organize horizontal exchange of information and electronic conversation among participants in the network. In the case of IVRP and TARAkendras, however, such activities were not popular, and apart from a handful of anecdotal references of horizontal exchange between participants and one-dimensional flow of information from the main centre to subcentres, there

Figure 4.2. IVRP's offline newspaper *Namma ooru Seythi* (Our Local News).

(The images are of the issues released on 15 March 2002 and 1 July 2002 providing lead news about women's rights in the police station and welfare schemes for fishers respectively. The logo of the paper shows the village enabled by computer-generated messages transmitted through the speaker system across the village.)

was hardly any networking among participants. Gyandoot reported more instances of participants engaging in information exchange.

Third, Castells mentions the access to online networking for individuals and organizations that have been long outside the Internet. In this respect, too, TARAkendras, IVRP and Gyandoot did not appear to be making a remarkable showing, although, given the facilities, the potential for offering these services was indeed bright.

Nevertheless, the initiators of these projects often attempt to portray them as holding out emancipatory potential and the image of social movements. The examples, which are often quoted to support this, were at best exaggerated and distorted accounts of inconsequential incidents or at worst, mere figments of imagination. The degree of distortion and exaggeration increases with each iteration of the example. The story relating to MSSRF's Embalam centre is a case in point. As in the case of many other MSSRF centres, the space for housing the information shop was provided by the Temple Trust in this village. The room given by the temple was one adjoining its outer wall near the main entrance. This aroused the imagination of the correspondent of the *New York Times*, who reported this as follows:

Embalam, India – In this village at the Southern tip of India, the century old temple has two doors. Through one lies tradition. People from the lowest castes and menstruating women cannot pass its threshold. Inside, the devout perform daily poojas, offering prayers. Through the second door lies the Information Age and anyone can enter. In a rare *social experiment*, the village elders have allowed one side of the temple to house two solar-powered computers that give this poor village a wealth of data, from price of rice to the day's most auspicious hours. (Dugger 2000)

As a matter of fact, the temple does have more than one door (see Figure 4.3). However, the second door mentioned in this passage (the roll-down shutter door to the left of the temple gate, which is the first door referred to) does not open to the temple, but to the 'information age' room only, and this room does not even have ventilation facing the temple. The emphasis on menstruating women is far off the mark, since all temples in India prohibit their entry, with this temple being no exception. The temple had allowed entry to Dalits several years before the project was conceived, according to accounts of the villagers, including volunteers at the kiosk. In fact, a Dalit representative was a sitting member of the board of trustees of the temple, and Dalit meetings were often held within its premises. However, by the time the jury of the Stockholm Challenge Award interpreted the *New York Times* report, the story had developed further:

Because of this project, some traditional barriers have fallen. For example, a temple that formerly excluded low-caste people now opens *its doors to everyone so they may use computers*. This project is a wonderful example of the benefits of IT, and of the power of information and opportunity. (Quoted in MSSRF 2002, 137, emphasis added).

The member of the temple's trust, who was also a party to the decision to let the kiosk use its outer room, is now a portrayed as a beneficiary of the social transformation brought about by the project. Surprisingly, the functionaries of MSSRF use this imaginary social action to consolidate the organization's image as a crusader against caste iniquities. Quoting Dugger, Arunachalam (2002) explains: 'Caste-based division is still a problem in southern India despite strict laws in force; our knowledge centre at Embalam has made a minor dent.'

My own enquiry provided additional information contradicting most of the claims about ICT-based CSOs initiating social action in rural India. Nevertheless, rather than scrutinizing the truth behind several such claims, we may raise the question of the potential of these CSOs to emerge as social movements. The CSOs operate under conditions predicated by the social and economic institutional structures and their ability to react is inherently limited by the nature of mediations into which they enter while seeking legitimation. They work closely with the village elites, intermediaries or

Figure 4.3. The 'two doors' and the Embalam kiosk.

temple trustees. This crucial factor is often undermined in the exaggerated accounts of ICT-based CSOs as vehicles of social transformation. However, it may be pertinent here to point out that ICTs were being increasingly used by organizations and movements with specific social and political objectives such as human rights movements and secular collectives. In the next section, a glance at one such initiative is provided to illustrate a contrasting experience.

Participation in Net-Based Social Action

In order to draw a comparative picture, we take a quick look at the operation and politics of a relatively lesser-known CSO, working in the arena of human rights, trying to use ICTs, albeit in a limited sense, to scale up its influence and scope. I have chosen HOPE (Holistic Approach for People's Empowerment), based in Pondicherry, for this purpose.[13] HOPE was founded in 1996 with the objectives of documenting and disseminating information pertaining to human rights issues, with a special focus on minorities and communal tensions. HOPE did not hesitate to seize the opportunity offered by the Internet to further its goals. Thus, it began to publish an e-bulletin called 'Human Rights Newsletter'. This was followed by e-group initiatives with open membership and moderated postings, called 'Communalism Watch'.

Although the organization was involved in online activities in a major way, it looked at its own cyber presence as supplementary to grassroots-level activities and offline awareness campaigns initiated with an intention to mobilize resources and people against communalism and human rights violations. It worked closely with movements and organizations at the national level and helped to coordinate their programmes in Pondicherry. One of the major initiatives in this respect was a successful linking up with the Human Rights Education Movement of India (HREMI) to organize a lawyer's collective named 'Human Rights Lawyers Forum' in Pondicherry.

However, the major ICT initiative launched by HOPE was its project to offer free web presence to all South Indian CSOs.[14] The website was designed with the help of 'online volunteers' and it is run with the meagre resources of the organization and little external funding. The website was actually designed by a person who was not personally known to any of the activists of HOPE:

> Online volunteers are available for similar projects. Here what we did was to register for at a net-aid website requesting assistance of an online volunteer to design our website. When HOPE registered and announced its political motivations, several people volunteered to help us. We settled for Mr. Sundar Swaminathan after continued correspondence for about a year.[15]

Resource crunch was a major problem inhibiting the organization in its e-ventures. One of the first offers of help actually came from the state. The Small Industrial Development Bank of India (SIDBI), Pondicherry, approached HOPE after the announcement of the launching of the website in the newspapers. The manager of SIDBI wrote a letter to HOPE stating that:

> As part of our support to NGOs, SIDBI has designed a special scheme to assist NGOs for acquiring Internet connection and hosting websites. The outlay for Internet connectivity can include license fee for Internet connection, hosting website, cost of hardware, computer modem, etc.

The letter also mentioned that the source of its information about HOPE's activities was a local newspaper that reported the initiative. The manager of SIDBI wanted HOPE to contact them for availing assistance under this scheme. Although HOPE holds up an anti-establishment political outlook, it was not initially averse to receiving this support. However, the offer could not be accepted because of some technical problems that arose as a result of HOPE not being able to meet some of the criteria for funding under the scheme. Since the project did not have any funding it was not possible to contact CSOs directly. A printed form for organizations to fill out was circulated through informal channels and at training centres for CSO activists. Some 180 CSOs had already registered on the site.[16]

HOPE was a politically oriented organization with membership in the Indian National Social Action Forum (INSAF). It was also associated with the People's Union for Civil Liberties (PUCL). HOPE's activists worked with people at the grassroots level, mobilizing resistance against human rights violations and creating awareness of human rights. Its activities also included issues such as child labour and women's empowerment. HOPE was planning a project called 'Internet for Social Advocacy' that essentially aimed at training CSOs in undertaking/handling human rights issues.

However, the use of computer-mediated technology for campaigning and mobilization had not led HOPE to define its activities as essentially driven by technology. The activists were aware of the limitations of this technology on two counts: (1) its potential to be used by dominant actors to propagate their hegemonic ideas and (2) the fact that in a hierarchically organized social setting, technology itself becomes a mode of revealing social divides. As noted by one of the activists:

> We do not believe that the success of our campaigns depend upon [the] use of advanced technology. But we will try to use it wherever possible to reach out [to the] maximum number of people. Depending solely on computer technology for ideological struggles would leave [out] a vast majority of people who are underprivileged. Our resources are meagre and we have to use them prudently. We are not certain if attempts to take information technology to rural areas have yielded positive results.[17]

As Castells points out, social movements in the Information Age are mobilized around cultural values:

> The struggle to change the codes of meaning in the institutions and practice of society is the essence of struggle in the process of social change in the new industrial context. (Castells 2001, 140)

Ideological affirmation thus becomes a crucial factor in identifying the social movement content of any organization. Hence, in conclusion, I will try to provide a comparison of some crucial elements that highlight the ideological leanings of MSSRF, TARAhaat and HOPE. I argue that the nature and focus of HOPE enables us to look at it as a social movement of the Information Age, while MSSRF and TARAhaat are social enterprises contesting within the realm of civil society. Table 4.6 provides a comparison of these three projects on the basis of some crucial indicators of their ideological attributes. It can be seen that the developmental CSOs have a very limited scope in engaging in transformative praxis using ICTs, whereas social movements have the opportunity to leverage ICTs for widening their scale of activities and area of operation. One of the basic differences between organizations striving to use ICTs for developmental action and those making it instrumental in direct social action, is with respect to their ideological orientation. Organizations such as TARAhaat and IVRP view technology as a medium as well as a goal. A loosely defined idea of developmentalism underlies their strategies and action at the grassroots level. Information technology is seen as essential in solving developmental maladies. In the most extreme cases it propounds a naïve technological determinism, in that it holds technology as the key for social change as well as economic development in rural areas.

The concept of sustainable livelihood, for example, would now be seen as a possibility, where computer-mediated technology is used in a local context to enable villagers to access crucial information. Organizations that try to use new technology for advocacy, on the other hand, might not uncritically adopt a deterministic position on the uses of technology. Organizations like HOPE would see the campaigns that they undertake via the net as supplementary to the grassroots-level efforts for social mobilization that they undertake. Creation of a technically skilled section of the rural population did not appear to be an agenda of action for HOPE. HOPE would rather oppose the technological domination of everyday life that permeates hierarchically organized social ensembles.

In terms of funding requirements and sources of funding, there are apparent differences between these organizations; while the developmental CSOs are in a better position to avail state funding and funding from foreign donors, organizations like HOPE would have to remain satisfied with donations and contributions from its well-wishers and fellow-travelers. While TARAhaat and IVRP benefit from either direct or indirect state subsidies, the offer of help extended to HOPE by a state-owned bank did not materialize due to technical reasons. The organizational structure and internal management of developmental CSOs are becoming increasingly bureaucratized, and such a vertically organized form of internal governance does not appear to appeal to the ideology as well as the mode of political action that organizations like HOPE uphold. Moreover, HOPE was not run by salaried staff, but social activists with a cause, while the key personnel involved in TARAhaat and IVRP were salaried staff. The kiosks in the case of IVRP were managed by volunteers, who are mostly unpaid, and TARAhaat managers were franchisees who had invested their capital in setting up their kiosks. These differences have an important bearing in defining their relations with the state. While

Table 4.6. Ideological milieu of civil society-based ICT initiatives.

Features / Project	IVR Project	TARAkendras	HOPE
Location	Pondicherry and Dindigal	Bundlekund and Bhatinda	Pondicherry
Objective	ICT for development	ICT for development	ICT for advocacy
Orientation	Developmental initiatives for poverty alleviation and food security	Market-based developmental initiatives for economic growth	Protest movements and social action
Social perspective	Developmentalism	Developmentalism	Social radicalism, humanism
Target group	Local community	Local community	CSOs/social activists, citizens
External funding	Availing	Availing	Not availing
Government funding	Availing	Availing	Not Aavailing
Relation with other CSOs	Weak	Weak	Strong
Management	Vertical and bureaucratic	Vertical and bureaucratic	Informal
Human resources	Salaried staff and local volunteers	Salaried staff and franchisees	Social activists
Specific ICT intervention	Collection and dissemination of locale-specific information relating to agricultural prices, central and state government schemes, health care, cattle diseases, weather, etc. User fees nominal.	Delivering education, information, services, and online marketing for rural consumers via the Internet and kiosks. Providing cost-effective gateway for larger corporations to rural markets. Depends on user fees, membership fees and commissions for profit.	Collection and dissemination of information on human rights violations, communal tensions, social problems, etc. Imparting training and building databases for CSOs working in South India.

Technology	Motorola VHF business radios for instantaneous communication and data transmission between the villages and the hub. 'Spread Spectrum Technology' introduced in three kiosks.	Extended C-Band VSAT units initially to connect 10 computers in six rural kiosks currently subsidized by Hughes-Escorts. This is optional and supplements phone connections or WLL connections already in vogue in kiosks.	Launching discussion groups, websites and e-newsletters in borrowed cyber space.
Current thrust	Withdraw from existing projects; move on to other regions	Consolidate existing projects and move on to other regions	Launch Internet-based training on advocacy for CSOs
Relationship with state Agencies	Weak	Weak	Conflicting
Links with private sector	Weak	Strong	Nil
Sustainability	Conditional	Conditional	Conditional

the developmental CSOs envisage a smooth and cordial relationship with the state and its agencies as the ideal environment for them to operate in (although in most cases this ideal is not accomplished), HOPE attempts to highlight the policy failures as well as state positions that they think create communal tensions, and protest against the human rights violations in which the state is covertly or overtly involved. Moreover, HOPE was committed to setting up effective organizational mechanisms, such as lawyer's collectives, to oversee the state's record on human rights and communalism.

ICTs and Limits of Developmental CSOs

MSSRF and TARAhaat are social enterprises operating within the realm of civil society, while Gyandoot is a semi-autonomous NGO with notional relationship to civil society. These developmental CSOs and quasi-NGOs appear to have a very limited scope in engaging in social transformative praxis using ICTs. Organizations such as TARAhaat, Gyandoot and MSSRF view technology as a medium as well as a goal, with a loosely defined idea of developmentalism motivating their strategies and actions at the grassroots level. These organizations tend to view information technology as the most crucial factor in solving developmental maladies and social inequality. The concept of sustainable livelihoods, for example, would now be seen as a possibility, where computer-mediated technology is used in a local context to enable villagers to access a crucial lack of information.

The question of actual participation by vulnerable and marginalized communities in ICT-based developmental projects has not received serious attention from most commentators of these initiatives in rural India. More often than not, the claims made by the CSOs on behalf of the underprivileged, including women, are considered to be valid in confirming the hypothesis that information technology is a gender and caste equalizer in the context of rural South Asia. The corollary is that the emerging rural network society is less hierarchical and inclusive than the existing social organization in these societies. A reality check in terms of actual participation and an analysis of the dimensions of nonparticipation has been enormously revelatory. Nonparticipation would imply social exclusion as the Internet becomes the dominant domain of the public sphere as well as the site of governmental action and service delivery. Computer illiteracy may emerge as a structural disadvantage, as computer-mediated communication and action becomes more widespread in the everyday life of villagers in shaping the contours of a rural network society.

Contrary to the conventional wisdom that the question of inclusion is fundamentally a matter of choice rather than structure, and the belief that the only means to overcome the problem of social exclusion is added emphasis on the role of awareness building, conscious design and incorporation of gender concerns, our study reveals that the overarching structures of social barriers appear to be far more constraining in the Indian rural setting. Developmental NGOs have inherent limitations in donning the role of social movements. In the Indian context, the analysis of the patterns of inclusion in rural cyber-kiosks shows that nonparticipation, particularly of women, is a critical drawback in ICT-based projects. Contrary to popular belief, these social enterprises are not inclusive enough, and the social factors that perpetuate inequalities in rural areas are in fact reinforced by the projects – rather than eliminating them. The participation of women and the underprivileged in these projects is abysmally low and this is in striking contrast to the projected image of these initiatives as being overtly sensitive to issues of gender and social divisions. Therefore, ICT-based NGOs are often wrongly credited with social achievements that decades of social and political interventions and struggles have been striving to attain, such as reducing gender inequalities and mitigating caste oppression. The trajectories of these organizations clearly suggest that such claims are devoid of genuine historical and empirical support.

One rather less-explored area of ICT based intervention is in the domain of social action that aims at consolidating ideological and political perspectives to combat social maladies such as human rights violations and communalism. While the potential for using the Internet as a medium through which social action could be mobilized, its success depends heavily upon factors of resource availability and participation. But unlike CSO initiatives such as IVRP, TARAKendras and Gyandoot, the nature and focus of initiatives like HOPE enables us to look at them as social movements of the Information Age.

Chapter 5

INNOVATING FOR THE RURAL
NETWORK SOCIETY

The Appropriate Technology for the Masses

One of the important questions that CSOs attempting to play a pivotal role in moulding a rural network society had to address was that of technology innovation. There were at least two major questions that they needed to answer in this domain. The first was the way in which existing technology could be adapted for the rural environment. The second was with respect to the need for promoting a series of inventions and innovations wherever the existing technological mix was found to be inadequate to launch the carefully planned ICT projects. However, the powerful and pervasive discourse on the use of ICTs that captured the imagination of a wide spectrum of academics, technicians, CSO activists and development practitioners in India, was not followed up with adequate coordinated efforts to understand the needs of each community and to evolve suitable technological packages that attended to their specific requirements. Nevertheless, many organizations and 'social venture capitalists' realized the need for developing appropriate technology for rural masses to get inroads into the markets at the 'bottom of the pyramid' (BoP). It was believed that the social bottlenecks in reaching the poorest of the consumers could be addressed by the developing imaginative and cost-effective ICT innovations.

The ICT-based activities of CSOs were characterized by a focus on providing individuals direct access to technology, and the protocols of their delivery mechanisms were dominated by a high level of technology applications. Consequently, the thrust on developing a series of inventions and innovations formed the major aspect that defined the character of many of the CSO initiatives. At least from the point of view of the scale and intensity of operations that the CSOs mapped for themselves, it was evident that the technological content of the proposed projects was understood to be playing a crucial part in facilitating the interventions. Almost bordering on a technological determinist position on the role of technology in ushering in social transformation, these organizations began to realize that legitimation for their development initiatives had to emerge from their potential to demonstrate that cheap but effective ICTs could indeed be made available for rural masses. The slogan 'ICTs for social development' emerged as irresistibly appealing. Not surprisingly, the notion of development was underproblematized in these mostly propagandist discussions and hence, the fallacies in conceptualizing ICT as an enabling artefact for national development (Sein and Harindranath 2004), and the dilemmas of democratic design of ICTs at the global level (Iversen et al. 2004) and regional level (Parthasarathy and Srinivasan 2008) did not receive adequate attention in the literature on ICT innovations during the early phase.

In order to facilitate ICT revolution in rural India, it became imperative that inventions and innovations had to be generated at three different levels (see Table 5.1). First it was necessary to create the appropriate software and value-added information, either identified/imagined by the organizations themselves as essential for the masses or recognized in the course of the launching operations of the projects through need-assessment exercises. The second imperative was to develop/adapt terminal equipment for user interface. The third level involved organizing/managing equipment and arrangements for transmission, such as wireless or wire-line connectivity. Each of these

Table 5.1. ICT requirements of early CSO interventions.

Level of invention/ innovation	Type of gadget/ technology	Practical forms	Specific technology developed/ used	Agencies involved
Level 1	Navigation	Web page, Intranet, software, content and packaging	Local language interface software, horoscopes	Private firms, CSOs, state
Level 2	Terminal equipments for user interface	Computers, printers, phone	PCs, istation, Simputer	University, CSOs, private firms
Level 3	Equipment/ arrangements for transmission	Wireless/wire-line connectivity	VSAT, WLL	University, CSOs, private firms

levels, however, was a problem area in its own right, causing complications at practical field-level operations of the CSOs. Who will initiate the innovations/inventions was an important question that required an answer. The market logic of facilitating innovations appeared to be in conflict with the fact that there was no immediate market for them. The market had to be created, and development of a market for the innovations relied on creating an awareness and a stimulus among the poor to purchase the new information products and services. CSOs were obviously not part of the conventional National Innovation System (NIS) that could generate the feedback loops and benefit from a positive response from the major elements of the system, such as the state-owned research and development (R&D), University/Institute R&D, or Industry R&D. It was realized that operational dynamics at all these levels demanded a certain degree of coordination of CSOs with the major traditional players of the NIS. It is important to ask whether these processes eventually resulted in the integration of CSOs with the NIS and directly or indirectly influenced the formation of the proto-forms of rural network societies in rural India. In this chapter, an attempt is made to address these questions against the backdrop of two major innovative initiatives at Level 1 and Level 2 – namely, the Simputer and the corDECT WLL (Wireless Local Loop).While the Simputer was hailed as the ultimate technology created by 'Gandhi and marketed by Steve Jobs', corDECT WLL was celebrated as possessing the 'Midas touch' for India's rural telecom scene. This chapter discusses the complex social processes that eventually resulted in the collapse of the euphoria and the gradual restoration of realism and pragmatism. There is also a deep sense of disillusionment that e-topia has been defeated.

The next section will discuss the theoretical debates on the process of innovation, asking the question whether CSOs can be considered an emerging actor in the NIS along with the conventional players like the state, the market and the university. The discussion based on Table 5.1 indicates that this is indeed a theoretical and practical possibility. In the section that follows, I will further explain the rationale of this integration with a focus on the dynamics of the triple helix model of innovation. It is also important to understand the tensions and conflicts that integration of CSOs into the structure of the NIS will engender. Then the next section will provide an overview of some of the projects and attempt to critically review the assumptions upon which the possibility of scaling up these initiatives in rural India is often imagined. The subsequent sections will focus on two case studies. First, I attempt to analyse the story of the Simputer, widely held by the proponents as well as the media to be a solution to the technological constraints and economic burden of using personal computers for rural development. This is followed by an analysis of the politics of innovation in the case of corDECT WLL, which was described as an indigenous technological innovation for creating appropriate cost-effective transmission standards for the emerging rural network society. The final section will provide some concluding observations.

Innovation and CSOs in Rural ICT Interventions

Evolutionary theory in economic thinking has been a major source of stimulating debates in the literature on technical change and innovation (Dosi, et al. 1988; Hodgson 1993; Metcalfe 1997). One of the major insights of this approach has been the notion that innovation and diffusion are inseparable processes and that technical change and economic change are concomitant (Metcalfe 1997). Understood as national or regional innovation systems, these approaches emphasize the role of interaction of major institutions such as industry, the state, and research institutions (Edquist 2001; Elam 1997; Freeman 2000; Johnson 1997; Lundvall 1998; Felker 1999). Commonly known as the triple helix model, a new variant of the innovation systems approach has brought in the role of academia as central to this modelling, and provides immense insights into the complex network of scientific practices leading to innovations with systemic features (Benner and Sandstrom 2000; Castro, et al. 2000; Etzkowitz and Leydesdorff 1997 and 2000; Leydesdorff 2000). Nevertheless, social process that shape feedback mechanisms underlying the complex interconnections are not often given their due in the literature on innovation systems (Khan 1998).

The prime concern of orthodox development theory since its beginnings in the 1950s had been the economic growth in developing countries. In the wake of the decolonization process, several genres of theoretical approaches have attempted to understand and interpret social transformation in postcolonial societies. These approaches are cast within widely differing technological, political, economic and social paradigms. The techno-determinist models highlighted the role of capital accumulation and technical changes as important indicators of economic growth (Ayres [1944] 1962; Harrod 1952; Domar,[1957] 1982; Rostow 1960; Solow 1956). In Chapter 2, I discussed the context of the relative neglect of critical development theories in ICT4D literature. The political economy approach of the dependency school emphasized the role of international economic and technological division of labour and the specific core/periphery linkages and location of developing countries within the world order as playing a fundamentally determining role in shaping the processes of development and underdevelopment (Amin 1974; Baran 1957; Chilcote and Johnston 1983; Frank 1967; Slater 1987). The paradigms that based the analytical understanding of development on the social dimensions of governance and distributive justice looked closely into the internal dynamics of economic and technological policies and practices of national and regional governments (Bellah et al. 1991; Gasper 1996; Marglin and Marglin 1990 and 1996; Sen 1989, 1999; Sen and Nussbaum 1993).

Underlying models of innovation processes that inform these approaches are closely linked to their methodological and epistemological foundations. The growth theories of the modernization genre placed greater emphasis on a free-market economy with limited and clearly specified roles for the state. The approaches based on global equations of economic relations attempted to spell out the essential features of dependent technological development and technology transfer that constrain the innovation processes in developing countries. The models framed in line with reasoning akin to economic sociology borrowed their notions of technical progress and innovation from growth theoretic approaches. One of the major drawbacks of these models was their failure to understand technical change and innovation as an autonomous process moulded by the interrelationship that evolves among a welter of institutions taking lead roles in defining the contours of technological development in developing countries. The paradigm of NIS viewed innovation processes in a nation or region as an interrelated system of knowledge creation, diffusion and use in an attempt to overcome the limitations of approaches in which technical change and innovation were considered as residual. The NIS approach was initially developed in the context of developed economies, but later, the theoretical framework was used as a heuristic template for analyzing the processes of innovation in developing countries as well. In fact, it has been argued that the theory itself had taken some of its essential elements from early literature on economic development in less-developed countries.

The context of information technology expansion in developing countries provides an interesting backdrop for some empirical and theoretical reflections on innovation processes and economic development. It has to be recognized that there are several dimensions to the problem of ICT expansion that require closer attention. Many countries of the developing world, particularly the countries of South Asia, are now formulating policies and strategies to generate scientific synergy and economic productivity through the development of information technology. It can be seen that there are at least four major actors actively participating in this process: the State, Industry, Research (University), and Civil Society Organizations (CSOs).[1]

CSOs have also come to play an important role in facilitating ICT expansion in developing countries. Their relationship with the basic actors of the triple helix is particularly important. CSOs have become major vehicles in the implementation of government programmes for governance and poverty alleviation. With the expansion of ICTs, there are at least two major developments that deserve specific attention: First, many CSOs have started using ICTs on a large scale, creating a new pattern of demand for these technologies. Second, many CSOs use ICTs directly for developmental activities that they undertake. These ICT-based CSOs focus their attention on the dissemination and use of ICTs in the rural sector. The ICT-based CSOs thus attempted to create a milieu of innovation where cost-effective ICTs for developmental activities were being generated to cater to the rural demand for these products. The case of the Simputer is a typical example. There were also several other similar experiments, although they did not manage to gain the prominence of the Simputer. Further, the activities of CSOs in the area of ICTs have another major catalytic role in shaping government policies in this sector. In the triple helix model, innovation is essentially viewed as a technocratic phenomenon. It does not attempt to capture the grassroots-level dynamics of technology diffusion and the feedback that can ultimately influence the pattern and direction of innovation processes. ICT expansion, given the nature of infrastructure problems in developing countries, was destined to remain an urban phenomenon in the absence of an effective agency that could mediate and negotiate technology diffusion. With the massive proliferation of CSOs in the area of rural ICT expansion, rural connectivity has been brought into the governmental agenda with the urgency it deserves.

The state also requires the active participation and involvement of CSOs in implementing ICT-related projects such as e-governance. In the neoliberal political setting, the state does not aim to undertake the massive task of familiarizing the illiterate and semiliterate masses of developing countries with the use of ICTs. Collaboration between the state and CSOs on the one hand, and CSOs and universities on the other, become vital to this process. Industry is also assumed to play an important role in this context. The new demand for specialized packages and services created as a result of grassroots-level understanding of the real needs of rural areas can best be attended to by involving the industry. Nevertheless, how the dynamics of this new collaboration would unfold depends on the degree and scale of integration of CSOs into the traditional structure of the triple helix model.

CSOs and the Triple Helix Model

The major pillar of argument that supported the innovation system approach was its characterization of innovation as a nonlinear process based on analytical advances in economic reasoning contributed by the evolutionary theorists. Its point of departure from various theoretical schools of thought such as the classical political economy of Smith and Ricardo, Marxian economics, neoclassical economics, and Schumpeterian development economics was the primacy it attributed to the degree of interrelationships and linkages between the state and the private sector in determining the growth direction and patterns of innovation in a national or regional economy. The major actors in the national system of innovation were the state and industry, with historically specified roles and intermediation delivering a collective system of projects and processes leading to scientific knowledge production as well as innovations. The NIS approach comprised two different types of conceptualizations; one strand hinging on an understanding of the innovation process where the lead role among the actors was attributed to the state, while the other ascribed it to industry.

An implied concept of double helix, the analytic of a coevolution between two dynamics of state and industry in the NIS approach, has been found unsatisfactory in the context of the diminishing role of the state and industry's increasing dependence on the academia for powerful innovative interventions leading to the emergence of what is commonly termed as triple helix configuration of innovation. The new model reconfigures the national system of innovation approach to integrate the role of universities in shaping production, dissemination, and use of new ideas and concepts. The three-way interaction envisaged in the triple helix model adds to the description of institutional arrangements and policy dynamics where the university encompasses a third mission of economic development in addition to the state and industry.

The new phase of globalization is marked by changes in technological fix in the case of information technology, biological technology, and materials technology has indirectly influenced a more encompassing theorization of the innovation process in national and regional contexts. The industrial era was characterized by techniques of data storing in the analogue form using electricity and electronics. The new technology manipulates data in digital form with the aid of microelectronics, optronics and associated software. Biological technologies have been revolutionized. In the industrial era, industrial fermentation using enzymes and microorganisms formed the core of its technical package while emerging technologies in this field apply microbiological techniques to microscopic engineering of living organisms.

The triple helix model captures this moment of assent of new generic technologies with their excessive dependence on universities in the creation of innovative and entrepreneurial talent. The political economy of changes in the conditions of knowledge production necessitated a reconfiguration of state-industry relations and state-university relations, where the state's withdrawal from investment in projects for innovation compelled both industry and the university to come closer for more meaningful associations. The major actors seemed to have adapted to the new regime of innovation protocols defined by the emergence of a triple helix of state-industry-university interaction with universities taking a central place in the overall configuration. The model has not only given a new dimension to the innovations system approach, it successfully incorporates several institutional and structural aspects of the process of technological change that a coevolutionary model of state-industry relations was unable to comprehend. A striking example of this analytical advance is reflected in the new focus on the internal changes in interactions and cross-linkages between these institutions, and the cumulative and recursive effects of these changes.

Nevertheless, the extension of the triple helix model to the problems of innovation in developing countries is fraught with an array of institutional and structural problems. In the context of well-developed innovation systems, the specific interlinkages as well as the benefit stream that might accrue from it are clearer and more tangible. On the other hand, the usefulness of the model in capturing the holistic dimensions of innovation processes in developing countries is less apparent. The dependent relations of the industry with the international order, the financial limitations of the state, the quality of education in universities etc. are only some of the aspects that appear on the surface. If one digs deeper, one will be perplexed by the complexities of institutional and organizational rigidities that envelope the processes of scientific research and innovation in developing countries.

The state's role remains fundamental, having close linkages and interaction with all the other participants (Baark and Sharif 2006; Sharif 2010). Obviously, the triple helix of innovation had a significant role to play in the development of ICTs in developing countries. There is a widespread belief that international technology spillovers are becoming increasingly transparent and smoother with the new phase of globalization and liberalization of domestic economies in developing countries. But in reality, the 'digital divide' – as the gap between developed in countries in ICTs is sometimes referred to – is widening. This could be due to a reinforcement of the patterns of global economic processes, which historically and politically hindered the development of low-income countries, or the result of more deep-rooted structural problems of domestic economies in interaction with the rapid changes in the international technology market. The strategic significance of these aspects is underscored by the differential progress made by low-income countries in reaping the benefits of global information economy expansion. Consequently, a development-oriented interventionist state remains an important element of the innovation system in developing countries, facilitating the activities of other agents of change besides directly involving itself in capacity building and knowledge dissemination.

Industry also had a key role to perform. The increasing visibility of the information economy and the proliferation of technopoles the world over were beginning to receive academic attention and consequently, a large corpus of analytical studies had been generated. Majority of the new technopoles were situated in the United States, England, continental Europe, and the newly industrialized countries (NICs) in Southeast Asia and Japan. Castells and Hall (1994) argue that technopoles exemplified the reality that cities and regions were increasingly being modified in their structure. They were also conditioned in their growth dynamics by the interaction of major global historical processes. These included a technological revolution based on information technologies (including genetic engineering), the formation of a global economy that works as a unit in a worldwide space built for capital, management, labour, technology, information or markets and the emergence of new forms of economic production and management where horizontal networks substitute vertical bureaucracies and flexible specializations replace standardized mass production (ibid.). However, the strong drive of many regions to become the 'next Silicon Valley' failed. Castells and Hall (1994) argue that the magic formula often worked out by opportunistic consultants – namely, a small dose of venture capital, a university or technology institute, fiscal and institutional incentives to attract high technology firms etc. wrapped in a glossed brochure and futuristic name, did not help build a new technopole. According to them, what we see is a world 'littered with the ruins of all too many such dreams that have failed or have yielded meager results at far too high costs' (ibid., 8).

The triple helix model, in a sense, responded to this issue by bringing to bear the central role of educational institutions, that of creating a social space conducive for technical change and innovation. There are two types of interactions involved in this process. On the one hand, while the historical relationship between the state and the university is under siege, it is still important in many developing countries. On the other hand, the industry-university relationship had not been particularly strong and visible in developing countries. But this scenario is gradually changing, leading to much greater integration between these two actors, for reasons discussed earlier.

It is against this backdrop that the role of CSOs has to be critically assessed (Sreekumar 2003; Parayil and Sreekumar 2004). The issues of economic development and technical change in developing countries have to be addressed without ignoring the impact of human agency in effecting these transformations. In the case of ICTs, a huge number of CSOs have become major mediators of development in rural areas, expecting to enhance demand for ICTs and thereby acting as positive feedback loops in influencing innovation processes. While the importance of the triple helix configuration is well recognized, the activities of CSOs in the area of ICT-related activities entail the potential to demonstrate the grassroots-level impacts of new technology, and the feedback mechanisms it generates could probably influence policy priorities of the state, industry and the university. The manner in which a field of innovation becomes operative in the case of a rural ICT intervention shows that processes of innovation and diffusion are not based on a simple linear model as is sometimes assumed.

The concepts of the 'iStation' and the Simputers were telling examples of innovative initiatives that sprang up in response to CSO involvement in using ICTs for development.[2] The 'iStation' offers email connectivity at the plug of a phone line through appropriate software and a linked email service. This was priced around USD 150, enabling many rural users and CSOs to acquire it. The Simputers were available for USD 250–480. This was imagined as a pocket device that can read a SIM card, simultaneously possessing advanced audio and text processing capacity in several Indian languages. In the following section, I will look at the trajectory of the innovation of the Simputer and the subsequent technical and organizational crises that help us understand some of the key structural issues that are pivotal in addressing the question of ICT innovations in the rural network society.

The Simputer: 'Gandhi's Invention, Steve Jobs' Ad Campaign'

No other gadget has received as much attention as the the Simputer in the context of discussions on cost-effective and efficient computers for bridging the digital divide in India by both resolving the need for connectivity and providing a friendly user interface for the illiterate/semiliterate villager (Fonseca and Pal 2004; Lie 2004; Saxena 2009).

The 'Simputer' is a neologism meaning 'simple computer', indicating a hand-held computer conceived by a group of Indian scientists in 1999. It is a piece of equipment that received global attention, mainly because of the fact that its designers claimed that its potential to bridge the digital divide stems from the fact that it is both low cost and specifically designed for the unskilled rural user. So it was widely seen as a technology that would become highly useful in projects and programmes for poverty alleviation by replacing high-cost PCs as the major infrastructure for initiating ICT-based development programmes in rural areas. Its proposed highly user-friendly interface was considered remarkable for its simple and easy-to-grasp-and-operate facilities.

The Simputer, as a hand-held device, had, admittedly, very close resemblances to a Palm Digital Assistant (PDA). But the major difference that had been highlighted by The Simputer Trust, the CSO that promotes the gadget, was not particularly technical but social. The Simputer, they pointed out, was essentially designed for the rural user, particularly small and medium farmers who are either semiliterate or illiterate. It was claimed that the wide range of functions that that the equipment is able to perform revolves around an understanding of the needs of the poor farmer who is exploited by rich farmers, middlemen, and other rural magnates due to the nonavailability of vital market information, including wholesale and retail prices of farm products in distant markets. The Simputer, thus, was designed to resolve the three major problems that perpetuate the digital divide – namely, questions of access, content, and capability.

The Simputer attempted to tackle the question of access by reducing costs as well as suggesting a community-based use of the machine. The retail showroom of PicoPeta, the private firm that produced and marketed the products, had three different models priced at USD 240, USD 300 and USD 480 (see Table 5.2). It is reasonable to assume that a small farmer or an agricultural labourer who earns less than one US dollar a day may not be able to afford even the least-priced model. So, the Simputer Trust imagined a network society where a community of users would be availing the facilities provided by the machine by sharing the one-time cost of purchasing the Simputer. They assumed that just as it is common in rural and urban South Asia for people to use a shared public phone booth, the community could commonly own and use a Simputer. As regards content, the Simputer claimed to provide local language interface and translation along with icon-based interactive functions that should make it attractive to the literate or semiliterate farmers. Moreover, they hoped that the technical simplicity of the gadget would also make it easy for the villagers to handle the equipment.

The concept of the Simputer emerged from a genuine practical requirement, as described by a banker to an academic in November 1998. The banker was the managing director of the Karad Urban Co-op Bank with nearly 30 branches spread over five districts in Maharashtra. The academic was Dr. Vinay Deshpande of IISc, Bangalore. Deshpande remembers that when they had a chance meeting at a family wedding, the banker told him of a practical problem he faced in handling their rural thrift programme called 'Pygmy Deposit Scheme'.[3,4] As per the scheme, agents of the bank were engaged in daily door-to-door collection of small sums of money paid in daily or weekly instalments of probably two cents to three cents or a quarter of a US dollar in remote villages. The payees were given paper receipts on the spot and later, when the money was transferred to the bank, the agents had opportunities to cheat by altering the counterfoil of the receipts and entering smaller amounts than what was actually paid by the villager. The sheer cost of detecting this

Table 5.2. Amida Simputers: Comparison of the marketed models.

Model \ Accessory	Amida 1200	Amida 1600	Amida 4200
Processor	206 MHz	206 MHz	206 MHz
Permanent storage	16 MB	32 MB	32 MB
RAM	32 MB	64 MB	64 MB
Display	Greyscale (STN: 16 shades of grey)	Greyscale (STN: 16 shades of grey)	Premium Colour (TFT: 64K colours)
USB ports	2	2	2
USB Flash stick (Chikki)	– Model Accessory	16 MB	32 MB
Serial port*	Yes	Yes	Yes
Infrared port	No	Yes	Yes
Built-in speakers	No	Yes	Yes
Built-in microphone	No	Yes	Yes
Flip-flop motion sensor	Yes	Yes	Yes
SmartCard slot	No	Yes	Yes
Bundled software	Limited – Email, Browser	All features**	All features
Internet connectivity	Not included	Sify Gold (20 hrs.)	Sify Gold (20 hrs.)
POP3 email account	Not included	Free	Free
Intl. pricing (excluding shipping)	USD240 INR 9950***	USD300 INR 12450	USD480 INR 19950
Modem	Not available	Not available	Not available

Source: Compiled and edited from www.simputer.com; retrieved on 23 December 2003. The site is no longer accessible.
* 4 pin RS232.
** Email, Internet browser, news headlines, photo album, mp3, music player, voice recorder, Khatha calendar, games, paper, e-library, address book, notebook, Bhasha notebook, stop clock, world clock, education panchanga, health manager, conversion calculator, smartcard and calculator.
*** Excluding taxes and shipping charges.

malpractice and the time lag involved in the process were frustrating for the banker. When the banker came to know about the background of Deshpande, he wondered whether it was possible to design an electronic gadget with a receipt printer attached to it and capable of storing and transmitting the information to the bank's main office without delay that would solve this problem. He promised that he would buy 10,000 machines if the cost was not above USD 200.

Deshpande was inspired by this suggestion from a banker in the co-operative sector, and it caught his imagination that an electronic device with functions similar to a PC – but costing much less – capable of being used for the development needs of the rural sector in India could possibly be a leap towards bridging the digital divide. This led him to form a team of engineers and academics for designing the gadget that the banker wanted. They eventually struck upon the idea that the machine could in fact be a multipurpose one with many more functions than the banker had initially thought of. The discussions and experiments led to the concept of a hand-held device with functions similar to a PC, but cheaper and capable of running on AA batteries, thus cutting the Gordian knot of power problems faced by rural households in operating electronic devices.[5] The new device was also supposed to provide the facility to use 'smart cards', since it was mostly going to be shared by a number of users who could store personal information and retrieve the data whenever required. Further, it was also felt that the device should provide Internet connectivity to farmers who wanted market information that was often unavailable to them due to the lack of effective channels of information, leaving the small, illiterate farmer at the mercy of middlemen and arbitrary prices set by them. It was felt that the instrument, if it was to be useful for semiliterate and illiterate farmers, should also have a language interface that they could understand. This necessitated the creation of icons and local language-based interface with facilities for translating web information in English into Indian languages so that they could listen and understand the information available on the Internet. Therefore, the new equipment had to provide user interfaces based on sight, touch and audio, to be achieved through a browser for Information Markup Language (IML). If this was crucially pertinent, then the gadget had to have a built-in modem. Moreover, a device with all these operational facilities had to be inexpensive. Even though the banker was prepared to pay USD 200 for a simpler gadget, Deshpande and his team thought the ideal price line for the new device with the properties mentioned above should still be the same amount. To reduce costs, a GNU Linux-based platform was used; it was named 'The Simputer'.[6]

As soon as the concept was introduced, it received wide attention and appreciation. The two promised aspects that caught the attention of those interested in using ICT capabilities for social change were low cost and simplicity. The idea kindled a hope that it was possible to build a computer smaller than a PC and portable, but at the same time maintaining the technical standards and basic functionality that a PC can provide, but at about half the cost. The project looked reassuring for those who believed that the unskilled, illiterate, low-income segments of the rural peasantry in India entering the seamless web of worldwide information was a cost-effective technological possibility. The project received instant international acclaim and the prototype was hailed as a solution to the problems of underdevelopment, thereby reducing, or even bridging, the digital divide. In the interviews given by the scientists who designed the gadget, as well in independent reviews that appeared in numerous periodicals and journals in the early phase of the development of the product, it was emphasized that it was meant for the Third World poor.

> When the prototype was first announced two years ago by researchers at the Indian Institute of Science in Bangalore, the Simputer captured imaginations across the world. It was heralded as a way to help the poor and illiterate join the information age, and many predicted it would bridge the digital divide in a country with a billion people, but only a few million computers. (Noronha 2003)

In a short span of time, the adulation for the device and its unique qualities that mark it as a poor–friendly technology were featured in English, Italian, French, Swedish and a host of other language press, as well in visual media, such as the BBC. Its reputation spread to other Asian countries and many developing countries contemplated possible future collaboration with Simputer Trust and promised to buy the tool as soon as it was ready for the market. In 2002 it was recorded that the marketing of the product on a large scale had almost materialized. Harvey wrote with confidence in the *Scientific American*:

> I recently got a chance to evaluate one of the pre-production models that have been put together by the Simputer Trust, a non-profit organization based in Bangalore, India. This year Encore Software, a Bangalore based company that licensed the technology from the trust (not to be confused with the California software company of the same name), plans to sell thousands of the handheld devices, capping an effort that began in 1998. (Harvey 2002)

Periodicals such the *New York Times*, *Asia Week*, the *Times*, the *Economic Times*, the *Guardian* etc., apart from a host of publications in India (both in the English language as well as vernacular press), carried highly optimistic reports on the new technology and its prospects. Harvey specifically noted that 'it was designed to meet the needs of the rural villagers in countries such as India, Malaysia, Nigeria and Indonesia'. Soon after the Simputer bagged the Government of India's Dewang Mehta award in September 2001 for innovation in information technology, the *New York Times* nominated it as a significant innovation of 2001. Bruce Sterling wrote:

> The most significant innovation in computer technology in 2001 was not Apple's gleaming titanium PowerBook G4 or Microsoft's Windows XP. It was the Simputer, a Net-linked, radically simple portable computer, intended to bring the computer revolution to the Third World. The Simputer, officially unveiled last April and intended for mass production in India next March, is a small hand-held device designed for the rough conditions of rural India. It operates – without a keyboard – through touch, sound and simple visual icons. It translates English-language Web sites into local Indian languages, reading the content aloud to illiterate users. (Sterling 2001)

Sterling went a step further and affirming the poor-friendly attributes of the gadget, mentioned:

> The Simputer is expected to cost 9,000 rupees, or about $190; it is meant to be owned not by individual users but by village cooperatives. Each user carries a simple, tough, very cheap 'smart card', which will hold all his or her settings and data. No training is required; there are no upgrades, no broadband and no planned obsolescence. It runs on batteries. *This is computing as it would have looked if Gandhi had invented it, then used Steve Jobs for his ad campaign.* India has already largely succeeded in localizing cinema, satellite communications, cable television and radio. The Simputer is meant to do the same for the Internet. (ibid., emphasis added)

The whole mosaic of new technology and Gandhi's vision of appropriate technology fused into the imagination of reviewers, propelled by the description of the tool as one essentially designed for the poor for whom Gandhi cared most. The Simputer is represented as a product of modern technology that Gandhi disfavoured (an implied reading of Gandhi as essentially antimodern). Nonetheless, the Simputer, although a product of modernism, has successfully transcended its ideological biases, being poor friendly and cost effective and hence, would endear even Gandhi. Experts and scientists also claimed that the tool was easy to use, based on experiments and pilot testing among tribal school children as well as farmers in Indian villagers, testing that proved the user friendliness and ease of use among the illiterate and the unskilled.[7] Reporting on the readiness of the Simputer for in-the-field trials, Quereshi expressed, in the *Indo Asian News Service*, the belief that 'India's common man's PC, the

Simputer, was ready for trials and the production would surge immediately after the trials:

The numbers will surge with non-governmental organizations (NGOs) waiting to use it in micro banking and world space radio and Picopeta Simputers for a pilot education project in the tribal belt of Bastar in Chattisgarh. (Qureshi 2001)

While these discourses shared an optimism that local bodies such as panchayats, municipalities, farmers cooperatives, self-help groups in microbanking, and a host of other similar organizations in the realm of civil society were ready to purchase and use the machine as soon it was marketed, Indian newspapers carried news about the possibility of major IT firms such as Wipro and TVS coming forward to license the manufacturing of the Simputer.[8] It was also stated that many provincial governments (states) in India were also interested in buying Simputers in bulk, which would have a street price of less than USD 200, with the cost of production per unit dropping to as low as USD 100 (Saxena 2001). In fact, Banerjee (2001) reported that the Simputer would soon be launched in the Middle East and African markets.[9]

During the two-year period between the development of the concept of the Simputer in 1999 and the launching of the preproduction model in 2002, the gadget had been able to attract enormous national and international attention. However, during the next two-year period between the production of the model and its eventual marketing in 2004, a number of questions were raised on the uniqueness of the product, its use of the technology, its licensing policies, application and usefulness and the organizational structure set up to promote it. Venture capital had almost shied away from the project. At the level of technology in use, it has been pointed out that it was not much different from the PDAs that were available at the time. Branded gadgets like ipaq, Kaii, Zaurus sl 5000, Agenda VR3, LART, Pengachu PDA and a host of similar products marketed in India and elsewhere had architecture that closely resembled the Simputer. Moreover, unsubstantiated claims that gadgets similar to the Simputer were being independently developed and marketed in countries like China and Brazil also flashed in online ICT news groups. The price range for these PDAs also looked more or less equivalent to the market retail prices for the Simputer. In addition, most of these products were also Linux-based, which helped them to quote a lower price compared to Palm, which worked on the proprietary Palm OS developed by the company Palm, Inc. However some of the technological capabilities, like the smart card and storage facilities, appeared to give the Simputer an edge over its competitors. However, according to its progenitors, the ideal Simputer was different from other PDAs not just in terms of the technological content. They believed that the Simputer was essentially a technology for the rural masses in an emerging rural network society. This was precisely the reason that when the Simputer was finally brought to the showroom and advertised as the gadget for the urban middle class, several eyebrows were raised.

The first critical conflict that the CSO initiating the innovation had to address came from the domain of software freedom. The advocates of free software and open software viewed the original licensing policy of Simputer Trust as one that contradicts the basic principles of technology use and sharing under the GNU-GPL conventions. The trust was intending to charge a one-time license fee of USD 25,000 from firms wanting to manufacture Simputers if they were based in a developing country and USD 250,000 if it were based in a developed country. The Simputer hardware was, in theory, open source. Anyone who wanted to produce for noncommercial purposes was exempted from paying the license fee. The trust had admitted that its licensing model, called the Simputer General Public License (SGPL), deviated in important respects from the GNU-GPL model, although it shared the basic philosophy of GPL. It is:

(b)ased on the GNU General Public License but, due to the essential dissimilarities between the types of intellectual property being distributed, is significantly different. Everyone is permitted to copy and distribute verbatim copies of this license, but no one may change it or distribute changed versions under the same name.[10]

The position that the Simputer Trust would charge a license fee was viewed as problematic from two basic angles in the critiques posted in the 'open-membership-based' and unmoderated Yahoo! news group for discussions on the Simputer.[11] The first was that the license fees for both the developing and the developed world had been too high so that it would increase the cost of production of the Simputer, making it unaffordable for the masses. Second, it was also argued that the innovation had been the product of research by the members of the academic community of the Indian Institute of Science (IISc) and hence, only the IISc had the right to claim a license fee – if one was to be levied at all. The trust clarified that the innovation was made possible by private financing by the individuals involved in the project and, further, that IISc had been made an equal partner of the trust along with Encore Software Ltd (Bangalore). It was argued that:

With great wisdom and sagacity and what should be regarded as a unique experiment in academic- industrial interaction, IISc and Encore have

deposited any intellectual property on the Simputer from their respective
sides with the Trust.[12]

So what had emerged was a new model of innovation process where Simputer
Trust, a nonprofit civil society-based organization, was integrated into
the conventional framework of the NIS. It turned out that there were two
licensees for the Simputer – PicoPeta Simputers Pvt Ltd and Encore Software
Ltd. There have always been doubts about the claim that the Simputer would
help bridge the digital divide by making computer technology available for
the rural poor at affordable rates. Trial experiments were conducted in tribal
areas when the prototype of the gadget was developed. However, when the
product was finally marketed, it targeted a completely different set of potential
users – as evident from the mode of marketing drive used for Amida models of
the Simputer. The pricing of Simputers itself became an issue of contention
when multiple models with differential features hit the market. The basic
model, which remained low cost, had less than fifty per cent of the features
of the higher priced models (Table 5.2). From conception to development, the
idea of the less than USD 200 Simputer that would become the computer for
the poor masses appeared abandoned (Ganapathi, 2003).

The picture gallery of the Amida Simputer (http://amidasimputer.com/
gallery; note: the site appears to be closed[13]) had displayed half a dozen
pictures of potential users of the machine. The photos were indicative of
the change in market expectations. The first picture showed a teenage urban
girl walking past the shopping malls in M. G. Road, Bangalore in jeans and
a top, listening to music using the Simputer as an MP3 player. The second
picture showed the Simputer with the monitor filled with the picture of a girl
and it informs us that Amida has a photo album to store pictures. The third
picture was also of an urban teenager who was shown surfing the Internet
and sending email using his CDMA mobile phone via the Simputer. Another
image was that of a well-clad senior citizen in a cozy house reading stories
from Amida's e-library to his granddaughter. Similarly, the next two pictures
showed a rich housewife planning her party expenses on the Simputer and an
executive, sitting comfortably in his car scheduling his day using the Simputer.
The images of rural farmers, agricultural labourers and tribals earning less
than a dollar a day (as widely published in the national and international
media) and in whose names the gadget had received international attention
and acclaim, were curiously missing from the gallery. During the trial run of
the prototype, the media had published several pictures of tribal villagers,
possibly provided by the Simputer Trust itself, familiarizing themselves with
the Simputer. These images, however, failed to find a place in the picture
gallery of the firm that finally manufactured the product. At this point, Encore

Technologies reportedly tried to underplay the significance of the massive publicity campaign of the Simputer as a technology for the poor. The CEO of the company was quoted as arguing that the portrayal of the gadget as the computer for the poor and the widely circulated pictures of farmers in India holding Simputers were just part of a publicity strategy (Liu 2003).

The story of the Simputer reveals the complex processes that underlie the trajectory of social innovations. The Simputer has traversed the hype-cycle model that characterizes most innovations in the IT sector. The hype cycle provides a snapshot of the position of a set of technologies or innovations in the cycle of hype and disillusionment that characterizes a technology's path to maturity (see Figure 5.1). According to the Gartner group, the hype cycle depicts the progression of technologies from inception and overenthusiasm, through a period of disillusionment to an eventual phase of maturity. It highlights patterns of overreactions, typically originated by unrealistic expectations and reinforced by media effects. The original model was developed in the context of the triggering and diffusion of ICTs in industry. There was initially a technology or innovation trigger, which created significant interest in the community as well as media consequent on the emergence of a new possibility of ICT use for rural development. A better understanding of the rural economic dynamics and grounded reality through the interactions in the field of innovation may result in a more realistic and defensible project that is far less hyped than the original. If this organizational and technological innovation ingrained in the model demonstrates its capacity to produce tangible results, it may survive. Still, the survival will be conditional.

Figure 5.1. The hype cycle of innovations.

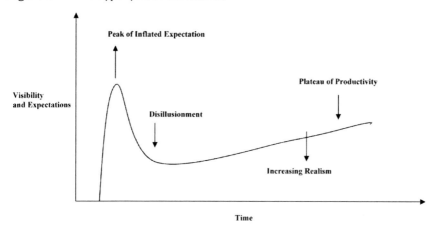

Source: Adapted from Linden and Finn (2002).

The Case of CorDECT WLL: 'The MIDAS Touch'

Another major innovation for speeding up rural telephony and Internet connectivity was an initiative of the Indian Institute of Technology (IIT), Chennai, which indigenously developed a Wireless Local Loop (WLL) technology called corDECT, based on the Digital Enhanced Cordless Telecommunication (DECT) standard specification of the European Telecommunication Standards Institute (ETSI).[14] It was described by its progenitors as an advanced wireless access system providing access solutions integrating both voice and Internet services. It was presented as a cost-effective WLL system that provides simultaneous toll-quality voice and 35 or 70 kbps Internet access to wireless subscribers. CorDECT was developed by IIT, Chennai in collaboration with Midas Communication Technologies and Analog Devices Inc., USA. WLL technology was originally developed to support developing countries with inadequate telecommunication infrastructure by supplying narrowband telephone services. It was supposed to help connect subscribers to a public network using radio signals in place of the traditional copper wires, and thus was regarded as a technology suitable for low-income regions where laying copper wires could be too expensive (James 2003, 90).

The corDECT system is best described as containing three subsystems: namely, the DECT Interface Unit (DIU), compact base stations (CBS), and subscriber access units such as fixed wall sets or portable handsets (ATIP 1997). The DIU is both an interface switch between the public switch telephone network and the CBS (a small, pole-mounted or wall-mounted electronic unit that provides 12 simultaneous speech channels) and the base station controller, connected to a maximum of 20 CBS with CBS serving between 30 and 70 subscribers. It is connected to the public switch telephone network through standard E1 lines and controls functions such as base station powering, call controls, PCM/ADPCM transcoding, and calls set up and tear down. The DIU also performs system operation and maintenance, and remote fault monitoring functions. Each CBS can be located up to four kilometres from a DIU. Each CBS serves one microcell, with a typical microcell radius ranging from 50 metres to 1,000 metres, and is connected to the DIU through standard twisted-pair copper links that carry data in the ISDN (Integrated Services Digital Network) format. CBSes installed without the need for frequency planning are equipped with antennae for 'talking' to subscriber wall sets or handsets. The radio transceiver in the base station could operate in any of the ten DECT frequencies on any of the 12 slot pairs. The subscriber access unit (handset or wall set) searches for access to the strongest base station and locks on to the quietest channel through the dynamic channel selection procedure. This ensures interference-free communication. Encryption in the air interface protects from eavesdroppers. The handset was a small, portable, battery-operated unit that allows subscribers limited mobility at pedestrian speed. The subscriber can have access to any CBS connected to one DIU. The wall set was a wall-mounted unit with an external antenna powered by mains, but with a standby battery pack. A wall set can be used three kilometres from a CBS while a handset can be operated up to 200 metres from a CBS, depending on the obstacles. The wall set can be connected to a standard fax machine or a modem. It was argued that its features made it competitive with rivals such as CDMA or PHS (see Table 5.3).

It is evident that the corDECT WLL system was capable of providing a relatively low-cost, yet rapid installation of telecom services in rural areas.[15] The corDECT system offered an Internet access speed of 35/70 kbps. The cost per line was estimated to be approximately INR 18,000 (USD 396), but the innovators hoped to bring it down subsequently to INR 10,000 (USD 220) per line (Krikke 2004). The effectiveness and utility of the technology, stemming from its unique architecture, soon caught the attention of the media as well as the state. The innovation was the result of the collaboration between the private sector and academia, although the state's presence could be seen in the fact that IIT – like IISc – is a public institution. Civil society organizations were also not involved in the innovation process. However, the politics of technology played out in the sector in the form of a continued

Table 5.3. Comparison of DECT, PHS and CDMA.

Feature	DECT	PHS	Feature	DECT	CDMA
No. of simultaneous calls	12	3	Frequency planning	Not required	Required
No. of supported base stations	20	68	Power planning	Not required	Complex power planning
Total subscribers/ base station	240	204	Voice quality	32 kpbs	9.6– 13 kpbs
Power at base station	Not required	Required	Subscriber density	Very high	Low
Services supported	Voice/ fax/ modem	Voice/ fax/ modem	Services supported	Voice/ fax/data/ N-ISDN	Limited data handling

Source: Compiled from Table 3 and Table 4 provided in ATIP (1997).

tussle between the indigenous innovator and foreign providers of competitive substitutes that had already entered the market following the liberalization of the telecommunication sector. The corDECT technology needed the state as an arbitrator, if not as a collaborator, when in the technology's diffusion and eventual popularization, the indigenous innovator had to compete with foreign multinational corporations (MNCs) under a liberalized telecommunication policy regime.

The major problem faced by the team of innovators was the opposition from the MNCs that were allowed to operate in India as a result of the drastic policy changes during the 1990s leading up to the liberalization of the telecom industry. They invariably used the Global System for Mobile (GSM) technology, a standard that evolved in Europe to universalize the usage of the mobile handset (TRAI 2000). According to Krikke, the launch of WLL services in the late 1990s resulted in:

> (d)ramatic decline in the value of India's GSM stocks, generated heated political debate, and resulted in a legal battle that has reached the Indian Supreme Court...WiLL is a typical representative of a 'disruptive technology'. Over four million Indian consumers are using WiLL instead of cellular GSM services. WiLL uses radio waves to connect customers to the nearest telephone exchange. (Krikke 2004)

The first wave of opposition from the MNCs was in the form of a bad-mouth campaign that the corDECT technology is obsolete (Jhunjhunwala 2001). The negative campaign intensified when the sops given to the MNCs in the form of import duty concessions were withdrawn by the government in 1999, which directly helped the corDECT manufacturers. The corDECT team maintained that the withdrawal was well in order, since they had always thought that sops were unjust and the timing of the announcement of the sops had in fact coincided with the successful field trial of the corDECT technology. It was reported in the media that the corDECT team had always resented the concessions given to MNCs. They argued that it was not a mere coincidence that the sops were given out to MNCs:

> (j)ust when our field trial was getting completed and the production was starting? The concessions were announced not for all telecom equipment, but for WLL. Was this done because the indigenous development in this area was to be thwarted?[16]

In fact, the withdrawal of the concessions, which infuriated the MNCs, was the result of massive campaigning by the corDECT team, which believed that the 'removal of this injustice became a Herculean task'. The mood of the corDECT team and their response to the announcement of the sops and their eventual withdrawal was summarized by the *Hindu* as follows:

> The entire who is who of the North Block and the Communications Ministry was approached by the winner of the prestigious Shanti Swaroop Bhatnagar award for innovative research in telecom technology last year. A large number of scientists also rose in support and even met other political leaders such as Mr. L. K. Advani and Mr. M. M. Joshi in this regard. The re-imposition of CVD and removal of concessional customs duty, according to Dr. Jhunjhunwala, should not be viewed as extraordinary. Since no concessions were enjoyed by other imported telecom equipment such as switches, telephone equipment etc., he wanted to know why WLL should be treated differently.[17]

However, the manufacturers and suppliers of substitutes continued to voice their concern over the government's volte-face in terms of the concessions.[18] Again, when a number of fixed-line carriers, including Bharat Sanchar Nigam Ltd (BSNL), launched the service in several urban areas, it was objected to by the MNCs and they opposed it within the Indian telecom Industry. It was noted that:

> GSM carriers, united in the Cellular Operators Association of India (COAI), cried foul. They protested that fixed-line operators used WiLL to enter the mobile market through the back door while they had paid huge fees for exclusive mobile licenses. (Kirkke 2004)[19]

Dr. Jhunjhunwala has stated that the opposition to the technology ranged from total disbelief in the ability to develop R & D indigenously in this sector to a more direct and open attack to ensure that it was never deployed:

> Egged on by competing companies, all kinds of obstacles were put up to prevent the product from being commercially deployed in India. One suddenly found out that the spectrum in which we were asked to develop the product was not even available with the telecom department. Specifications were framed for the Wireless [in] Local Loop product making it as different as possible from the indigenous product. Competing (and expensive) imported products were given tax concessions such that a locally manufactured product paid more taxes than imported ones. Questions were raised whether the product was really Indian and investigations were started. Court cases were filed to prevent the telecom

department from placing even a meagre order, claiming that our system was an obsolete analog wireless technology, when in fact it was a fully digital system. (Jhunjhunwala 2001)

He also maintained that while on the one side there were frantic attempts to tarnish the image of the whole project, there were several moves to buy them out (ibid.). The initial belief of the originators was that a liberalized policy regime in the telecom sector would work out to their benefit also did not turn out to be completely correct:

> We had hoped that the privatization of telecom services would solve our problem, as private operators should definitely prefer a lower-cost higher performance system. We were obviously novices in business. We had no understanding of the role that finance plays in such decision-making. Vendor financing was key to such sales, especially to cash-starved private operators, and financial institutions kept us mostly at bay. (ibid.)

The state and the judiciary had been sympathetic to the cause of this innovative technology, although final decisions regarding some of the crucial issues had a more protracted history of negotiations. In 2001, the Telecom Regulatory Authority of India (TRAI) apparently ruled in favour of the fixed-line players, arguing that WLL services were not outside the ambit of their licenses, being like a supplementary or value-added service, similar to the supplementary and roaming services being provided by cellular operators (Krikke 2004). GSM operators immediately lodged a complaint with the Prime Minister's Office, lamenting that their huge investment of over INR 200 billion (USD 4.4 billion) in cellular infrastructure was made redundant by the new policy. They felt that the government was violating rules of fair play and hurting business confidence, and scaring international investors (ibid.). Although the case was subsequently taken up by the Telecom Disputes Settlement and Appellate Tribunal (TDSAT), the GSM companies' views were disregarded by its ruling that the government cannot deny benefits of new technology to the consumer on the pretext that the policy decision framed earlier does not permit advent of a new technology, and 'the attempt to segregate wireless technology and wired technology into rigid compartments cannot be sustained' (Krikke, 2004).

WLL went on to enjoy a reasonable market share. The corDECT WLL technology was licensed to four of the major telecom equipment manufacturers in India – namely, Crompton Greaves Ltd, Bangalore;

Electronics Corporation of India Ltd, Hyderabad (with a tie-up with ITI for corDECT); Himachal Futuristic Communication Ltd, New Delhi; and Shyam Telecom Ltd, New Delhi. These manufacturers marketed corDECT WLL systems. Their buyers included MTNL, BSNL and many basic service operators in India and abroad.

The corDECT technology, nevertheless, did not become popular among CSOs. While MSSRF was not using the corDECT technology, Gyandoot, the e-governance initiative, had enthusiastically embraced corDECT. I have discussed this in Chapter 3. The technology did enjoy a reasonable export success also. It was exported to some African countries and Fiji. It also cleared the tests by telecom standardization bodies in Argentina, Brazil, Europe (ETSI), Kenya, Angola, Tunisia, and Nigeria. Field trials were successful in Iran, Egypt and Yemen. Apparently, commercial corDECT systems are also operational in Argentina, Brazil, Tunisia and Nigeria.

ICT Innovations, CSO and the State

In this chapter I discussed the various dimensions of the processes of ICT innovations contributing to the emergence of a rural network society in India. I have tried to analyse the dynamics in terms of the fissures and contradictions that mark the NIS, traditionally comprising the state, university and the private sector. One of the important aspects of the ICT innovation system as it emerges in India is the presence of CSOs, integrating themselves into the system through various points. In many cases, they trigger innovative processes by creating unique locale-specific demands for ICT products in rural areas. In the case of the Simputer, the private sector–academic collaboration has resulted in the birth of a CSO, the Simputer Trust, which provides licenses to the manufacturers. Although Gyandoot is the major project in the rural sector to make use of corDECT, many private sector players have begun to use this technology in moulding a rural network society by linking their kiosks with the help of corDECT.

The case of the Simputer highlights the difficulties in innovating for the poor. The story of the chance origins of the Simputer in 1998, and its long journey into the showroom of PicoPeta, illuminate several interesting aspects of ICT-related innovation processes aimed at the welfare of the rural poor in South Asia. The huge mismatch between rhetoric and reality is evident in the evolutionary trajectory of this gadget. It took an unusually long period for the product to reach the market from the laboratory. When finally arrived, it failed to live up to the expectations and imaginations that it had kindled in the minds of several of its supporters. From the idealized description of a technology for the rural poor, it has come to envisage a niche market of urban youth and the petit-bourgeois class. The product had clearly traversed a hype cycle.

It can be seen that state support at critical junctures has been vital for the success of WLL. While it is true that a harmonized relationship between the state, the private sector, and academia lies at the root of a successful National Innovation System, the fissures and contradictions in the system sometimes play a crucial role in undermining its effectiveness. The basic problem in the case of corDECT had been an unfavourable policy regime, which still continues to disrupt its potential. While the team of innovators had affirmed their faith in the working of a free-market economy, they felt themselves helpless against bigger players in the market and rushed to the state protection that they were able to receive, albeit on a limited scale.

The case studies, as well as my own modelling of the process of innovation in the ICTs catering to the demand generated by the development initiatives in rural areas, amply reveal that the tensions in the innovation systems are highly significant and capable of determining the course of technological trajectories. One of the important aspects of this complex process is the role of the state in arbitrating the tensions, which emerged as a critical variable, obliquely in the case of the Simputer and more directly in the case of diffusion of corDECT technology.

Chapter 6

ICT AND DEVELOPMENT: CRITICAL ISSUES

Civil Society, Community and ICTs

One of the consequences of the idea that ICT/community-based projects are necessarily virtuous was that most of the early approaches in ICT4D and Community Informatics did not critically examine how the historically formed social structures and social divisions within communities would impact the nature of ICT adoption and access. Ferdinand Tönnies, in his seminal study, made a distinction between communities (*Gemeinschaft*) and civil society (*Gesellschaft*) as two basic types of social groups (Tönnies [1887] 2002). He defined a community as an absolute unity that excludes the distinction between the parts; it is an indistinct and compact mass, an aggregate of consciousness bound in such a way that the parts cannot be separated. This is important because it does not allow any fragmentation within the community. This would then also mean that concepts such as class are not relevant for the community. Tönnies' definition tends to ignore class differences. The concept of community will thus be hiding social divides. It would then also mean that there would be no class consciousness – that consciousness be of the same nature, or very similar, is a necessity; the community is essentially the blood community, and family is identified as its nucleus. The advent of the Internet resulted in a renewed interest, both online and offline, in the study of community formation. ICTs were identified as a tool that can be effectively used to foster communitarian networks (Beamish 1995; Jones 1995; Foster 1996; Rheingold 1993 and 2000; Shrum 2005). How ICTs change the various dimensions of community dynamics such as socio-cultural, political and economic contexts of community networks, management of communities' techno-organizational architecture and intracommunity relations soon became a focus of research leading up to the emergence of community informatics as an important area of scholarly attention (Gurstein 2000; Keeble and Loader 2001; O'Neil 2002; Blattman et al. 2003). While it is increasingly recognized that 'online sociability is a fact of everyday life' (Feenberg and Bakardjieva 2004, 37), critique of techno-utopianism inherent in virtual community theories and approaches has also been emerging (Robins 1996 and 1999; Wellman 1999; Webster 1999; Sarukkai 2008). Nevertheless, ICT/community projects in developing countries were singularly based on an optimistic overassessment of the potential of these technologies for community development and networking. Looking into the varied dimensions of the social contexts of ICT4D projects was thus an area that required specific academic attention. The present study has been a modest attempt in this direction.

The advent of ICTs into the Indian rural landscape in the form of telekiosks was a sociotechnical process of great import and multiple meanings. It arrived in rural India roughly after a decade-and-a-half of experimentation in rural Europe. It is facile, but important to point out that the backdrop, lived experiences and the historical sociocultural and economic impacts of the phenomenon as a techno-social innovation varied widely in these two differing spatial/temporal coordinates of rural Europe and rural India. The differences were in many ways fundamental in terms of technological contours, resource mobilization, achievements, organization and impacts. At the same time, there was a common thread of rhetoric of the hope, aspirations, motivations, ideological ramifications and expectations that unite these efforts. Nevertheless, the story of the diffusion of the telecentre experiment in India has always been narrated as a unique and distinct phenomenon keeping the global tales of the rural telecentre movement 'untold'. One of the reasons why the European origins of the telecentre movement was suppressed or dismissed as 'a lost piece of trivia' (Patra et.al. 2009, 357) could be due to the fact that the ICT initiatives in India in the form of telekiosks appeared at a time when a new set of beliefs and convictions of ICT expansion, which Wade (2002) calls 'groupthink', had become a powerful global discourse. This groupthink, according to Wade, hinges on some key assumptions about the emerging global reality of ICT expansion, the foundations of which are deeply suspect. In his critique of groupthink, Wade points out that it maintains the position that the digital divide is the site of a major unequalizing force in the contemporary world economy. As a corollary, it assumes that this divide could be bridged by supplying more ICTs to developing countries. Groupthink also views ICTs as an 'inherently enabling metatechnology that can bypass or leapfrog institutional and infrastructural obstacles' (Wade 2002, 460). This would, in turn, imply the fallacious position that the standard cost/benefit comparisons are irrelevant in the case of ICT projects since ICTs form the fulcrum of a new paradigm of social and economic development. Accordingly, and with loyalty to these convictions, groupthink admits no failures, as a rule; exceptions are when they could be brushed aside as a lag in rectifying training inadequacies, tackling cultural constraints or eliciting political will. In practical terms, it promotes the belief that 'the spread of computers and Internet access itself will cause efficiency gains in firms and public administrations and lower transaction costs to all' (ibid.). The ways in which the major actors in the Indian story conceived and executed ICT-driven developmental initiatives provide a strong enough basis to believe that they attempted to spread the ideological slogan that more ICTs will strengthen democracy at the roots, while no policy solutions that challenge existing political structures and property relations were being deliberated (Gill 2004).

In this study, I took up four major aspects of ICT expansion in rural India that have contributed to a conflict-ridden and precocious formation of a rural network society. I have looked at the inner tensions and contradictions that marked its evolutionary trajectory through an analysis of the interplay of various elements that constituted its formative structures. I have argued that one of the important aspects of the telekiosk movement as it emerged in India was the identification of civil society as the major site of intervention, particularly in the early phase. There were several political, ideological, historical and practical reasons for this development. By the turn of the century, civil society had taken a predominant position in discourses on development and democracy, mainly due to the recognition that the state, for widely differing reasons and with varying repercussions, had failed in the capitalist, socialist and mixed economies to deliver the goods people expected of it. In the 1980s, with the dramatic political developments that culminated in the fall of the socialist world, civil society had earned a reputation as a site of rebuilding the ruptured fabric of a nation torn by totalitarianism and relative underdevelopment. In the capitalist world, liberal democracy was tested for its effectiveness and found wanting in many respects, leading to the belief that associational aspects of everyday life have taken a back seat in the structures and processes of social and political life, resulting in a deterioration in the quality of democracy experienced by the vast majority of its populations. In the Third World, in the wake of the failures of decolonization, the postcolonial states faced serious crises in terms of legitimation, and consequently witnessed mass upheavals against demoralized democratic regimes or military dictatorships. The weakening of the state in general is identified by many analysts as a reason for the growing relevance of understanding civil society as a site for social action where, at least in its ideal form, the tyrannies of the market and the state are absent.

Arguing that the other master institutions of modern society cannot function without the state, Evans (1995) points to the contradiction between the necessity of the state and the continuous imperfections with which the state performs as a fundamental source of frustration in modern society. His response is to analyse what makes some states more effective than others, focusing on only one of the state's tasks – namely, promoting industrial growth, and with a specific empirical discussion on the growth of local information technology (IT) industries in newly industrializing countries (NICs), in particular Brazil, India, and Korea during the 1970s and 1980s. The underlying aim is to understand state structures and roles, relations between state and society, and how states contribute to development. In addition to the classic roles of the state (both ancient and modern) – namely, making war and enforcing internal order, a third role has become increasingly central to the role of the state in modern times – namely, the responsibility for economic transformation, which has become a source of legitimacy in itself. Being involved in economic transformation has two different facets: first, it means becoming implicated in the process of capital accumulation, and second, the corresponding responsibility over welfare and distribution. In this process, welfare and growth easily become entangled. Moreover, states increasingly view the international system as a division of labour, and economic transformation is inescapably defined in global terms. Evans suggests replacing 'sterile debates' about 'how much' states intervene – pointing out that in the contemporary world, 'state involvement is a given' (Evans 1995., 10) – with arguments about what kind of involvements and their effects, which must be built around the historical examination of particular states. He chooses Brazil, India, and Korea as examples of undeniable state involvement in industrial transformation, examples suitable for answering the 'what kind' of question on state involvement. The IT sector in these countries is chosen because 'it is the sector most likely to spark a twenty-first century conspiracy in favour of development' and provides a good context to test the proposition that 'state involvement can affect a country's place in the international division of labour' (ibid., 11). Starting with the premise that variations in involvement depend on variations in the states themselves (predatory or developmental), Evans defines a state as developmental only when 'autonomy' (corporate coherence) and 'embeddedness' (bound to society in a concrete set of social ties) are joined together (ibid., 12). For him, this apparently contradictory combination of corporate coherence and connectedness, which he calls 'embedded autonomy', provides the underlying structural basis for successful state involvement in industrial transformation. Nevertheless, it has also been argued that the contemporary strategy of governance has proven to be increasingly incapable of coping with the aspirations of civil society, in its search for 'articulating a new mode of state-society relations that outgrows the conventional model of citizenship (Ku 2009, 506).

As I discussed in Chapter 2, the reinvention of civil society as a possible domain to counter the tyrannies of the market and the state provided the political setting for the ICT interventions in India in the late 1990s to be located in this realm. Consequently, CSOs took a major role in popularizing the concept of village telekiosks in India and elsewhere during this period. The disquiet over the bureaucratic state's eroding credibility as a reliable agency of initiating social change, led donor agencies to channel their funds through CSOs, prompting the government to sponsor independent organizations in the domain of civil society in the form of QUANGOs, which are, in a technical sense, autonomous CSOs, but controlled by the state through administrative and managerial structures.

Although there was a rather uneasy consensus on the need for finding alternatives to the state and market in the domain of civil society, it was not really clear whether these organizations were in fact capable of accomplishing the tasks they so willingly undertook. In the case of the ICT-driven initiatives, I have argued that the CSOs failed to deliver the grand promises made either by themselves or on their behalf. In an attempt to explore the contemporary practice of CSOs in using ICTs as a medium of social and economic change, based on a close analysis of the promises and shortcomings of CSOs such as MSSRF's Village Knowledge Centres (Pondicherry) and DA's TARAkendras (Bhatinda), I have shown that a wide chasm separated the expectations and actual benefits of ICT-oriented CSO initiatives in rural India. The popular belief that these social enterprises were rooted in the resources of the local economy had turned out to be an assumption devoid of a clear understanding of the grassroots-level realities. Further, it was also found that the potential for CSOs to evolve into replicable developmental models capable of drawing on local community resources for their sustenance was virtually nonexistent. Local economic regeneration through creation of jobs, developing local services and markets, providing training for enskillment and entrepreneurship, building social capital etc. – the professed benefits of these initiatives – were, at best, extremely limited. While incremental values such as exposure to new technology, skill development for poor children who can access the facilities in the kiosk, etc., that these initiatives could create in rural areas, appeared significant, it could also be noticed that both the service-oriented model and the market-based model systematically overstated their achievements, leading to a superficial glorification of the potential of ICT-based initiatives.

Structure and Agency

If the internal structural deficiencies of these models were important in explaining their overall failures, it was equally interesting to note that the state-civil society relations in ICT projects were marred by innumerable tensions and contradictions. The social enterprise models of CSOs had varying degrees of failure in making the state respond to their signals. Instead of building a strong alliance with CSOs, the state decided to ignore them in most cases, signifying a growing fissure in state-civil society relations. One of the reasons why these social enterprise models have failed to impress was in the area of external resource generation, due to their excessive dependence on direct and indirect subsidies by donor agencies, and their failure to check the capture of new technology deployed in villages by local elites. There are two important aspects of this reasoning that deserve mention. First, it was the Arthiyas, Natanmais and upper-caste temple trustees forming the creamy layer of the rural social setting who were more enthusiastic in assisting the CSOs in the implementation of the projects. Second, in the absence of external funding, the financial viability and economic sustainability of the projects depended on the network's capabilities to reap the benefits of the economies of scale – Metcalfe's law, which states that the value of any complete network grows with the square of the number of users, as opposed to a linear growth. However, the gross limitations of resources, coupled with a low demand for IT-enabled services, have effectively crippled the option of expanding operations. In other words, the rural network society, as it emerged in India – consequent on the proliferation of ICT-oriented CSOs – appeared to be grossly limited in scope and prospects despite the production of a highly pitched rhetoric on its immense benefits. The parables of success were less than sufficient to stand in for the tall claims of achievements made on behalf of these organizations.

Some of the concerns about the dynamics of the emerging rural network society, as seen in the case of the social enterprise model, were found to be relevant in the quangocratic models as well. QUANGOs specialize in delivering the promises of better governance through networking, using ICTs in varied forms. An understanding of e-governance as a technical process involving the transformation of traditional forms of governmentality was limited in many respects. Rather, e-governance is a contested arena of social forces shaping the trajectory of the evolution of this technocratic innovation. In the case of some prominent QUANGOs, such as Gyandoot, it would probably end up in the consolidation of and centralization of power in the hands of those who directly or by proxy, own, control or manipulate the technology. One critical issue that needs revision is the assumption of neutrality of technological processes enmeshed in the notion of e-governance. Technical processes defining e-governance are deeply embedded in the structures of power that reinforce the power relations in rural areas, where the local magnates play a key role in its implementation and admittedly benefit from this public good. As in the case of social enterprise model, the hold of the village elites on the projects was highly visible, and their collaboration was seen as a major factor for the survival of the projects.

While many of these projects are floundering and have been unable to break the initial inertia, the concept of networked governance has sown the seeds of a network society in some rural areas. Gyandoot's Intranet is a typical example of an emerging rural network society with scattered but conjoined nodes and a decentralized delivery system. Nevertheless, it cannot be forgotten that the micropower structures and technological aspects, such as connectivity where power relations get inscribed through modes of negotiations, are important in defining its scope and prospects. The rural network society that developed as an offshoot of networked governance could at best be described as a techno-social network with a latent ability to enhance citizen to government and person-to-person communication in rural areas. But the expansion of the network society would depend on the project's capability to display a synergy to combine the forces of both civil society and the market. I have pointed out the fact that the efforts of the state to forge meaningful alliances with the private sector and civil society have not met with any considerable success. Concerns about the relationship between state and ICTs emerged as a central issue in discussions on public administration in the context of the developed countries before they became popular in the Third World (Dai 2000; Margetts 1999 and 2003; Hood 2000). Euphemistic descriptions of the uses and potential of e-governance are reported from the developed world as well. A book dealing with the regulatory initiatives in the domain of electronic government in advanced countries makes the following observation in the beginning of the first chapter on the digital governance experience of the US government:

In May 2001, an interesting article appeared in the newspapers: the US government was reported to be more successful in its sales on the Internet than Amazon.com. Whereas the US government was reported to have a turnover of 3.6 billion dollars on the Internet, the sales of Amazon. com amounted to only 2.8 dollars. The news suggests that the concept of electronic government has expanded enormously in the United States. (Prins et. al. 2002, 3)

There are two basic approaches that underline the understanding of the emergence and phenomenal growth of e-governance projects all over the world – namely, the developmentalist approach and the governmentality approach. Governmentality represents continuity in terms of rule of self, household and the state whose ruptures will cause and precipitate crises in governance (Baddeley 1997, 64). Hence, ICTs and government are thoroughly intertwined (Frissen 1997, 111). ICT-based e-governance initiatives thus entail a reinvention of government in terms of the relocation of artefacts for provision of utilities and services to the point of direct contact with citizens and lateral integration of official records, making them available for users. It also involves redesign of governmental institutions (Bellamy and Taylor 1994 (quoted in Frissen 1997, 68)). A closer look at the question of governmentality in its varying definitions and analytical frames that Foucault himself has provided would help us understand governmentality as a historical form of power. Foucault argued that institutions such as family, school, prison, mental asylum, poor homes etc. are important for defining the totality of society and they work according to a logic of their own, producing certain knowledge of individual members as subjects. He attempted a history of the organization of knowledge with respect to both domination and the self and called the contact between the technologies of domination of others and those of the self 'governmentality' (Foucault 1991).

From a developmenatlist perspective, e-governance is generally understood as a concept capable of transforming the quality of administration and hence, changing people's lives. Its successful implementation is expected to ensure better governmental performance by reducing corruption, increasing efficiency and creating a responsive and transparent administrative environment. It is sometimes argued that given the low level of development of communication infrastructure in most Indian states, the prospects of e-governance are overly bleak. Nevertheless, the experience of various state governments have clearly shown that barriers to the implementation of e-governance can be overcome through a focused and strategic approach aiming at specified targets and allowing reasonable time frame for attaining them. Even in situations where the initial conditions for trying e-governance appear to be nonexistent in terms of inadequate skilled personnel or weak infrastructure, a gradual, flexible and reflective approach can bring about drastic positive changes. The fundamental idea that would inform the formulation of such a framework would be the concept of a coevolving programme with several structural levels. More concretely, the framework thus conceived should comprise a sustained attempt to develop infrastructure, train human power, initiate policy changes and explore collaborations with the private sector as well as CSOs.

The developmentalist approach often characterizes the e-governance initiatives as providing limitless opportunities for achieving various development goals set by the state. The e-governance projects started at the local level are more often that not considered as providing a new fillip to the implementation of existing programmes, as well as leveraging a more efficient and participatory launching pad for new programmes. The approach essentially attempts to highlight the need for creating new awareness, particularly among the underprivileged, on the immense use of computer literacy so as to enhance the level of people's participation in these programmes. They also emphasize the need for making the locale-based programmes sustainable by generating resources through various user fees and also by seeking the possibility of generating revenue through innovative profit-oriented ICT-based product/ service development targeting local rural markets. A conviction on the success of this strategy appears to the fundamental assumption informing the belief that ICT based innovative projects could become self-sustainable. In this book I have taken issue with the developmentalist perspective as well as the governmentality approach. The essentialism ingrained in these approaches leads to a teleological and fatalist understanding of the process of e-governance, particularly in the context of third-world countries. Both approaches entail a deep belief that the introduction of ICTs involves reinvention of the essence of technology – rational control, efficiency, productivity and cost effectiveness – in day-to-day administration. In the case of governmentality, it emerges as a possible critique of e-governance.

Nevertheless, as Feenberg (1999, viii) notes, it bases its critique on the generalizations about technological imperatives such as rationality, efficiency, enframing, etc. Ironically though, it shares the technocratic assimilation of technology as essentially functional and oriented toward more efficient organization of resources. It is important to underscore the social and historical specificity of technological systems, the relativity of technical design and absorption to the culture and strategies of actors (ibid., x) in order to understand e-governance from a nonessentialist perspective. Social constructivism provides some provisional but meaningful theoretical foundation to look at e-governance in nonessentialist terms. One of the important conceptual endeavours, from the constructivist perspective, to understand e-governance initiatives would be to disaggregate the question of technology from the differential perspective of the dominant and subordinate subject positions of the actors involved. In the case of ICT-based networked governance, the possibility of the formation of a rural network society was imminent and its protoforms, with deep crevices and conflicting layers of incorporation of different actors, have appeared in the contexts of projects like Gyandoot, where the person-to-state interface and to a limited extent, person-to-person relations, are affirmed by the technology of the Intranet. The relatively weak, but undeniable structuration of the rural network society is manifested in the narratives of networking facilitated by the design of the project, with scattered nodes connected to a centralized service-monitoring centre. Nonetheless, the rural network society is a complex social domain of opposing interest groups and a space where some of the political and ideological conflicts in the larger society manifest in newer forms. The fact that the technology itself gets enmeshed in the relatively autonomous logic of the network society partly explains the inertia that stops the inevitable progress envisaged in the visions moulded by concepts informing both the governmentality and developmentalist perspectives on e-governance.

This has led us to the question of exploring the level of actual participation by vulnerable and marginalized communities, including women, in the ICT-based developmental projects. The relationship between gender and information technology, as it emerged in the context of developed countries, has shown that both increased participation and nonparticipation of women are marred by problems that require special attention to resolve. This is particularly important in the case of nonparticipation, since it would imply some kind of social exclusion as the Internet becomes a domain of the public sphere as well as a site of governmental action and service delivery. Computer illiteracy may emerge as a structural disadvantage as computer-mediated communication and action become more widespread in the everyday life of villagers, thereby shaping the contours of a rural network society. The hypothesis that information technology is a gender and caste equalizer in the context of rural South Asia, and its corollary that the emerging rural network society is less hierarchical and therefore more inclusive than existing social organizations, seems to be less than accurate once a reality check in terms of actual participation and an analysis of the dimensions of nonparticipation are conducted. My analysis of MSSRF's Village Knowledge Centres (Pondicherry), Development Alternative's (DA's) TARAkendras and the Madhya Pradesh government's Gyandoot clearly showed that nonparticipation, particularly of women, is a limitation of ICT-oriented projects. These projects are much less inclusive than they are believed to be, and the social factors that perpetuate inequalities in rural areas are in fact reinforced by the projects rather than eliminated by them. The participation of women in these projects is very low, and this stands in striking contrast to the popular image of the projects as gender sensitive. More interestingly, ICT-oriented CSOs are often credited with social achievements that decades of social and political interventions and struggles have been unable to achieve, such as reducing gender inequalities and caste oppression. Such claims lack empirical support, and developmental CSOs exhibit inherent limitations in assuming the role of social movements. So it could be argued that the state models as well as social-enterprise models have been systematically overstating their achievements, leading to a superficial glorification of the potential of ICT-based initiatives. However, in the domain of social action that aims at consolidating ideological and political perspectives to combat social maladies such as human rights violations and communalism, ICT-oriented social movements have made some modest successes that are worth considering. The focus and orientation of initiatives like HOPE, working in these domains of social action, enable us to understand them as social movements of the Information Age.

Finally, as I schematized in Chapter 5, the emergence of rural network society has created a demand for specific types of ICT innovations at different levels of technology applications. In this study, I focused on understanding the processes that underlie two typical ICT innovations pertaining to Level 2 and Level 3 (Table 5.1) respectively – namely, the Simputer and the corDECT WLL. The Simputer was expected to replace PCs in the kiosks and elsewhere without compromising the range of functions PCs could offer, but at a lower cost. The corDECT technology was expected to be a transmission technology that would link the kiosks that form the basic element of the emerging architecture of the rural network society. In the case of the Simputer, the huge mismatch between rhetoric and reality evident in its evolutionary trajectory highlights some aspects of the difficulties in innovating for the poor. It had taken an unusually long gestation period for the product to reach the market from the lab. When it finally arrived, it did not reflect the expectations and imagination that it evoked among several of its supporters in the initial phase, when it was claimed to be an exclusive ICT innovation for the illiterate and semiliterate subjects of the rural network society. From this idealized description of a technology for the rural poor, it has come to identify itself as being for a niche market of urban youth and members of the bourgeois class. The Simputer Trust, which now holds the right for distributing licenses for producing the Simputer, is in a legal sense a CSO. But its formation and its eventual interpretation of public licensing of free software characteristic of civil society involvement in innovation remains unconvincing for many who view elements of corporatization in these developments. The product thus clearly traversed a hype cycle. On the other hand, corDECT WLL, which enjoyed some moderate success, experienced tremendous difficulties in negotiating its survival in a liberalized policy regime where a threat perception by multinational corporations (MNCs) providing substitutes to corDECT WLL led to protracted lobbying and litigation that to date remains unresolved.

Technology and Sustainability

This discussion brings forth three important points worth mentioning in the context of the dynamics of the emergence of the rural network society. The first point is about the role of technology itself. The belief that ICTs are inherently an emancipating social equalizer appears not to be founded on the actual empirics of their social mediation in rural South Asia. ICTs get enmeshed in the complex ensemble of the rural social structure and are invariably amenable to capture by rural elites, depriving the poor and the underprivileged through covert and overt methods. The overwhelming enthusiasm displayed by the rural elites in unequivocally embracing the new technology, and the spiralling scepticism and nonparticipation of the poor and the marginalized in areas where these projects are initiated, support the idea that a possible elite capture of the projects was already underway. The second point is related to the sustainability of the projects. The belief that these projects, in the long run if not in the short run, would emerge as financially viable and economically sustainable consequent on the extraordinary flexibilities of the technology in question and its capabilities to create an ever-expanding and innovative supply-driven market for information goods and services, also appear to be based on fundamentally flawed premises and assumptions about the grounded reality under which they operate. Different types of institutional mechanisms that have sprung up in the context of ICT expansion in rural India have failed to evolve for themselves adequate methods to generate resources internally by selling goods and services or from the localities they operate. External support from donors, the state or industry provided the necessary lifeblood for most of these projects to survive. This was one reason why many of them continued to remain pilot projects even after many years of existence. Sometimes, the dependence on external funding affects expansion, as in the case of MSSRF's Village Knowledge Centres in Pondicherry, where an ambitious plan to extend it to several villages was rolled back, admittedly at the suggestion of the donor agency. MSSRF had made it clear that it planned to extend the work to Dindigal and that suspended expansion of operations in Pondicherry was due to donor agency's instruction to do so. In other words, there were serious resource constraints that limited the scope and prospects of these organizations and projects. The resource constraint argument draws support from the twin facts of funding impossibilities: one is the failure to generate adequate resources internally through the social enterprise model, and second is the inability of the local communities and their local self-governments to provide continued subsidies. This forced them to reprioritize their developmental activities and reallocate scarce resources such as electricity and the space that they command for the operation of the kiosks. The opportunity cost of subsidizing Internet kiosks makes it a less appealing option for them in the long run.

The final point pertains to the role of civil society, the site of many of these initiatives by default or by choice. One of the common themes that unite this discussion, apart from imagining the emergence of a rural network society marred by tensions, conflicts and contradictions, is the implied questioning of the civil society argument. The belief that civil society is a harmonious site of social action and association, and hence a problem-free domain where any search for alternatives to the state and market could seamlessly be experimented with or acted out as a powerful supplementary force for the state or market, does not reflect the ground realities within which these organizations and their projects operate. The recognition of this crucial fact is important in redefining the role of civil society, understanding its fractured relations with the state and market, and the meaning of its politicization. Civil society is not inherently a domain of democratic action. It is pulled by forces that could manipulate its order and substance. As a corollary, it may also be pointed out that the belief that civil society is a realm of social action inherently superior to the state or market in terms of reduced conflicts, cost effectiveness in project implementation and increased social participation is also somewhat naïve.

The fact that these projects have enjoyed media attention, appreciation and public support despite their colossal failures in achieving the twin objectives of moulding themselves into a viable alternative to the failed postcolonial state as well as generating replicable and sustainable micro models of ICT oriented developmental action and enterprises, points to the need for a basic critique of the discursive power of the rhetoric. It is important to question achievements and benefits conveyed through a groupthink that endlessly reaffirms faith in the enormous capabilities of the new technologies. The layers of stories, narratives and anecdotes of success that envelop these projects' descriptions in the mainstream media and publicity materials is indicative of an implied technological determinism that underlies the ideology of these initiatives.

It is interesting to note that iterations of the narratives had been more hyped than the previous one in terms of content and conviction. From the story of the computer kept in a small room adjoining the outer wall of the Hindu temple in Embalam, which came to be imagined as inside the sanctum sanctorum of the temple, making the computer a 'modern' idol to be worshipped, to the representation of Simputer, (a gadget that finally sought buyers in an urban market, shedding its initial self-descriptions as a pro-poor innovation for the masses) as almost an 'invention of Gandhi himself', we can see the bold contours of this narrative offensive that supported a hyped discourse of a superficial glorification of ICTs benefits and achievements.

In the Introduction, Chapter 1, I outlined three major analytical issues that emerged in the context of understanding ICT-oriented CSO initiatives in rural South Asia. The issues raised some key questions to be answered. The set of questions broadly fell into three groups – namely, issues relating to the domain of civil society, issues of technology, and the issue of problematizing the state. These issues were analytically significant, since they formed the central questions that a study of the developmental initiatives using ICTs sought to answer. The uniqueness of these social projects stemmed from the fact that they identified civil society as the major site of experimentation, attempted to use innovative and what can be generically called 'appropriate technology', and in the course of the projects' evolution entered into complex and practically significant relations with the state and its agencies. I have shown that the presumption that civil society is an inherently virtuous domain devoid of the disadvantages that are usually found germane to the institutions of state and market is completely misplaced. Just as we talk about market failures and state failures, it is possible that failures in the domain of civil society can be identified once an attempt is made to understand the ways in which the organizations operating in this domain carry out their activities, assessing them in terms of the actual benefits and physical and social costs.

The groupthink that ICTs are inherently an enabling metatechnology that does not need to address the standard cost/benefit parameters undermines the sociotechnological nature of these interventions and their impacts in the rural countryside. While the donor-CSO relations are important in terms of analyzing the dependency of these programmes and in assessing their sustainability, it is equally or even more important to understand the contexts of the implementation of these projects and the complex social relations that form the backdrop of these experiments. A contextualist analysis of the civil society-based nature of these experiments was thus extremely significant. The lessons that can be learned from the analysis include several issues that emerge at the confluence of state-market-civil society relationship. Civil society organizations are likely to fail because they tend to ignore the embedded nature of technology. Technology is not neutral and cannot exist independently of the local social forces and resources. It is necessary to ensure that ICTs are appropriated by the local community, including the creation of capabilities and solutions that ensure maximum participation in the projects. CSOs have often been unwilling to carefully assess the actual usefulness of the technology, and the actual demand for services required in a rural setting. A more careful analysis and understanding of the actual needs of potential beneficiaries is required. CSOs also have a tendency to be carried away by the hype surrounding ICTs. On the one hand, their activities are frequently funded by donors who are attracted to the project on account of the hype (and thus without the hype, donor resources might dwindle); on the other hand, ICT hype often acts as a self-reinforcing 'ideology' that helps maintain the enthusiasm of volunteers but unfortunately, also obscures the likely problems. It appears that many new projects are also bound to share the same ideology of technological determinism, despite the increasing awareness about the massive setbacks. Attempting an apparently linear periodization of ICT4D as evolving from ICT4D 0.0 to ICT4D 1.0 and ICT4D 2.0, Heeks (2008) reviews the weaknesses of the earlier models and assesses the strengths of the emerging model while sharing the optimism that underscored the approaches of the projects initiated in the initial years of the ICT euphoria.

Ongoing efforts have focused on developing the type of low-spec, low-cost, robust terminal device that could work in large numbers of poor communities. The most high-profile of these is the One Laptop per Child (OLPC) project's XO and, not coincidentally, a slew of relatively similar devices is spewing forth. Despite 20 years of overpromising and underdelivering—from the People's PC to the Simputer—it seems low-cost terminals will be a central part of ICT4D 2.0. (Heeks 2008, 27)

Heeks (2008) further argues that there are indeed increasing opportunities within ICT4D 2.0 for engagement with development studies and such engagement would help understand 'where digital technologies fit into development paradigms, processes, and structures'. However, as Thompson has pointed out:

If developmental discourse is an important topic for study because of the unequal power relations it embodies, then the power relations surrounding the development and use of ICT in developmental contexts can be seen as an important element of such discourse. Approaches to the relationship between technology and peoples' behaviour vary from technologically determinist at one extreme, where ICT is seen as having the power directly to affect peoples' actions, through relativist positions, to social constructivist views at the other. (Thompson 2004, 104)

Thus, the second important analytical issue that I have sought to address relates to the questions of technology itself. I have shown that many of the projects consciously tried to use new technologies in ways that become useful for the poor. Although the concept of appropriate technology was not popular among the ICT-oriented CSOs, they implicitly looked towards gaining ground in the village areas by adapting and innovating ICTs in a way that was attractive and useful for the rural areas. From value additions such as information in the form of local language translations to the manufacture of terminal gadgets like the Simputers or transmission equipment like corDECT WLL, the attempts to provide appropriate technology for the masses were visible in CSO initiatives, making them part of the National Innovation System (NIS) along with industry, university, and state. However, technology is not a neutral force in society, and the failures of some of the major initiatives point to the fact that lapses in appreciating aspects of technology-society interaction could contribute to the stagnation and lower level of participation than these projects would have otherwise been able to elicit.

It is possible that, as the case of corDECT WLL illustrates, international market pressures and policy environment can often be an obstacle to innovating for the rural masses. Innovations with a social content emanating from CSO-university collaborations in developing countries would have to compete with MNCs for a niche in the market, and the liberalized policy regime may stand in the way of their attempts to penetrate the rural market. Support of the state in terms of policy interventions such as taxation and regulations may become absolutely necessary for innovations from developing countries to take root. Finally, the role of the state and the question of civil society-state relationship form an important subset of analytical issues to be addressed in this regard. It is probable that the failures of the state or failures of civil society can in certain cases be located in the deep crevices in the relationship between these two entities.

The fractured nature of the state-civil society relationship often forms one of the major reasons for the inertia experienced by the projects initiated by both the state and CSOs. The role of the state in building key infrastructure and creating an appropriate policy environment is also important. The milieu of civil society innovations cannot emerge without close collaboration and involvement with the state and its agencies. Thus, creating partnerships and collaborations should become an important and urgent agenda for both the state and CSOs. Formation of QUANGOs, an organizational platform different from government departments, basically initiated in the domain of the civil society, but most often indirectly controlled by the state, is often recommended as ideal entities for ICT-oriented development action and e-governance in rural areas. But these organizations have shown a tendency to degenerate into bureaucratic structures leading to 'red-tapism', nepotism and corruption, usually considered the hallmarks of governmental administration. Although QUANGOs are formed to integrate civil society into the state's activities, thereby closing the possibilities of degeneration through vigilance and participation, this goal is rarely achieved.

While addressing these central analytical issues, this study has, in its own modest way, attempted to penetrate this thick layer of hyped discourse, and based on field observation and reinterpretation of available sources of information, provided a more realistic picture of the emerging rural network society in South Asia. The study is however, limited in several respects. The number of projects selected for the study in each category is smaller than ideal. Nonavailability of critical secondary literature, coupled with the amoral familism (mistrust for outsiders) of the CSOs in sharing their closely guarded data and information imposed further limitations on the study. Moreover, in sharpening the focus and formulating a viable working framework to conceptualize the problems, the vastness of the issues involved presented intellectual and scholarly challenges that could only be inadequately attended to. Nevertheless, this study has certain clear pointers to future research in this area. Regarding the working of the social enterprises, the ways in which they get deified as harbingers of social change needs further analysis and interpretation. This would perhaps help to unravel the problems that restrain their working in rural areas in a more realistic manner and help to formulate correctives to their erroneous focus, orientation and convictions. Future research could also possibly throw light on the ways in which internal reorganization and administrative and managerial aspects of these organizations could be improved. Similarly, in the case of QUANGOs, future research could bring forth the reasons for projects' failures from the point of view of their internal logic and logistics of operation and offer correctives. Another future area of research that could entail from the analysis of the social innovation for ICTs discussed in this book is the conceptualization of civil society as a constituent of the NIS along with state, industry and university. This fourth sector has not been integrated fully and organically into the NIS. The problem of incorporation of civil society in the NIS and an understanding of the ramifications of such an inclusion offer an interesting, and yet largely unexplored, domain of future research. Another area of future research is the interface between donors in the North and CSOs in South Asia, where the politics of dependency inscribed in the postcolonial story of technology transfer and development aid for modernization is witness to a postmodern turn in the rhetoric of ICT expansion in the South for 'bridging the digital divide'.

The prime concern of development theory since its beginnings in the 1950s has been economic growth and social change in developing countries. In the wake of the decolonization process, several genres of theoretical approaches attempted to understand and interpret the momentous changes taking place in postcolonial societies. These approaches are cast within widely differing technological, political, economic and social paradigms. The techno-determinist models highlighted the role of capital accumulation and technical changes as integrative indicators of economic growth. The political economic approaches emphasized the role of transmuted international economic and technological division of labour, and the specific linkages and positions of developing countries within the international economic order as playing a fundamentally determining influence in the processes of development and underdevelopment. The paradigms that based their analytical understanding of development on the social dimensions of governance and distributive justice looked closely into the internal dynamics of economic and technological policies and practices of national and regional governments.

Underlying models of innovation processes that inform these approaches are closely linked to their methodological and epistemological foundations. The growth theories of the modernization genre placed greater emphasis on a free-market economy with limited and clearly specified roles for the state. The approaches based on global equations of economic relations attempted to spell out the essential features of a dependent technological development and international regimentation of dissemination of technical know-how delimiting innovation processes in developing countries. The models framed in line with reasoning akin to economic sociology borrowed its notion of technical progress and innovation from the growth theoretic approaches, although they, in the last instance, were interested in the way in which technology and innovation mediated social justice with economic growth.

One of the major drawbacks of these models was their failure to understand technical change and innovation as an autonomous system moulded by the interrelationship that evolves among a welter of institutions taking lead roles in defining the contours of technological development in developing countries. Even within an overarching regime of global technical processes, the national and regional innovation processes had assumed unique features with legitimate claims for targeted analytical studies. The paradigm of the NIS viewed the innovation process in a nation or region as an interrelated system of knowledge creation, diffusion and use in an attempt to overcome the limitations of approaches in which technical change and innovation were considered residual. The NIS approach was initially developed in the context of developed economies; later, its theoretical framework was used as a useful heuristic template for analysing the processes of innovation in developing countries as well. In fact, it has been argued that the theory itself had taken some of its essential elements from early literature on economic development in less-developed/wealthy countries.

Rural Network Society: The Politics of Transformation

The notion of e-governance as it is practiced and promoted in Third-World contexts has close resemblances with scenarios of neoliberal discourses of new media technologies that Armitage (1999) powerfully criticized as a 'pan-capitalist theory and practice of explicitly technologized, or "telematic", societie'. He argued that this discourse is primarily 'concerned with legitimating the political and cultural control of individuals, groups, and new social movements' through 'production, promotion, distribution, and consumption of new media technologies', both at the material and ideological levels. Rhetoric of e-governance and the euphoria over the social enterprise initiatives of CSOs and the state in the Indian context was also deeply enmeshed in a larger discourse of cyber-libertarian developmentalism that brought together the idea of economic development and neoliberal discourse of technology arbitrarily to rationalize ICT-based state and civil society interventions for social and economic transformation in the rural setting, a point that I have discussed in Chapters 2 and 3 (also see Sreekumar 2003).

Following Armitage (1999), and basing the analysis on the Foucauldian notion of governmentality, Navarria (2006, 126) argues that 'the concept of e-government does not only signify efficiency gains and economic benefits – for both the government and its subjects', but in the long run, 'the overall e-government project, broadly understood as a product of the neo-liberal discourse of technology and the contemporary development of pan-capitalism, could represent a greater and long lasting threat for citizens' life and freedom'. The mapping of the social and political constraints that marginalized communities and individuals encounter in their interface with e-governance projects, perhaps, has implications for the optimistic political vision of new media technologies as a decolonizing force facilitating development of 'cyborg skills' required for their survival under techno-human conditions theorized in the cyber-feminist approaches to new technologies (Haraway 1991; Sandoval 1995). Identifying the structural factors that envelop human/technology interaction in the rural setting in South Asia is thus an inevitable step in understanding social innovation and its impacts either initiated by the state or by civil society or by state-civil society partnerships.

Besides the ambivalent role that ICTs play in providing rural livelihoods, health and education, and access to markets, information and power for the marginalised and the disadvantaged people in rural South Asia, the deeper political issues of consolidation of local power relations and reinforcement of social divides including gender divide within the rural social setting created by technological interventions need further research and critical evaluation. Critical studies that look at what happens in the field provide empirical richness to the theoretical debates. Recent studies on technology, particularly *technofeminist* approaches (Wajcman 2004) have attempted to stress that while technology is viewed as producing and perpetuating social divides, it should also be understood as both a source and consequence of social relations. Wajcman's (2007: 4), analysis charts that identity and marginality are in fact constitutive for what is understood as technology and both marginality and its discourses are produced simultaneously with (new communication) technologies. Wajcman's attempt is to critique an essentialized view of both identity and technology with a focus on gender roles. It is argued that this approach emphasises both agency and capacity for empowerment of the subaltern subjects. The basis of Wajcman's observation rests on the assumption that the "new information technologies do not simply embody the same old social relations, values, and goals" and that they are "inherently more flexible than many of the old technologies and open to new meanings and uses" (Ibid: 4). Nevertheless, changes are mediated within specific contexts of historically given social equations and neither the inherent flexibility nor the new relations, values and goals embodied in new technologies call for overly optimistic assumptions about their social consequences. The cases I examine this book provides an opportunity to look at the trajectories of technological interventions as social processes involving multiple levels of mediation and representation. It must be emphasized that the advent of ICTs is an important technological process that sparked off debates about the future development options that lay before developing countries, which has some connection to the earlier discussions on the relationship between technology and development. The widely criticized techno-determinist model of ICT diffusion called ICT4D (information and communication technologies for development) has been a spin-off of the spectrum of ways in which the emerging relationship between ICTs and development were imagined and represented in the discourses on the limitations and technological possibilities of ICT innovations. The idea of 'leapfrog', a notion that sums up the euphoria generated by ICTs, provides the backdrop for understanding the nature of the relationship between ICTs and development in the ICT4D literature. The ICT4D approach maintained that developing societies would be to be able to overcome decades of underdevelopment and economic backwardness if they positioned themselves strategically in a technological regime that leveraged ICTs and promoted ICT-based innovations. A moderate critique of this position pointed to the faulty presumptions of the approach, while more forceful criticisms challenged the premises of its theoretical and ideological underpinnings. While some of the criticisms are still valid, and the new notion of ICTD (information communication technologies and development) has provided a relatively restrained understanding of the link between ICTs and development, the changes in the technological assemblage of ICTs in the last decade has necessitated a new look at the question of innovation processes and their impacts on development. The leapfrog model has remained largely idealistic and devoid of empirical examples to corroborate its historical validity. At the same time, several advances in some areas of new media technologies have been groundbreaking. The incremental innovations in these spheres have integrated hitherto quiescent areas of the developing world into a global network society, enabling them to share some of the new opportunities opened up by the emerging globalist economy.

The key to understanding the complex set of issues in the domain of ICT innovation is a perspective that helps place them in the context of a theoretical position that views innovation as primarily social rather than technical. The question of ICT innovation cannot be discussed in isolation from a range of political economy issues such as the changing nature of technology transfer, division of international labour, emerging patent regimes, spatial dynamics of clusters and cities and the circulation of capital. Equally important is to place the question in the local cultural and social milieu where some of the innovations are greatly impacted. This is an important concern, since both micro and macro aspects of ICT innovations have had policy implications as well as political consequences. At the macro level, ICT innovation has been associated with changes in infrastructure that would connect everyone to the global economy (Sawhney 2009). In a recent report on the digital scenario in the Asia-Pacific region, it has been noted that one of the important conditions for economic development in developing countries is ICT infrastructure development (Nair and Shariffadeen 2009).

It is argued that infrastructure spending not only generates a wide range of ICT products and services, but also creates spillover benefits such as the formation of virtual community associations, implying, in my view, that it's imperative for the accumulation of social and cultural capital necessary for economic development. Besides, Nair and Sharaffadeen (2009, 28) also argue that for nations to move up the innovation value chain they must focus on intellectual capital development, reinforcing interrelationships among key players such as industry, the state, and research institutions, adhere to good practices of governance, incentivize innovation and promote legal and regulatory institutions for social networking.

None of these processes can happen in a vacuum of political and social policy initiatives that would define the nature of the relations that each country holds with the international order. The problem with the ICT4D approach, in the context of innovation studies, is that it neglects the political, cultural and social dimensions that influence the direction of innovation. When we look at the micro level, the deep impacts that ICT innovations have at the grassroots must also be understood in terms that are not one-dimensionally instrumental. The technologies can influence the complex set of social relations at the local level in various ways. More ICTs do not necessarily mean more local democracy, participation or more happiness. ICTs affect the systems of power relations, social structures, and social divides negatively if they remain unmediated. State agencies and civil society organizations have traditionally been major actors in the social sector, thus it is not surprising that they were in the forefront of social and developmental initiatives based on new technologies as well. However, recent experiences indicate increasing involvement of for-profit corporations in ICT-driven social development projects. The marketing notion of the 'bottom of the pyramid' (BoP) has captured the imagination of corporate entities, inspiring them to explore rural markets for high-value products (Prahalad 2005).[1]

It is indeed true that the emergence of rural network societies has created a demand for specific types of ICT innovations at different levels. This discussion brings forth some important points worth mentioning in the context of the dynamics of the emergence of the rural network society. The first point is related to the sustainability of the projects. The belief that these projects, in the long run if not in the short run, would find themselves financially viable and economically sustainable consequent on the extraordinary flexibilities of the technology in question and its ability to create an ever-expanding and innovative supply-driven market for information goods and services, also appears to be based on fundamentally flawed premises and assumptions about the grounded reality in which they operate. Different types of institutional mechanisms that have sprung up in the context of ICT expansion in developing countries have failed to evolve for themselves adequate methods to generate resources internally by selling goods and services or from the localities in which they operate. External support from donors, state or industry provides the necessary lifeblood for most of these projects to survive. This is one reason why many of them still remain pilot projects even after many years of existence. The resource constraint argument draws support from the twin facts of funding impossibilities: one is the failure to generate adequate resources internally through the social enterprise model and second is the inability of the local communities and their local self-governments to provide continued subsidies. This forces them to reprioritize their developmental activities and eat into scarce resources such as electricity and the space they command. Second is about the role of technology itself. There are reasons to be sceptical and cautious: the belief that ICTs are inherently an emancipating social equalizer appears not to be founded on the actual empirics of their social mediation in developing countries. ICTs get enmeshed in the complex ensemble of the rural social structure and are invariably amenable to capture by rural elites that deprive the poor and the underprivileged through covert and overt methods. The overwhelming enthusiasm displayed by rural elites in unequivocally embracing the new technology, and the spiralling scepticism and nonparticipation of the poor and the marginalized in areas where these projects were initiated, support the idea that a possible elite capture of the projects is already underway.

In this book, the emergence of ICTs as a leading technological assemblage central to the discourses on development and social transformation, involving the state, civil society and the market, has been viewed as a political context of power plays, tensions and contradictions of technology diffusion and acceptance. The contemporary history of the rural network society is marked by partial successes of social innovations, failures of the organizational models created by the state, market and the civil society and the disappearance of the initial euphoria about the emancipatory potential of new technologies. Many of the fundamental questions in the debate on technology, development and social change were neglected in the early debates on the social impacts of ICTs in general, and in ICT4D literature in particular. Institutional critique has a special place in unravelling the complexities of such historical trajectories. Technology, posited as the sole solution to social problems, tends to reinforce determinism of both varieties – technological and social. The cracks and crevices that I have pointed out in the articulation of the contemporary rural network society in India, indicate dominant modes of ICT diffusion promoted on the basis of a deterministic understanding of technology and social change can be detrimental to the democratic assimilation of emerging technological innovations. Moreover, they also tend to take no notice of the larger political and economic forces of neoliberal globalization that define the contemporary nature of sociotechnical and organizational innovations for rural transformation.

NOTES

Chapter 1. Introduction: Exploring the Rural Network Society

1 This is not to refute the moments of social upheavals in Europe and their consequences for redefining citizenship, as has happened in the case of intense uprisings such as the 1968 students movement, the workers struggles or new social movements like the peace and green movements. Nevertheless, it remains a fact that the village in Europe is not the same as the village in Asia in terms of social and economic foundations as well as capabilities and entitlements of its inhabitants.

2 Qvortrup et al. (1985) provides a snapshot of the IT-based social experiments in Europe that became popular in the late 1970s and early 1980s. Articles in the volume discuss analytical and practical issues relating to such experiments in agriculture, rural areas, health care, local communities, social services, etc. The book was based on the papers presented in a seminar titled 'Social Experiments with Information Technology' at Odense University, Denmark during 13–15 January 1986.

3 For brief discussions on the history of the early phases of the European telecentre movement, see Bihari and Jókay (1999), Short and Latchem (2000), Murray (2001), Roman and Colle, (2002), Jókay (2002) and Rothenberg-Aalami and Pal (2005). For a comparative perspective of Hungary and India, see Dixit (2007).

4 In the Third World context also, rural kiosk experiments are being increasingly described as the 'telecentre movement' (Carvin and Surman 2008; Toyama and Keniston 2008).

5 For a discussion on fatalism and determinism of beliefs about ICTs in cross-cultural settings, see Licker (2001).

6 This section partly draws on Sreekumar and Rivera Sanchez (2008).

7 Dalit (lower caste) is a pan-Indian word that approximately means 'the oppressed', preferred by a wide section of underprivileged castes in India as opposed to the official expression 'Scheduled Castes' or 'Harijan' (God's Children) coined by M. K. Gandhi.

8 For example, the 'mode of production' debate (on the process and nature of transformation of feudalist relations in Indian agriculture) in the 1970s and early 1980s captures the social and economic changes brought about by the Green Revolution in rural India (Patnaik 1990). For a representative literature that analyse the political economy of agrarian changes in India in the wake of Green Revolution, see Rudra (1970), Patnaik (1971), Chattopadhyay (1972), Banaji (1972), Byres (1972), Bhaduri, (1973), Alavi (1975), Mencher (1978), Omvedt (1981), Bardhan (1982) and Sau (1984). Omvedt (1981) argues that the central question of concern to most participants of the mode of production debate was best expressed in the catch phrase, 'Will the Green Revolution turn into a red one?'

9 Chandhoke (2003) provides a detailed discussion of the set of issues related to the civil society argument. Also see Walzer (1998) for an exposition of the conceptual problems of the civil society argument.

10 See, for a useful discussion of the issues of democracy and civil society in Eastern Europe, Pelczynsky (1988), Wesolowski (1995); Glenn (2001). Some authors believe that the CSOs caused the downfall of the communist regimes. Tismaneanu (1990), for example, argues:

> But the rapid and apparently irreversible decline of communist power in Eastern Europe did not occur overnight. Nor is it the result of a sudden and inexplicably generous decision by those in power to accept a democratic model imported from abroad. It is, instead, the result of long struggle by a constellation of informal, voluntary, nongovernmental associations often referred to as 'civil society', a political concept that has become part of the story in Eastern Europe.

11 For a discussion, see Putnam (1993 and 1995) and Fukuyama (1995). Also, see Cohen (1999) for a critical evaluation of the notion of social capital.

12 Correspondingly, there has been a debate around the concept of the global civil society. For a critical appraisal of the concept, see Brown (2000), Kaldor (1999), and Scholte (2000). Scholte argues that the recent emergence of the global civil society is momentous, but what it augurs depends heavily on conjunctures. It is argued that the phenomenal growth of the global civil society necessarily challenges the authority of the nation-state (Scholte 2000).

13 For a closer look at the highly controversial struggle against the construction of India's largest system of dams in the Narnada River, see Baviskar (1997). For a passionate and informed account of the struggle and what the dams mean for the indigenous people who are being displaced, see Arundati Roy's commentary 'The Greater Common Good' in Roy (1999).

14 It has been noted that foreign aid programmes of many of the developed capitalist countries 'have identified civil society as the key ingredient in promoting democratic development in the economically less developed states of the "south"' (Jenkins 2001, 252). Also see Hudock (1999) for a discussion of the issue from the viewpoint of southern NGOs whose development endeavours are 'thwarted' by donors.

15 For a discussion on the virtues of civil society as embodied in a concept of civility within liberal democratic polity, see Shils (1997).

16 The discussion on social capital has generated a huge literature on its varied dimensions history and uses. The most influential and controversial exposition of the concept has been provided by Putnam (1993 and 1995). Harriss (2001) provides a useful discussion of the origins of the idea of social capital tracing its varied definitions in the work of Coleman (1988), Bourdieu (1977) and Putnam (ibid.). He argues that the concept of social capital has been used by agencies like the World Bank to depoliticize the notion of development by systematically undermining the structures of power manifest in the social relations in the South.

17 See the concept in Mitchell (2000, 5) as he attempts to imagine an urban e-topia in the wake of the information revolution that replaces 'old social fabrics- tied together by enforced commonalities of location and schedule'.

18 See Cohen, S. (1999 and 2001) and Williams (2001) for a philosophical discussion on contextualism.

19 This is a Yahoo! news forum where the members are free to discuss any aspect of the Simputer, including technical, legal and political/ideological issues relating to the production, marketing, improvisations, etc. The forum gives an opportunity for the trustees of the Simputer Trust, as well as the private licensees of the Simputer, to get feedback and provide their explanations.

Chapter 2. Civil Society and Cyber–Libertarian Developmentalism

1 This concept captures the role of individuals who are CSO leaders willing to make the necessary social and financial investment in profit-oriented social economy projects. Satish Jha, CMD, James Martin & Co., who has invested in TARAhaat and Drishtee, described himself as a social venture capitalist. Discussion, 6 August 2002, New Delhi. See also, Rangaswamy (2006).

2 For a review of the growth of rural information kiosks in India, see Sood (2003). For an early attempt to explain the proliferation of telecentres, see Rogers and Shukla (2001). A recent study reviews diffusion of information for telecentre use and sustainability (Pick and Gollakota 2010).

3 For an interesting collection of articles on varied aspects of community informatics, see Gurstein (2000) and Keeble and Loader (2001).

4 J. Petras (1999b 434–35) observes that the shift involves an attempt to divert attention from the sources and solutions of poverty. For him, 'To speak of micro-enterprises instead of the exploitation of overseas banks as a solution to poverty is based on the false notion that the problem is one of individual initiative rather than the transfer of income overseas.'

5 W. W. Rostow's Stage Theory (Rostow 1960) has been a favourite standard explanation of this transition within the modernization paradigm. The stage theory frames the societal evolution from a backward, traditional agrarian economy to a stage of high mass consumption when preconditions for 'take-off' in the primary sector trigger the 'take-off' stage and subsequently an industrial society. Rostow's book was ironically subtitled *A non-communist manifesto*.

6 A new philosophy of gradual betterment of civic life in poor countries is projected as the underlying rationale of this global programme executed locally and thought globally, faithfully following the dictum from an old Oxfam poster. CSO professionals have seen in this new philosophy a vindication of their work in the past and present. The following words by Muhammad Yunis, founder of the Grameen Bank in Bangladesh, aptly capture this mood:

> When I was arguing that helping a one-meal family to become a two-meal family, enabling a woman without a change of clothing to afford to buy a second piece of clothing, is a development miracle, I was ridiculed.That is not development, I was reminded sternly. Development is growth of the economy, they said; growth will bring everything. We carried out our work as if we were engaged in some very undesirable activities. When UNDP's Human Development Report (HDR) came out we felt vindicated. We were no longer back-street operators; we felt we were in the mainstream. (UNDP 1999, 15)

While HDRs are much more than a vindication of CSO professionalism in the third world, it may be noted that it is representative of a new phase of developmentalism.

Moreover, it is supplementary to a more compelling mode of economic thinking popularized by international financial organizations such as the IMF and World Bank.

7 The debate on globalization has produced a voluminous literature. Nevertheless, the critical points of contention revolve around four fundamental issues pertaining to the extent, nature, constraint and impacts of globalization (Held et al. 1999,18). There are also authors who believe that 'imperialism' is, analytically as well as heuristically, a better word to capture the phenomena that 'globalization' claims to describe (for example, see Petras 1999a). For a more reasoned analysis of the ideas of development, imperialism and globalization, see Sutcliffe (1999).

8 Harvey (1989, 82) attempts to capture these developments in three interrelated concepts – namely, time-space compression, flexible accumulation and accelerating turn over time in production. He states: 'Improved systems of communication and information flow, coupled with rationalization in techniques of distribution (packaging, inventory control, containerization, market feedback, etc.), made it possible to circulate commodities through the market system with greater speed. Electronic banking and plastic money were some of the innovations that improved the speed of the inverse flow of money. Financial services and markets (aided by computerized trading) likewise speeded up. So as to make, as the saying has it, "twenty-four hours a very long time" in global stock market'. Dyer-Witheford (1999, 130–31) clarifies this point through Marx's own words that 'capital "by its nature drives beyond any spatial barrier" so that "the creation of the physical conditions of exchange-of means of communication and transport-the annihilation of space by time-becomes an extraordinary necessity for it."' Dyer-Witheford reminds us that Marx's statement was made in the context of observing telegraphs, railways and steamships of his age. For a comprehensive discussion also see Castells (2000).

9 For a discussion of the spatial geography of Bangalore's emergence as a technopolis, see Parthasarathy (2004). Also, for a critique, see Nair (2000). Chapter 5, in Spivak (2008) provides a postcolonial analysis of the Bangalore Megacity project and the subject positions of the 'southern citizen of the virtual megacity'.

10 Global media, both print and TV, have been in the forefront of publicizing the virtues of these initiatives. Many international magazines have run cover stories or main stories glorifying the major projects launched in India. For example, *Asiaweek* (29 June 2001) captioned its cover story on the MSSRF's Village Knowledge Centres and the Simputer as 'Heroes of the Digital Divide' (Ghahremani 2001). *Businessworld*, in a cover story, described TARAhaat as the 'Rising star of the rural market place' (Jishnu et al. 2001, 30).

11 For a critical appraisal of the declared usefulness of the set of information provided by the MSSRF's Village Knowledge Centres, see Saith (2008).

12 The MSSRF was already planning to extend the project to other parts of southern India. We will discuss this aspect later in the chapter. Dindigal, in Tamil Nadu, was one of the new regions of their operation.

13 The project was initially conceived as one, which would set up info-shops. Although the project has changed its name more than once, the basic model remains the same, the multipurpose kiosk attempting to cater to the information needs of rural population.

14 Discussion with K. G. Raj Mohan, Administrative Coordinator, on 26 July 2002. According to his account, this has been rather difficult with mixed outcomes. In certain cases, the panchayaths (local bodies) had agreed to provide the necessary resources and in certain other cases, different temple trustees had taken an interest. The ambivalence

of the rural elite as well as the commoners was understandable if seen in the light of the allocation dilemmas of resource-poor villages forced to invest in projects with uncertain opportunities.

15 For details of the Bio-Village Project in Pondicherry, see MSSRF (c.2001, 85–88). The UNDP supported project was entering a new phase envisaging 250 villages in Pondicherry to be transformed into bio-villages by 2007. Not surprisingly, some of the first local enthusiasts for the Village Knowledge Centres were people who have been associating with the bio-village Project.

16 Literal meaning is 'the ruler of the land'. They are not always democratically elected, but constitute the local political and caste elite. An attempt to conduct elections to the local bodies in Pondicherry has been initiated by the government recently.

17 Discussion with K. G. Raj Mohan, op. cit.

18 Interview with Kankeyan, Village Head, Veerampattinam on 27 July 2002.

19 'They ask for INR 2,000 to 3,000 as salary. MSSRF and panchayat are not willing to pay. So this centre is managed by women alone' (interview with a woman volunteer, *Embalam* centre). Ironically, the CSO had interpreted this lack of cooperation of the educated male youth in Embalam differently. The project that operated with the help of a total of 30 volunteers across twelve centres used to claim that 50 per cent of them were women. But it is never pointed out that ten of them were volunteers in the Embalam kiosk. According to my informant, this overcrowding was the result of male non-cooperation: 'As women we are afraid to sit in the kiosk alone. Hence, for each shift, five of us take turns.'

20 Satish Jha would call this 'social venture capital'. See also note 1.

21 Discussion with Ranjith Khosla, CEO, TARAhaat, 6 August 2002, Delhi.

22 Peterson et al. (2001) is a curious study conducted with support from Microsoft and the Markle Foundation showing unsubstantiated optimism in the success of the project, primarily based on the internal projections of the CSO and at very early stage of its implementation.

23 Interview with TARAhaat's Field Operation Executive (FOE), 9 August 2002, Bhatinda.

24 *Aarthyas* are powerful middlemen in the villages.

25 Interview with TARAhaat's FOE, op. cit. The process is indicative of the welter of influences the village elite, particularly the middlemen, can wield in the implementation of the project. There is a striking similarity here with the process of formation of MSSRF's kiosks supported by temple trustees and village elite.

26 The equivalent for one United States Dollar (USD 1) in early 2011 was approximately 46 Indian Rupees (INR 46). The rate of conversion for INR against USD has wavered approximately between INR 40 to INR 50 in the last decade.

27 Interview with IVRP Volunteer on 28 July 2002.

28 Same as above.

29 Same as above.

30 Interview with IVRP volunteer, on 29 July 2002.

31 Same as above.

32 Nevertheless, such projections abound in the literature on ICT diffusion in rural India. The statement by the chairman of the Tamil Nadu Institute of Information Technology is a typical example: 'Approximately 13,000 kiosks are expected to be set up and operated by private agents under the community Internet Kiosks Project in Tamil Nadu. More than 10 percent of them will be operational from the very beginning. The whole state

will be interconnected by microwave, optical fibre and satellite links' (Vasagam 1999, 23–24). Needless to say, nothing of this has materialized in the following six years.

33 For a discussion of the state-industry-civil society interaction in ICT innovations in rural India, see Sreekumar (2003).

34 Interview with Paul Adrien, Director, Department of Agriculture, Pondicherry, 30 July 2002.

35 *Asiaweek* reported in 2001, on the basis of an Interview with M. S. Swaminathan, that 'The Pondicherry Government wants the foundation to extend its network to 208 villages, which to Swaminathan would be a good start. He predicts millions of jobs can be created in rural India as early pioneers spread knowledge to others.' Kapoor (2001, 36). After four years, the project was still stuck with 11–12 kiosks and the government had mooted its own e-farm clinics, detaching itself completely from the CSO.

36 Interview with Paul Adrien, op. cit.

37 Discussion with Ranjith Khosla, op. cit.

38 Discussion with Satish Jha, op. cit.

39 QUANGOs are defined as organizations that essentially undertake the responsibility of implementing state-sponsored programmes or public policies, funded by the state, but operating at arm's length of the executive without an immediate hierarchical relation with it (Van Thiel 2001, 5). The formation of QUANGOs is part of the general strategy adopted by the states, informed by the logic of civil-society mediation, as pointed out in the Pliatzky Report (quoted in Flinders 1999, 29).

40 For a philosophically informed recent critique of postdevelopment studies, see Parfitt (2002).

Chapter 3. Decrypting E-Governance

1 Heeks and Bailur (2007, 244), reviewing relevant literature, state that 'the term 'electronic government' seems to have first come to prominence when used in the 1993 US National Performance Review, whereas 'e-government' seems to have first come to prominence in 1997'.

2 Probably with the hindsight of retrospective reflection, Madon (2008, 269) considers these early attempts at computerization as 'e-government' initiatives. Based on the Government of India (GOI) *Seventh Five Year Plan* (1985), it is explained that 'in the first phase, efforts to develop e-government were concentrated on the use of IT for in-house government applications with a focus on central government requirements such as defence, research, economic monitoring and planning and certain data intensive functions related to elections, conducting of national census, and tax administration'.

3 The strategy of import substitution governed the development and planning regime of the Indian State during the 1950s, '60s and '70s. The public sector was envisaged as playing a major role in the growth and development of the Indian economy during the period.

4 For a critique of the technocratic dimensions of the good governance programmes of the Indian State, see Joseph, S. (2001). For critical review of the relationship between governance and development in e-governance projects in the states of Gujarat, Karnataka and Kerala in India, see Madon (2009).

5 Also see www.ciol.com/content/services/egov. The conference was one of the highlights of the Bangalore IT.com 1999 event.

6 One such example was the project announced by the IT Secretary of Kerala for computerizing and networking relevant applications for 1,214 local bodies that claimed

development of software for the payment of welfare pensions and a database that can be used for procuring building licenses, license fees and taxes. The secretary was confident that the system would help people living in rural areas to 'find out what quotas they are entitled to, what schemes are applicable to them, or in the case of land records, where they are located and whom to contact' (Katakam 1999, 79). Several years after the announcement, the project has not yet taken shape!

7 The Warna wired project in Maharashtra is perhaps a significant counter-example. It covers 70 contiguous villages, providing information and knowledge to increase efficiency and productivity of the sugar cooperatives. It aims to support the cooperatives with agricultural and medical information besides setting up a constellation of facilitating centres for continued enskilling and education. The National Informatics Centre (NIC) of the government of India and the state's education department collaborated with the cooperatives to launch a strong network of fiberoptic cables, V-SATs, PCs, and other ICT equipment.

8 Gyandoot was a joint winner of the Stockholm Challenge Award in the category 'Public Services & Democracy' along with the Australian initiative 'Technology for Social Justice'.

9 Discussion with Sanjay Inamdar, Regional Manager-Sales (Western Region) of n-Logue Communications Pvt Ltd, Chennai, on 13 August 2004 at the headquarters of the Gyandoot Samiti. He considers the collaboration as being mutually beneficial. See also Chapter 5 for a detailed discussion of the corDECT WLL technology.

10 For discussion of the uses of the services often offered by these types of village kiosks, see Saith (2008). The author attempts an outsider's evaluation of the utility of the services to farmers in the case of MSSRF, based on the list of services provided on its website. He wonders how some of these could be relevant or result in any material gains for the poor.

11 For a discussion of the popularity of QUANGOs among bureaucrats see Flinders (1999). In India QUANGOs are preferred due to a variety of reasons: First, it provides the façade of an NGO for an otherwise bureaucratic set up run by civil servants deputed by the government. Second, utilization of funds will not be scrutinized by legislative bodies as the budget allocation of nongovernmental organizations does not require the approval of the parliament. Third, it provides a suitable channel to receive foreign funding that can be routed only through NGOs.

12 The uptake of the Gyandoot and Drishtee services was not at the optimum level and it was unlikely that they contribute to any digital levelling. Sriramesh and Rivera (2006) argue that e-governance can promote citizen participation and symmetrical communication only if the political system provides greater levels of supports for public influence in governance.

13 In many Kiosks, additional software for preparing astral birth chart and horoscope based on the Indian system of Astrology was available. The standard rate per copy of the birth chart was INR 50. The soochak in the Nagda centre reported that he had purchased the software programme called 'Kundli 2000' from Indore and rates the demand for this service, which was essential for match making for arranged Hindu marriages, as relatively high. Interview with soochak, 14 August 2002.

14 Interview with the soochak, 14 August 2002.

15 We would be discussing this case subsequently in this section.

16 Interview with the soochak at the Amjera Kiosk, 12 August 2004.

17 Interview with the soochak at the Badnaver (1) kiosk, 14 August 2002.

18 Naveen Prakash, Project Manager, admitted that the distance between 2 kiosks varies between 8 to 40 kilometers. The catchment area of 12 to 15 villages in the case of each kiosk was seen as unviable. He believed that catering to a population of 5000 would be ideal. This would mean increased proliferation of Gyandoot centres in rural Dhar, the prospects of which did not seem to be feasible at the time. Interview on 12 August 2002.

19 The CEO of the Tribal Block Development Office, S. C. Sharma, verified the statement by the soochak and added that the Block availed services from the kiosk and paid for them. Interview on 12 August 2002.

20 One of the students at the kiosk, however, said he does not know about AISECE and that they award the degree. Interview with Rithu Raj Sing on 14 August 2002.

21 Interview with Naveen Prakash, Project Manager, on 12 August 2004.

22 Retrieved from http://www1.worldbank.org/publicsector/egov/gyandootarticle.pdf in April 2004.

23 NDTV January 27, 2003. Archived at http://www.apnic.net/mailing-lists/s-asia-it/archive/2003/02/msg00013.html.

24 Ibid.

25 During my visits, one of the three centres in Badnaver was closed during office hours. Incidentally this one was housed in the Block headquarters itself!

26 The initial investment for the Government was INR 2,500,000, which was collected from the local bodies (Interview with Sanjay Dubey, District Collector, Dhar District on 12 August 2002). The District Council established the Server with a cost of INR 500,000 spending INR 150,000 on the machine and another INR 150,000 for software. The District Council also financed the training of the soochaks that were selected to run the kiosks. Moreover, the subsidy of INR 16,000 for each entrepreneur is also borne by the District Council.

27 The soochaks were asked to pay INR 60,000 for procuring the machine and setting up the centre in addition to a license fee of INR 5,000 payable to the Gyandoot Samiti. It was likely that they incurred an amount of INR 8,000–10,000 as other expenses including purchase of stationery to get the kiosk operational. (Interview with Naveen Prakash (Project manager) and the soochak, Tirla Centre, 12 August 2002).

28 Interview with Naveen Prakash, 12 August 2002.

29 Interview with Naveen Prakash, Project Manger, 12 August 2002.

30 Interview with the soochak, 14 August 2002.

31 Interview with the soochak on 14 August 2002.

32 It was just less than two hundred metres from his kiosk.

33 Ibid.

34 This model, originally identified in Sreekumar (2002a) based on the Indian experience, has been found to be relevant in the contexts of understanding e-governance initiatives elsewhere (see Sokolova 2006).

35 The potential of using the Gyandoot kiosks for market expansion has been explored by corporate organizations like, HLL, Tata Trust, Mahindra Tractors, Jain Irrigation, and S. Kumars.

36 Discussion with Sanjay Dubey, District Collector, on 12 August 2003 at Dhar.

37 Based on Naveen Prakash's presentation 'Gyandoot and HLL: Looking for Strategic Partnership' at the Gyandoot headquarters on 12 August 2003.

38 There is an increasing involvement of for-profit corporations in ICT-based social development projects. It is argued elsewhere (Sreekumar and Sanchez 2008) that the

marketing notion of the 'bottom of the pyramid' (BoP) has captured the imagination of corporate entities, inspiring them to explore rural markets for high value products (Prahalad 2005; Kuriyan et al. 2008). It has also generated an accumulated literature in the light-weighted ICT4D genre. Hewlett-Packard's e-Inclusion initiative, 'which builds and runs telecentres in ten countries to support local digitally enabled social and economic development ventures' (Boas et al, 2005, 107) is widely discussed initiative. Schwittay (2008, 175) addresses the main shortcomings of Hewlett-Packard's three-year i-community programme in India aimed to provide access to ICTs in rural Andhra Pradesh and argues that ICTs are 'not neutral tools of development as conceptualized by practitioners of ICT4D, but are commodities produced by corporations with the ultimate aim to increase the corporate bottom line'.

39 Discussion with the Marketing Manager, Rural-New Ventures, Hindustan Lever, Mumbai on 12 August 2002 at Dhar.

40 Ghatak (2002, 10) describes the ITC strategy as follows: 'ITC, which exports INR 7 million worth of agricultural commodities (and hopes to increase this to Rs. 2,000 crore by 2005), has discovered a way to bypass the age-old mandi system and buy directly from farmers. Launched in June 2000, 'e-Choupal', has already become the largest initiative among all Internet-based interventions in rural India. 'E-Choupal' services today reach out to more than a million farmers growing a range of crops – soybean, coffee, wheat, rice, pulses, shrimp – in over 11,000 villages through 1,900 kiosks across four states (Madhya Pradesh, Karnataka, Andhra Pradesh and Uttar Pradesh)'. Also see, Kumar 2004.

Chapter 4. Cyber-Kiosks and Dilemmas of Social Inclusion

1 See for example, a special issue of *i4d* (Information for Development), Vol. 1, 3) on gender and ICTs. The magazine devotes considerable attention to various aspects of ICTs in rural development.

2 Interview with Akhil Jain, 14 August 2002. There are several studies analyzing the socioeconomic characteristics of female-headed household (FHHs). The studies are based mainly on region-specific surveys or macrolevel information from sources such as National Sample Survey (NSS Data). Visaria and Visaria (1985) and Dreze and Srinivasan (1995) are early attempts to understand the social dynamics of FHH in India. The two major trends that emerge from empirical studies are that the FHHs are relatively poor compared to male-headed households and that the number of FHHs is increasing at a rapid rate. See for example, Barros, Fox and Mendonca (1997) and Buvinic and Gupta (1997). This is probably because of the fact that in many countries, including India, the incidence of female-supported household appears to be high in the case of relatively underprivileged groups and marginalized communities. It is a known fact that in the United States, about 5 percent of non-Hispanic, white, and Asian households were headed by women with children, while the corresponding figure for African Americans is 22 per cent of all black households. The percentage of Hispanic households headed by women with children is about 14 percent and the last 25 years has seen the percentage of female-headed households with children increasing, particularly rapidly among blacks. For a recent reappraisal of the poverty-FHH link in India, see Gangopadhyay and Wadhwa (2003).

3 Interview with the soochak, 12 August 2002. However, the status of tribal women in the Indian context has to be understood in its diverging contexts. Anthropological literature on tribal customs and values in India have pointed to the fact that tribal women in general enjoy better social status within their communities than women belonging to caste groups associated with the Brahmanical Hindu order. Singh and Rajylakshmi cite Furer-Haimendorf (1943), Hutton (1921), Hunter (1973) and Firth (1946) as examples of studies that report a high social status for tribal women among Tharus of U.P., and the Nagas and Garos of the North East. These studies recognize that child marriage, stigmas regarding widowhood etc. are not practiced by many tribal groups. Tribal women are also able to enjoy greater choice in marriage, divorce, and remarriage. Nonetheless, Singh and Rajyalakshmi (ibid.) also point to some of the grim scenarios of tribal social life:

> However, there are many facts which indicate a low status for the tribal woman. For example, she does not have property rights except in a matrilineal society which is a small proportion of the tribal population. She is paid less as wages than her male counterpart for the same work. Several taboos discriminating against tribal women exist in certain tribal groups implying impurity and low status. The tribal woma?n cannot hold the office of a priest. There are taboos related to menstruation as in non-tribal communities. The Kharia woman cannot touch a plough nor can she participate in roofing of a house. The Oraon women are also prevented from touching a plough. The Todas of Nilgiri Hills do not touch a menstruating woman for fear of destruction of harvest. In certain tribes only the males can participate in ancestor worship (Satyanarayana and Behera 1986). The Toda and Kota women in southern India cannot cross the threshold of a temple. The Santal women cannot attend communal worship.

Nonetheless, tribal customs cannot solely explain the antipathy and indifference of tribal women in attending the kiosks. For a recent analysis of the socioeconomic status of tribal women in India, see Tripathy (2002). For a comparison of the situations of tribal and non-tribal women, see Sahay (2002).

4 Interview with Naveen Prakash, 12 August 2002.

5 See the article at http://www.sdcn.org/webworks/cases/usability_da1.htm

6 This PowerPoint presentation, previously available at www.developmentgateway.org/download/123055/TARAhaat.ppt (accessed in 2003), highlighted the major strategies and potential of the initiative as understood in the initial phase of its implementation.

7 Interview with the kiosk manager 9 August 2002. However, many franchisees of TARAhaat would not have been able to afford this because of financial constraints as well as limitations imposed by scarcity of electricity. Even in the kiosk in question, it does not appear sustainable.

8 Ibid. Many franchisees expected more aggressive marketing strategies from the top-level management of the TARAhaat. They believed that only the synergy created by local initiatives in conjunction with regional-level drive for expanding the market can help build awareness among women and marginalized groups.

9 Interview with the kiosk manager, 9 August 2002.

10 *News Pondicherry* 4, no.14 (19–25 March 2000). http://www.pondy-central.com/grapevine/msg00063.html#D10

11 Interview with a female volunteer, 29 August 2002.

12 Ibid.

13 The new website of HOPE can be accessed at http://www.vrhope.org/. The letter that was circulated to the CSOs mentioned clearly that it was a participatory project, and that HOPE did not intend to use materials available from secondary sources in the website, but would use only information that is voluntarily supplied by the CSOs.

14 See 'South Indian NGOs on Net', in *Pondicherry News*, 18–24 June 2001. The news report mentions that the site has a searchable database and offers options for selective viewing.

15 Interview with P. Joseph Victor Raj, 28 July 2002, Pondicherry. The major objectives of hosting the website are: to provide an opportunity for CSOs to get free web presence to propagate their activities, to enable CSOs to interact with each other for resource sharing, networking and mutual solidarity; to assist CSOs to liaison with nodal agencies and support service institutions; to help enhance capacity building and training efforts; to provide state and donor agencies with a comprehensive idea about CSO presence in a particular locality; and to plan their involvement with an understanding of the organizations in case they intend to build partnerships.

16 Ibid.

17 Same as in note 16. Some of the documents published by HOPE make its views on technology quite explicit. For example, a paper prepared as part of the resource materials for a programme called 'Strategic Planning for the Trócaire Partners in Tamil Nadu' it is stated that 'Technologies which will increase the productivity of the labour is (sic) welcome and not the one which will replace labour' (Raj, 1998).

Chapter 5. Innovating for the Rural Network Society

1 This section draws on Sreekumar (2003).

2 iStation was conceived as a low-cost e-mail device which allows multiple language usage to be developed indigenously by the iNabling Technologies, Bangalore. For details, see http://www.pcworld.com/article/53923/bringing_email_to_the_masses.html

3 Pygmy was the name of a small savings scheme for low-income households. Such schemes have been part of the state-sponsored drive for increasing rural domestic savings, encouraging very poor households to practice thrift and save small sums of money on a daily or weekly basis.

4 Discussion with Vinay Deshpande on 2 August 2002, Trivandrum, Kerala.

5 They eventually used Nickel Metal Hydride (NiMH) rechargeable AAA batteries.

6 Vinay Deshpande says that the name was suggested by Vijay Chandru, who later became the marketing director of the PicoPeta marketing the Simputer, probably as an acronym for Simple, Inexpensive, Multilingual Computer. Discussion with Vinay Deshpande on 2 August 2002, Trivandrum, Kerala.

7 Discussion with Vinay Deshpande on 2 August 2002, Trivandrum, Kerala.

8 See, for example, Saxena (2001). It was reported that some companies were in advanced discussion with the Simputer Trust for procuring the license to undertake large-scale production of the Simputer.

9 Regarding its mass production in India, Banerjee writes in the same report in November 2002 that the Simputer 'is expected to hit the domestic market in a big way next month'.

10 http://www.simputer.org/simputer/license/sgplv1.3.php

11 www.groups.yahoo.com/simputer
12 Message number 711 at www.groups.yahoo.com/simputer
13 The shift in the tone of marketing pursued by Amida Simputers was noted by Lie:

> With the coming of the new Amida model of the Simputer in April 2004, the market also seems to have shifted a little bit to the urban rich and urban young who cannot afford to buy an expensive PDA, but can afford to buy a Simputer. For them the Simputer could be an interesting alternative as the price is more interesting. This shift in markets is emphasized by the way the Simputer is advertised (for instance on the website of the Simputer itself. (Lie 2004)

14 DECT uses a bandwidth of 20MHz in the 1880–1900 MHz range. It does not require prior frequency planning necessary in conventional mobile cellular systems ATIP 97.002 (1997).
15 A corDECT system should be within the reach of local businesspeople at a combined cost of around USD 25,000. It is believed that most operators – known as local service providers (LSPs) – will be able to get 500–700 subscribers within a 25 km radius, making the investment worthwhile (Jayaraman 2002, 359).
16 Dr. Jhunjhunvala, quoted in the *Hindu* ('Telecom sops withdrawal in order') 23 January 1999).
17 The *Hindu* ('Telecom sops withdrawal in order'), 23 January, 1999.
18 *Times of India*, for example, reported on 31 May 1999 that the 'Basic telecom operators … mounted pressure on the government to roll back duty hike on wireless in local loop (WLL) equipment, saying that it would raise their project cost and impose on them an outdated technology in the name of promoting local industry.' For an intellectual defence of corDECT WLL project in the controversy, see Indiresan (1999).
19 Also see Laishram, (2003), who noted that 'the cellcos are fighting hard to keep WLL's wings clipped'.

Chapter 6. ICT and Development: Critical Issues

1 The notion of the 'bottom of the pyramid' (BoP) has captured the imagination of corporate entities, inspiring them to explore rural markets for high value products. Hewlett-Packard's e-Inclusion initiative is one such initiative. Schwittay (2008, 175), critiquing HP's three-year i-community programme in rural Andhra Pradesh, India, argues that ICTs are 'not neutral tools of development as conceptualized by practitioners of ICT4D, but are commodities produced by corporations with the ultimate aim to increase the corporate bottom line.

BIBLIOGRAPHY

Abirafeh, L. 2002. 'Afghan Women One Year Later: Creating Digital Opportunities for Afghan Women'. *dgCommunities*. http://topics.developmentgateway.org/afghanistan/sdm/previewDocument.do~427938

Adam, A. 2005. *Gender, Ethics and Information Technology*. Basingstoke, Hampshire: Palgrave MacMillan.

Alavi, H. 1975. 'India and the Colonial Mode of Production'. *The Socialist Register*, 12:160–197.

Albrechtsen, H. 1987. 'Tele-Cottages in the Nordic Countries'. *Canadian Journal of Educational Communication* 16 (4): 327–333.

Amin, A., A. Cameron, and R. Hudson. 2002. *Placing the Social Economy*. London and New York: Routledge.

Amin, S. 1974. *Accumulation on a World Scale: A Critique of the Theory of Development*. New York: Monthly Review Press.

Antony, P., and G. Vasudevan. 2008. 'Ricocheting Gender Equations: Women Workers in the Call Centre Industry'. In *ICTs and Indian Social Change: Diffusion, Governance, Poverty*, edited by A. Saith, M. Vijayabaskar, and V. Gayathri, pp. 290–319 India: Sage Publications.

Armitage, J. (ed.). 2000. *Paul Virilio: From Modernism to Hypermodernism and Beyond*. London, Thousand Oaks, and New Delhi: Sage Publications.

Armitage, J. 1999. 'Resisting the Neo-liberal Discourse of Technology: The Politics of Cyberculture in the Age of the Virtual'. *Ctheory - Theory, Technology and Culture* 22 (1–2) Article No. 68, http://www.ctheory.net/articles.aspx?id=111

Aron, R. 1967. *18 Lectures on Industrial Society*. Trans. M. R Bottomore. London: Weidenfeld and Nicholson.

Arora, P. 2010. *Dot Com Mantra: Social Computing in the Central Himalayas*. Farnham, UK: Ashgate Publishing.

Arun, S., R. Heeks, and S. Morgan. 2004. *ICT Initiatives, Women and Work in Developing Countries: Reinforcing Or Changing Gender Inequalities in South India?* Manchester: Institute for Development Policy and Management, University of Manchester.

Arun, T. G., and S. Arun. 2002. 'Gender, Development and ICT: Software Production in Kerala'. *Journal of International Development* 14(1): 39–50.

Arunachalam, S. 2002. 'Reaching the Unreached: How can we use ICTs to Empower the Rural Poor in the Developing World through Enhanced Access to Relevant Information?' Paper presented at the IFLA General Conference, August 18–14, Glasgow.

ATIP (Asian Technology Information Programme). 1997. 'corDECT- A New Indian Wireless Local Loop System', ATIP97.002. http://www.atip.org/atip.reports.97/atip97.002r.html

Avgerou, C., and G. Walsham. 2000. *Information Technology in Context: Studies from the Perspective of Developing Countries*. Aldershot, UK: Ashgate.

Avgerou, C., C. Ciborra, and F. Land (eds). 2004. *The Social Study of Information and Communication Technology: Innovation, Actors and Contexts*. Oxford, UK: Oxford University Press.

Ayres, C. E. [1944] 1962. *The Theory of Economic Progress: A Study of the Fundamentals of Economic Development and Cultural change*. New York: Schocken Books.

Baark, E., and N. Sharif. 2006. 'From Trade Hub to Innovation Hub: The Role of Hong Kong's Innovation System in Linking China to Global Markets'. *Innovation: Management, Policy and Practice* 8 (1–2): 193–209.

Baddeley, S. 1997. 'Governmentality'. In *The Governance of Cyber Space: Politics, Technology and Global Restructuring*, edited by B. Loader, pp. 64–96. New York and London: Routledge.

Bagga, R. K., K. Keniston, and R. R. Mathur (eds). 2005. *The state, IT and development*. New Delhi: Sage Publication.

Balaji, V., K. G. Rajamohan, R. Rajashekhara Pandy, and S. Senthil Kumaran. 2001. 'Towards Knowledge Systems for Sustainable Food Security: The Information Village Experiment in Pondicherry'. *Proceedings of the Theme session Information Technology for Development –a Millennium Perspective*, edited by M. R. Das. XIII Kerala Science Congress, January 29–31, Thrissur.

Balsamo, A.1996. *Technologies of the Gendered Body: Reading Cyborg Women*. Durham and London: Duke University Press.

Banaji, J. 1972. 'For a Theory of Colonial Modes of Production'. *Economic and Political Weekly*, 7(52): 2498–2502.

Banerjee, P. 2001. 'What Does it Mean to Empower Informationally the Local Government! – Designing an Information System for a District Level Development Administration'. *International Journal of Information Management* 21 (6): 403–421.

Barak, A. 2005. 'Sexual Harassment on the Internet'. *Social Science Computer Review* 23 (1): 77–92.

Baran, P. 1957. *Political Economy of Growth*. New York: Monthly Review Press.

Bardhan, P. 1982. 'Agrarian Class Formation in India'. *The Journal of Peasant Studies*, 10 (1): 73–94.

Baron, S., J. Field, and T. Schuller (eds). 2000. *Social Capital: Critical Perspectives*. Oxford University Press, Oxford.

Barros, R., L. Fox, and R. Menonca . 1997. 'Female-headed Households, Poverty, and the welfare of Children in Urban Brazil'. Economic Development and Cultural Change 45 (2): 231–57.

Baviskar, A. 1997. *In the Belly of the River: Tribal Conflicts over Development in the Narmada Valley*. New Delhi: Oxford University Press.

Beamish, A. 1995. 'Communities Online: A Study of Community-Based Computer Networks'. Master's thesis, Massachusetts Institute of Technology. http://theses.mit.edu:80/Dienst/UI/2.0/Describe/0018.mit.theses/1995–35.

Bellah, R. N., R. Madsen, S. M. Tipton, W. M. Sullivan, and A. Swidler. 1991. *The Good Society*. New York: Alfred A Knoff.

Bellamy, C., and J. A. Taylor. 1994. 'Introduction: Towards the Information Polity? Public Administration in the Information Age'. *Journal of Public Administration* 72 (1): 1–13.

Beniger, J. R. 1986. *The Control Revolution: Technological and Economic Origins of the Information Society*. Cambridge Mass.: Harvard University Press.

Benner, M., and U. Sandstrom. 2000. 'Institutionalizing the Triple Helix: Research Finding and Norms in the Academic System'. *Research Policy* 29 (2): 291–302.

Best M. L., and C. M. Maclay, 2002. 'Community Internet Access in Rural Areas: Solving the Economic Sustainability Puzzle'. In *The Global Information Technology Report 2001–2002: Readiness for the Networked World*, edited by G. Kirkman, P. K. Cornelius, J. D. Sachs and K Schwab, pp. 76–88. Oxford: Oxford University Press.

Best, M. L., and S. G. Maier. 2007. 'Gender, Culture and ICT Use in Rural South India'. *Gender Technology and Development* 11(2):137–155.

Bhaduri, A. 1973. 'A Study in Agricultural Backwardness Under Semi-Feudalism'. *Economic Journal* 83(329): 120–137.

Bhalla, G. S. 1981. 'Green Revolution in the Punjab (India): Rural Structural Changes in Nonmetropolitan Regions'. In *Rural-Urban Relations and Regional Development*, edited by F. Lo, J. S. Edralin, and N. T. Dung. Regional Development Series; v. 5, pp. 195–216. Singapore: Maruzen Asia for United Nations Centre for Regional Development, Nagoya, Japan.

Bhatnagar, S. 1990. 'Computers in Developing Countries'. In *Information technology in Developing Countries*, edited by S. Bhatnagar and N. Bjorn Anderson. Amsterdam: North-Holland.

———— 2004. *eGovernment: From Vision To Implementation, A Practical Guide With Case Studies*. New Delhi : Sage Publications.

Bhatnagar, S., and N. Bjorn Anderson (eds). 1990. *Information technology in Developing Countries*. Amsterdam: North-Holland.

Bhatnagar, S., and R. Sechware (eds). 2000. *Information and Communication Technology in Development: Cases from India*. New Delhi, Thousand Oaks and London: Sage Publications.

Bhatnagar, S., and N. Vyas. 2001. 'Gyandoot: Community-Owned Rural Internet Kiosks'. Retrievable at: www1.worldbank.org/publicsector/egov/gyandootcs.htm

Bhushan, P. 2008. 'Connecting or Dividing? Examining Female Learners' Information and Communication Technology Access and Use in Open and Distance Learning'. *Open Learning: The Journal of Open and Distance Learning* 23(2): 131–138.

Bihari, G. and C. Jókay. 1999. Telecottages in Hungary: The Experience and the Opportunities. Budapest: IGE Ltd.

Blattman, C., R. Jensen, and R. Roman. 2003. 'Assessing the Need and Potential of Community Networking for Development in Rural India'. *The Information Society* 19(5): 349–64.

Boas, T., T. Dunning, and J. Bussell. 2005. 'Will the Digital Revolution Revolutionalize Development? Drawing Together the Debate'. *Studies in Comparative International Development* 40(2): 95–110.

Bourdieu, P. 1977. *Outline of a Theory of Practice*. Trans. R. Nice. Cambridge: Cambridge University Press.

Brousseau, E. 2003. 'E-Commerce in France: Did Early Adoption Prevent its Development?' *The Information Society* 19: 45–57.

Brown, C. 2000. 'Cosmopolitanism, World Citizenship, and Global Civil Society'. Contemporary Research in Social and Political Philosophy 3 (1): 7–26.

Buvinic, M. and Gupta, G. R., 1997, 'Female headed households and female-maintained families: are they worth targeting to reduce poverty in developing countries'. Economic Development and Cultural Change 45 (2): 259–280.

Bury, R. 2005. *Cyberspaces of Their Own: Female Fandoms Online*. New York: Peter Lang Publishing.

Byres, T. J. 1972. 'The Dialectics of India's Green Revolution'. *South Asian Review*. Vol. 5(2): 99–106.

Campbell, C. J. 1995. 'Community Technology Centers: Exploring a Tool for Rural Community Development'. Amherst: The Center for Rural Massachusetts, University of Massachusetts. Available at www-unix.oit.umass.edu/~ruralma/CTC2.html

Carnoy, M., M. Castells, S. S. Cohen, and F. Cardoso. 1993. *The New Global Economy in the Information Age*. University Park PA: Pennsylvania State University Press.

Carvin, A., and M. Surman (eds). 2008. *From The Ground Up (The Evolution of the Telecentre Movement)*. Canada: telecenter.org, c/o International Development Research Centre. www.epractice.eu/files/media/media2257.pdf

Castells, M. 2000. *The Information Age: Economy, Society and Culture Vol. I-The Rise of the Network Society*. Oxford: Blackwell.

————— 2001. *The Internet Galaxy*. New York: Oxford University Press.

Castells, M., and P. Hall. 1994. *Technopoles of the World: The Making of 21st century Industrial Complexes*. London: Routledge.

Castro, E., C. Rodrigues, C. Esteves, and A. R. Pires. 2000. 'The Triple Helix Model as a Model for Creative Use of Telematics'. *Research Policy* 29 (2): 193–203.

CEC (Commission of the European Communities). 2001. *Information and Communication Technologies in Development: The Role of ICTs in EC development policy*. Communication from the Commission to the Council and the European Parliament, Brussels.

CEG-IIMA. (Center for Electronic Governance, Indian Institute of management, Ahmedabad). 2002. *An Evaluation of Gyandoot*. Washington: World Bank.

Cereny, P. G. 2000. 'Structuring the Political Arena: Public goods, States and Governance in a Globalizing world'. in *Global Political Economy: Contemporary Theories*, edited by R. Palan. pp. 21–35, London; New York: Routledge.

Chakravartty, P. 2004. 'Telecom, National Development and the Indian State: A Postcolonial Critique'. *Media, Culture and Society* 26(2): 227–49.

————— 2008. 'Labor in or as Civil Society? Workers and Subaltern Publics in India's Information Society. In *Global Communications: Toward a Transcultural Political Economy*, edited by P. Chakravartty and Y. Zhao, pp. 285–307. Lanham: Rowman & Littlefield Publishers, Inc.

Chandhoke, N. 2003. *The Conceits of Civil Society*. New Delhi: Oxford University Press.

Chaterjee, P(artha). 2001. 'On Civil and Political Society in Postcolonial Democracies'. In *Civil Society:History and Possibilities*. Edited by S. Kaviraj, and S. Khilnani. Cambridge: Cambridge University Press, 165–178.

————— 2004. *The Politics of the Governed: Considerations on Political Society in Most of the World*. New York: Columbia University Press,

Chatterjee, P(atralekha). 2000. 'Internet Takes Root'. *MSNBC*, February 27. www.stockholmchallenge.org/project/data/gyandoot

Chaudhuri, B. 2010. 'Good Governance in India: Interplay of Politics, Culture and Technology in E-Governance Projects'. European Association of Social Anthropologists (EASA) Workshop: Crisis and imagination. (Indiascapes: reflections of contemporary India) Maynooth, August 24–27, 2010.

Cherny, L., and E. R. Weise (eds). 1996. *Wired Women: Gender and New Realities in Cyberspace*. Seattle: Seal Press.

Chilcote, R. H., and D. L. Johnston.1983. *Theories of Development: Mode of Production or Dependency*. Beverly Hills: Sage.

Cohen, J. 1999. 'Trust, Voluntary Association and Workable Democracy: The Contemporary American Discourse of Civil Society' in *Democracy and Trust*, edited by M. E. Warren, pp. 208–248. New York: Cambridge University Press.

Cohen, S. 1999. 'Contextualism, Skepticism, and the Structure of Reasons'. *Philosophical Perspectives 13, Epistemology*: 57–89.

Cohen, S. 2001. 'Contextualism Defended: Comments on Richard Feldman's 'Skeptical Problems, Contextualist Solutions'. *Philosophical Studies* 103: 87–98.

Cohen, S. S., and J. Zysman. 1987. *Manufacturing Matters: The Myth of the PostIndustrial Economy*. New York, Basic books.

Coleman, J. S. 1988. 'Social Capital in the Creation of Human Capital'. *American Journal of Sociology (Supplement)*. 95, S95–S120.

Conroy, C. 2006. *Telecentre Initiatives In Rural India: Failed Fad or the Way Forward?* Kent: Natural Resources Institute, University of Greenwich.

Cortada, J. W. c. 2002. *Making the Information Society: Experience, Consequences and Possibilities*. London: Financial Times/ Prentice Hall.

Cowen, M and R. W. Shenton. 1997. *Doctrines of Development*. London and New York: Routledge.

D'Mello, M. 2006. 'Gendered Selves and Identities of Information Technology Professionals in Global Software Organizations in India'. *Journal Information Technology for Development* 12 (2): 131–58.

Dahlberg, K. A. 1979. *Beyond the Green Revolution: The Ecology and Politics of Global Agricultural Development*. New York: Plenum Press.

Dai, X. 2000. *The Digital Revolution and Governance*. Aldershot, Burlington USA, Singapore and Sydney: Ashgate.

De Vaney, A., S. Gance, and Y. Ma (eds). 2000. 'Technology and Resistance: Digital Communications and New Coalitions Around the World. New York: P. Lang.

De, R. 2009. 'Caste Structures and E-Governance in a Developing Country'. *Lecture Notes in Computer Science* 5693, pp. 40–53.

Dekker, P. and E. M. Uslaner (eds). 2001. *Social Capital and Participation in Everyday Life*. London: Routledge.

Dembski, W. A. 1994. 'The Fallacy of Contextualism'. *The Princeton Theological Review*, October. www.arn.org/docs/dembski/wd_contexism.htm

Dixit, V. 2007.'Habermasian Public Sphere and the Telecentre Discourse'. In *Foundations of e-Governance*. Edited by A. Agarwal V. VenkataRamana, pp. 55–68 New Delhi: GIFT Publishing.

DN. (Pseudonym) 2001. 'ICTs in Rural Poverty Alleviation'. *Economic and Political Weekly* 36 (1): 917–20.

Domar, E. D. [1957] 1982. *Essays in the Theory of Economic Growth*. Westport Conn.: Greenwood Press. Originally published: New York: Oxford University Press.

Donner, J. 2008. 'Research Approaches to Mobile Use in the Developing World: A Review of the Literature'. *The Information Society* 24 (3): 140–59.

Dosi G., C. Freeman, R. Nelson, G. Silverberg, and L. Soete. 1988. *Technical Change and Economic Theory*. London, Francis Pinter; and New York: Columbia University Press.

Dreze, J., and P. V. Srinivasan. 1995. 'Widowhood and Poverty in Rural India: Some Inferences from Household Survey Data'. Discussion Paper No. 125, November 1995, Bombay: Indira Gandhi Institute for Development Research.

Dugger, C. 2000. 'Connecting Rural India to the World'. *The New York Times*, 28 May.

Dyer-Witheford, N. 1999. *Cyber-Marx: Cycles and Circuits of Struggle in High Technology Capitalism*. Urbana and Chicago: University of Illinois Press.

Edquist, C. 2001. 'The Systems of Innovation Approach and Innovation Policy: An Account of the State of the Art'. Paper Presented at the DRUID Conference, June 12–15, Aalborg.

Elam, M. 1997. 'National Imaginations and Systems of Innovation'. In *Systems of Innovation: Technologies Institutions and Organizations*, edited by C. Edquist. London and Washington: Pinter.

Eriksson-Zetterquist, U. 2007. 'Gender and New Technologies'. *Gender, Work and Organization* 14(4): 305–311.

Etzkowitz, H., and L. Leydesdorff (eds).1997. *Universities and the Global Knowledge Economy: A Triple Helix of University-Industry-Government Relations.* London and Washington: Pinter.

Etzkowitz, H., and L. Leydesdorff. 2000. 'The Dynamics of Innovation: From National Systems and "Mode 2" to the Triple Helix of University-Industry-Government Relations'. *Research Policy* 29 (2): 109–23.

Evans, P. 1995. *Embedded Autonomy: State and Industrial Transformation.* New Jersey: Princeton University Press.

Feenberg, A. 1999. *Questioning Technology.* London and New York: Routledge.

Feenberg, A., and M. Bakardjieva. 2004. 'Virtual Community: No "Killer Implication"'. *New Media and Society* 6(1): 37–43.

Felker, G. 1999. 'Malaysia's Innovation System: Actors, Interests and Governance'. In *Technology, competitiveness and the state: Malaysia's industrial technology policies*, edited by K. S. Jomo and G. Felker, pp. 98–147. London: New York: Routledge.

Fine, B. 2001. *Social Capital Versus Social Theory. Political Economy and Social Science at the Turn of the Millenium.* London and New York: Routledge.

Finn, J., and M. Banach. 2000. 'Victimization Online: The Downside of Seeking Human Services for Women on the Internet'. *CyberPsychology and Behavior* 3 (5): 785–796.

Flanagan, M., and A. Booth (eds). 2006. *Reload: Rethinking Women and Cyberculture.* Cambridge: MIT Press.

Flinders, M. V. 1999. 'Quangos: Why Do Governments Love Them?' In *Quangos, Accountability and Reform: the politics of quasi-government.* Flinders, edited by M. V. and M. J. Smith, pp 26–39. Great Britain: Macmillan Press.

Firth, R. 1946. *Human Types.* London: Nelson.

Flinders, M. V., and M. J. Smith. 1999. *Quangos, Accountability and Reform: the politics of quasi-government.* Great Britain: Macmillan Press.

Fonseca, R., and J. Pal. 2003. 'Bringing Devices to the Masses: A Comparative Study of the Brazilian Computador Popular and the Indian Simputer'. Final Report. ICT4B, December.

Foster, D. 1996. 'Community and Identity in the Electronic Village'. *Internet Culture, D. Porter* (ed), pp. 23–37. London: Routledge.

Foucault, M. 1991. 'Governmentality'. In *The Foucault Effect: Studies in Governmentality.* Edited by G. Burchell, C. Gordon, and P. Miller pp. 87–104. Hemel Hampstead: Harvester Wheatsheaf.

Frank, A. G. 1967. *Latin America: Underdevelopment or Revolution? Essays on the Development of Underdevelopment and Immediate Enemy.* New York: Modern Reader.

Freeman, C. 2000. 'The "National system of Innovation" in Historical Perspective'. In *Systems of Innovation: Growth, Competitiveness and Employment, Vol. I*, edited by. C. Edquist and M. McKelvey, pp. 41–60. Cheltenham and Northampton, MA: Edward Elgar.

Frissen, P. 1997. 'The virtual state: Postmodernisation, informatisation and Public Administration'. In *The Governance of Cyberspace.* Edited by B. D. Loader. London and New York: Routledge, pp. 110–125.

Fugita, K. 1988. 'The Technopolis: High Technology and Regional Development in Japan'. *International Journal of Urban Research* 12: 566–94.

Fukuyama, F. 1995. *Trust: Social Virtues and the Creation of Prosperity.* New York: Free Press.

Fuller, C., and H. Narasimhan. 2008. 'Empowerment and Constraint: Women, Work and the Family in Chennai Software Industry'. In *In an outpost of global economy: Work and Workers in an India's Information Technology* edited by C. Upadhyay, and A. R. Vasavi, pp. 190–210. Routledge: New York.

Furer-Haimendorf, C. von. 1943. *The Chenchus: Jungle folk of Deccan.* London: Macmillan and Company.

Gajjala, R. 2002. 'Cyberfeminist Technological Practices: Exploring Possibilities for a Woman-Centered Design of Technological Environments'. Background paper prepared for the INSTRAW Virtual Seminar Series on Gender and ICTs. www.un-instraw.org/en/docs/gender_and_ict/Gajjala.pdf

Ganapati, P. 2003. 'Simputer. Not a Common Man's Device Anymore'. *Rediff Online*, 17 September http://in.rediff.com/money/2003/sep/17spec.htm

Gangopadhyay, S., and W. Wadhwa. 2003. 'Are Indian Female-Headed Households More Vulnerable to Poverty?' India Development Foundation, Institute of International Studies, UC Berekely. http://globetrotter.berkeley.edu/macarthur/inequality/papers

Gasper, D. 1996. 'Culture and Development Ethics: Needs, Women Rights and Western Theories'. *Development and Change* 27 (4): 627–61.

Ghahremani, Y. 2001. 'Heroes of the Digital Divide'. *Asiaweek* 29 June: 31–41.

Ghatak. M. 2002. 'Use of Information Technology in Agriculture'. www.indiainfoline.com/bisc/itin.pdf

Ghosh, A. 2006. *Communication Technology and Human Development,* New Delhi: Sage Publications.

Gill, S. S. 2004. *The Information Revolution and India: A Critique.* New Delhi: Rupa.

Glaeser, B. (ed.). 1987. *The Green Revolution Revisited: Critiques and Alternatives,* London: Allen & Unwin.

Glenn, J. K. III. 2001. *Framing Democracy: Civil Society and Civic Movements in Eastern Europe.* Stanford: Stanford University Press.

GOI (Government of India). 1985. *Seventh Five Year Plan, 1985–90.* New Delhi: Government of India, Planning Commission.

GOP (Government of Pondicherry). 2002. *Uzhavar Uthaviyakam- Oru Arimugam* (Farmers' Support Centre: An Introduction) Pondicherry: Department of Agriculture. (Pamphlet in the possession of the author.)

Golding, P. 1996. 'World Wide Wedge: Division and Contradiction in the Global Information Infrastructure'. *Monthly Review* 48(3): 70–86.

Goyal, A. 2003. 'Why Women Lag and Why they May Lead'. *i4d: Information for Development* 1(3): 13–21.

Green, E., and A. E. Adam. 2001. *Virtual Gender - Technology, Consumption and Identity Matters.* London and New York: Routledge.

Green, L. 2002. *Communication, Technology and Society.* London: Sage Publications.

Gupta, P. P. 1981. 'Policy Framework for Development of Computer Technology and Applications'. In *Computers in Developing Nations*, edited by. J. M. Bennet, and R. E. Kalman. Amsterdam/New York/Oxford: North-Holland Publishing Company.

Gurstein, M. (ed.). 2000. 'Community Informatics: Enabling Communities with Information and Communications Technologies'. Hershey, PA: Idea Group Publication.

Gurumurthy, A. and P. J. Singh. 2006. 'Civil Society and Feminist Engagement at WSIS: Some Reflections'. In *Gender in the information society*, edited by A. Gurumurthy, P. J. Singh, A. Mundkur, and M. Swamy, pp. 15–26. Bangkok: UNDP-APDIP-Elsevier.

Gurumurthy, A., and R. Sarkar. 2003. *Poverty Alleviation through Tele-centre Initiatives*. Bangalore: IT for Change. http://itforchange.net/mambo/content/view/62/40/

Habermas, J. 1984. *The Theory of Communicative Action: Volume I*. Boston: Beacon Press.

Hafkin, N. 2002. 'Are ICTs Gender Neutral? A Gender Analysis of Six Case Studies of Multi-donor ICT Projects'. Background paper prepared for the INSTRAW Virtual Seminar Series on Gender and ICTs. www.uninstraw.rg/en/docs/gender_and_ict/Hafkin.pdf

Hafkin, N., and N. Taggart. 2001. 'Gender, Information Technology, and Developing Countries: An Analytic Study'. USAID. http://ict.aed.org/infocenter/gender.htm www.usaid.gov/wid/pubs/hafnoph.pdf

Hall, A. J. 1995. *Civil Society: Theory, History, Comparison*. Cambridge: Polity Press.

Hall, P., and P. Preston.1988. *The Carrier wave: New Information Technology and the Geography of Innovation*. London: Unwin Hyman.

Haraway, D. J. 1991. *Simians, Cyborgs and Women: The Reinvention of Nature*. New York; Routledge.

Harcourt, W. (ed.). 1999. *Women@Internet: Creating New Cultures in Cyberspace*. London: Zed.

Hård, M., and A. Jamison. 1998. 'Conceptual Framework: Technology Debates as Appropriation Processes'. In *The Intellectual Appropriation of Technology : Discourses on Modernity, 1900–1939*. Edited by M. Hård and A. Jamison. Cambridge, MA: MIT Press, pp: 1–16.

Hariss, J. 2001. *Depoliticizing Development: The World Bank and Social Capital*. London: Anthem Press.

Harrod, R. F. 1952. *Economic Essays*. London: MacMillan.

Harvey, D. 1989. *The Condition of Post Modernity: An Enquiry into the Origins of Cultural Change*. Oxford: Blackwell.

Harvey, F. 2002. 'Computer for the Third World'. *Scientific American* 287(4): 100–102.

Haywood, Trevor 1995. *Info Rich – Info Poor: Access and Exchange in the Global Information Society*. London: Bower Saur.

Hedström, K., and Å. Grönlund, 2008. 'The Quest for Development – Reviewing ICT4D Research'. *GlobDev* 2008. Paper 24. http://aisel.aisnet.org/globdev2008/24

Heeks, R. 2006. 'Theorizing ICT4D Research'. *Information Technologies and International Development* 3(3) 1–4.

———— 2008. 'ICT4D2.0: the Next Phase of Applying ICT for International Development'. *Computer* 41(6): 26–33.

Heeks, R., and S. Bailur. 2007. 'Analyzing eGovernment Research: Perspectives, Philosophies, Theories, Methods and Practice'. *Government Information Quarterly* 24(2): 243–165.

Held, D., A. McGrew, D. Glodblatt, and J. Perraton. 1999. *Global Transformation: Politics, Economics and Culture*. Stanford: Stanford University Press.

Held, D., and A. McGrew. 2000. *The Global Transformations Reader: An Introduction to the Global Debate*. Great Britain: Polity Press.

———— 2000. 'The Great Globalization Debate: An Introduction'. In Held, D., and A. McGrew (eds). op. cit., 1–48.

Hodgson, G. 1993. *Economics and Evolution–Bringing Life Back into Economics*. Ann Arbor, MI: Michigan University Press.

Holloway, S. L, and G. Valentine. 2003. *Cyberkids: Children in the Information Age*. London and New York: Routledge Falmer.

Hood, C. 2000. 'Where the State of the Art Meets the Art of the State: Traditional Public-Bureaucracy Controls in the Information Age'. *International Review of Public Administration* 5(1): 1–12.

Hudock, A. C. 1999. *NGOs and Civil Society: Democracy by Proxy?* Cambridge, UK; Malden, MA: Polity Press.

Hudson, H. E. 2006. *From rural village to global village: Telecommunications for development in the information age.* Mahwah, NJ: Lawrence Erlbaum Associates.

Hunter, W. W. 1973. *Orissa.* London: Smith Elder.

Hutton, J. H. 1921. *The Sema Naga.* London: Macmillan.

Huyer, S., and T. Sikoska. 2003. 'Overcoming the Gender Digital Divide: Understanding ICTs and Their Potential for the Empowerment of Women'. Synthesis Paper, Virtual Seminar Series on Gender and ICTs, United Nations International Research and Training Institute for the Advancement.

Indiresan, P. V. 1999. 'Import Duty and the MNCs'. *The Hindu*, May 29.

Itzigshon, J. 2000. *Developing Poverty: The State, Labour Market Deregulation and the Infomal Economy in Costa Rica and the Dominican Republic.* Pennsylvania: The Pennsylvania State University Press.

Iversen, J. E., T. Vedel, and W. Werle. 2004. 'Standardization and the Democratic design of Information and Communication Technology'. *Knowledge, technology & Policy* 17(2): 104–126.

Jafri, A., A. Dongre, V. N. Tripathi, A. Aggrawal, and S. Shrivastava. 2002. *Information Communication Technologies and Governance: The Gyandoot Experiment in Dhar District of Madhya Pradesh, India.* Working Paper160. London: Overseas Development Institute.

James, J. 2003. *Bridging the Global Digital Divide.* Cheltenham; Northampton, MA: Edward Elgar.

Jayakumar, R., G. Vijayaraghavan, and D. S. Sureshkumar (eds). 2001. *Information Technology for Development: A Millennium Perspective.* Thiruvananthapuram: STEC, Government of Kerala.

Jayaraman, K. S. 2002. 'India Online'. *Nature* 415 (24): 358–9.

Jenkins, R. 2001. 'Mistaking Governance for Politics: Foreign Aid, Democracy and Construction of Civil Society'. In S. Kaviraj and S. Khilnani (eds). op. cit., pp. 250–68.

Jessop, B. 1990. *State Theory: Putting the Capitalist State in its Place.* Cambridge: Polity Press.

Jhunjhunwala, A. 2001. 'Making the IT Revolution Work for Us'. *Technology Day*, IIT Chennai.

Jishnu, L., M. Anand, and P. Hari. 2001. 'India's Great Digital Hope'. *BusinessWorld*, 21 May: 28–41.

Johnson, B. 1997. 'Systems of Innovation: Overview and Basic Concepts'. In *Systems of Innovation and Technologies, Institutions and Organizations.* Edited by C. Edquist. London: Pinter, 36–40.

Jókay, K. Z. 2002. 'Telecottages and the Modernization of Public Services in Hungary: The Case of the Village of Jászkisér'. In *Public Management in the Central and Eastern European Transition: Concepts and Cases.* Edited by G. Wright and J. Nemec, pp. 457–471, Bratislava: NISPACEE.

Jones, S. G. (ed.). 1995. *Cybersociety: Computer-Mediated Communication and Community.* Thousand Oaks, CA: Sage Publication.

Joseph, K. J., and G. Parayil. 2008, January 5. 'Can Trade Liberalisation Bridge the Digital Divide?' Assessing the Information Technology Agreement. *Economic & Political Weekly* 43 (1): 46–53.

Joseph, S. 2001. 'Democratic Good Governance: New Agenda for Change'. *Economic and Political Weekly* 36 (12): 1011–14.

Kaldor, M. 2003. *Global Civil Society: An Answer to War.* Cambridge: Polity Press.

Kanungo, S. 2004. 'On the Emancipatory Role of Rural Information Systems'. *Information Technology & People* 17 (4): 407–422.

Kapoor, S. 2001. 'M. S Swaminathan: Brain Food for the Masses'. *Asiaweek* 29 June: 35–36.

Karan, K. (ed.). 2006. *Cyber communities in rural Asia: A study of seven countries*. Singapore: AMIC/ Marshall Cavendish.

Karat, P. 1984. 'Action Groups/Voluntary Agencies: A Factor in Imperialist Strategy'. *The Marxist* 2(2): 19–54.

Katakam, A. 1999. 'Towards E-Governance'. *Frontline* 16 (25): 78–80.

Kaul, M., N. Patel, and K. Shams. 1989. 'New Information Technology Applications for Local Development in Asian and Pacific Countries', *Information Technology for Development* 4 (1): 1–10.

Kaushik, P. D., and N. Singh. 2002. 'Information Technology and Broad-Based Development: Preliminary Lessons from North India'. University of California Santa Cruz 2000–02 Working Paper Series No. 522. July.

Kaushik, P. D., and N. Singh. 2004. 'Information Technology and Broad-Based Development: Preliminary Lessons from North India'. *World Development* 32 (4): 591–607.

Kaviraj, S. 2001. 'In search of civil society'. In S. Kaviraj and S. Khilnani (eds), *Civil Society: History and Possibilities*. Cambridge: Cambridge University Press, pp. 287–323.

Kaviraj, S., and S. Khilnani. 2001. *Civil Society: History and Possibilities*. Cambridge: Cambridge University Press.

Keane, J. 1988. *Civil Society and the State: New European Perspectives*. London: Verso.

Keeble, L., and B. D. Loader (eds). 2001. *Community Informatics: Shaping Computer Mediated Social Relations*. London and New York: Routledge.

Kendall, L. 2002. *Hanging out in the virtual pub: Masculinities and relationships online*. Berkeley: University of California Press.

Keniston, K, and D. Kumar (eds). 2004. *IT Experience in India: Bridging the Digital Divide*. New Delhi, Thousand Oaks and London: Sage.

Khan, F., and R. Ghadially. 2010. 'Empowerment Through ICT Education, Access and Use: A Gender Analysis of Muslim Youth in India'. *Journal of International Development* 22(5): 659–673.

Khan, H. A. 1998. *Technology, Development and Democracy: Limits of National Innovation Systems in the Age of Post-Modernism*. Cheltenham and Northampton: Edward Elgar.

Khanna, R. 2001a. 'TARAhaat at a Glance'. *Development Alternatives News Letter* 11 (7).

———— 2001b. 'TARAhaat: Achieving Connectivity for the Poor Case Study'. International Conference on Achieving Connectivity for the Rural Poor in India, Baramati, India, May 31 – June 3. http://siteresources.worldbank.org/INTPOVERTY/Resources/335642-1124115102975/1555199-1124741378410/tarahaat.pdf

Kiely, R. 1998. 'Neo liberalism Revised? A Critical Account of World Bank Concepts of Good Governance and Market Friendly Interventions'. *Capital and Class* 64: 63–88.

Kizza, J. M.1998. *Civilizing the Internet: Global Concerns and Efforts Toward Regulation*, London: Mc Farland and Company Inc. Publications.

Krikke, J. 2004. 'WiLL to Transform Indian Telecoms'. *Tele Dot Comm*. www.indiantelephones.com/News/20040202_2.htm

Krishnakumar, A. 2001. 'Changing Rural Lives'. *Frontline* 18 (24). www.flonnet.com/fl1824/18240990.htm

Kroker, A., and M. Kroker. 1997. *Digital Delirium*. New York: St. Martin's Press.

Ku, A. S. 2009. 'Contradictions in the Development of Citizenship in Hong Kong – Governance Without Democracy'. *Asian Survey* 49 (3): 505–27.

Kumar, D. 2006. *Information Technology and Social Change: A Study of Digital Divide in India*, Jaipur: Rawat Publications.

Kumar, R. 2004. 'eChoupals: A Study on the Financial Sustainability of Village Internet Centers in Rural Madhya Pradesh'. *Information Technologies and International Development* 2(1): 45–73.

Kumar, R. 2007. 'Why Institutional Partnerships Matter: A Regional Innovation Systems Approach to Making the ICT for Development Projects More Successful and Sustainable'. Paper presented at the CPRSouth2 Conference, Indian Institute of Technology, Madras, December 15–17, 2007.

Kuriyan, R., I. Ray, and K. Toyama. 2008. 'Information and Communication Technologies for Development: The Bottom of the Pyramid Model in Practice'. *The Information Society* 24 (2): 93–104.

Laishram, N. 2003. *GSM Operators: United They Fight.* www.voicendata.com

Lee, E. 1997. *The Labour Movement and the Internet: The New Internationalism.* London: Photo Press.

Leydesdorff, L. 200. 'The Triple Helix: An Evolutionary Model of Innovations'. *Research Policy* 29 (2): 243–55.

Licker, P. 2001. 'Gift from the Gods? Components of Information Technological Fatalism. Determinism in Several Cultures'. *Electronic Journal of Information Systems in Developing Countries (EJISDC)* 7(1): 1–17.

Lie, R. 2004. 'ICTs for Agricultural Development. An Exercise in Interdisciplinarity'. International Conference Communication and Democracy: Perspectives for a New World, IAMCR (International Association for Media and Communication Research), 25–30 July, Porto Alegre, Brazil (http://umramap.cirad.fr/amap2/logiciels_amap/uploads/Documents/idao/ICT%20for%20agri%20dev-%20Rico.pdf)

Lim, S. S., and Nekmat, E. 2008. 'Learning through "Prosuming": Insights from Media Literacy Programmes in Asia'. *Science Technology & Society* 13(2): 259–278.

Lin, C. A., and D. J. Atkin (eds). (2007). *Communication technology and social change: Theory and implications.* Mahwah, NJ: Lawrence Erlbaum Associates.

Linden, A., and J. Fenn. 2002. 'The Gartner *2002 Technology Radar Screen Gives You a Look Into the Future*'. http://watch.state.wi.us/Home/links/gartner/g100902-Hype%20Cycle.pdf

Loader, B. 1999. *Cyber Space Divide.* London and New York: Routledge.

Long, N., and M. Villarreal. 1993. 'Exploring Development Interface: From Transfer of Technology to Transformation of Meaning'. In *Beyond the Impasse: New Directions in Development Theory*, edited by F. J. Shuurman, pp. 140–158. London and New Jersey: Zed Books.

Lovink, G. 2007. *Zero Comments: Blogging and Critical Internet Culture.* New York: Routlegde.

Lovink, G., and S. Zehle (eds). 2005. *Incommunicado Reader.* The Netherlands: Institute of Network Cultures.

Lui, J. 2003. 'The Simputer moves upmarket'. *ZDNet*, 6 November. www.zdnetasia.com/the-simputer-moves-upmarket-39156876.htm

Luke, T. W. 1998. 'The Politics of Digital Equality: Access, Capability and Distribution in Cyberspace'. In *The Politics of Cyberspace*, edited by C. Toulouse, and T. W. Luke, pp. 120–43, New York and London: Routledge.

Lundvall, B. A. 1998. 'Why Study National Systems and National Styles of Innovation'. *Technology Analysis and Strategic Management* 10(4): 407–21.

Madon, S. 2008. 'Evaluating the Development Impact of E-Governance Initiatives: An Exploratory Framework'. In *ICTs and Indian social change: diffusion, governance, poverty*, eds. A. Saith, M. Vijayabaskar, and V. Gayathri, pp. 268–289 India: Sage Publications.

Madon, S. 2009. *E-governance for Development: A Focus on Rural India*. London: Palgrave Macmillan.

Magnet, S. 2007. 'Feminist Sexualities, Race and the Internet: An Investigation of suicidegirls.com'. *New Media & Society* 9 (4): 577–602.

Mansell, R., and U. When (eds). 1998. *Knowledge Societies: Information Technology for Sustainable Development*. New York: Oxford University Press.

Margetts, H. 1999. *Information technology in government: Britain and America*. London and New York: Routledge.

Margetts, H. 2003. 'Electronic Government: A Revolution in Public Administration'. In *Handbook of public administration*. Edited by B. G. Peters and J. Pierre. pp. 366–76 London, Thousand Oaks, Calif.: Sage Publications.

Marglin, F. A., and S. A. Marglin (eds). 1996. *DeColonizing Knowledge: From Development to Dialogue*. Oxford: Clarendon Press.

———— 1990. *Dominating Knowledge: Development, Culture and Resistance*. Oxford, Clarendon Press.

Marglin, S. A. 1990. 'Towards the Decolonization of Mind'. In Marglin, F.A. and S. A. Marglin (eds). op.cit. pp. 1–27.

Mazzarella, W. 2010. 'Beautiful Balloon: The Digital Divide and the Charisma of New Media in India'. *American Ethnologist* 37(4): 783–804.

McGuigan, J. 1999. *Modernity and Postmodern Culture*. Buckingham and Philadelphia: Open University Press.

Mencher, J. P. 1978. *Agriculture and social structure in Tamil Nadu: past origins, present transformations, and future prospects*. Durham, NC: Carolina Academic Press.

Mercer, C. 2004. 'Engineering civil society: ICT in Tanzania'. *Review of African Political Economy* 31 (99): 49–64.

Metcalfe, J. S. 1997. 'Technology Systems and Technology Policy in an Evolutionary Framework'. In *Technology, Globalization and Economic Performance*. Edited by D. Archibugi and J. Michie. Cambridge: Cambridge University Press, pp. 268–96.

Mitchell, W. J. 2000. *E-topia: Urban lLife, Jim–But Not as We Know It*. Cambridge, MA: MIT Press.

Molloy, A., C. McFeely, and E. Connolly. 1999. *Building a Social Economy for a New Millennium*. Derry, Guildhall Press/NICDA.

Montgomery, J. D., and A. Inkeles. 2000. *Social capital as a Policy Resource*. Boston: Kluwer Academic Publishers.

Moore, N. 1998. 'Confucius or capitalism? Policies for an information society', in B. Loader (ed), *Cyberspace Divide: Equality, Agency and Policy in the Information Society*. London and New York: Routledge, pp. 149–160.

Morahan-Martin. J. 2000. 'Women and the Internet: Promise and Perils'. *CyberPsychology and Behavior* 3(5): 683–691.

MSSRF (M. S. Swaminathan Research Foundation). n.d. 'Assessment of Impact of Information Technology on Rural Areas of India' http://portal.unesco.org/ci/en/files/5870/10352133010india.pdf/india.pdf

———— 2000. 'Reaching the unreached: Village Knowledge Centres in Pondicherry for Sustainable Food Security'. Video Documentary, Chennai, Tamil Nadu: Produced by A.K Films.

———— c.2001.Eleventh Annual Report, M. S. Swaminathan Research Foundation. Chennai; Chennai: Reliance printers.

———— c.2002. Twelfth Annual Report , M. S. Swaminathan Research Foundation, Chenna: Chennai: Reliance printers.

Mukhopadhyay, S., and V. B. Kamble. 2006. *Information and Communication Tecnology (ICT) and Gender*. New Delhi: VigyanPrasar, Department of Science and Technology.

Mukhopadhyay, S., and R. Nandi. 2007. 'Unpacking the Assumption of Gender Neutrality: Akshaya Project of the Kerala IT Mission in India'. *Gender Technology and Development*, 11 (2): 75–95.

Murray, B. 2001. 'The Hungarian Telecottage Movement'. In *Telecentres: Case Studies and key issues*. Edited By C. Latchem and D. Walker, pp. 53–64. Vancouver: The Commonwealth of Learning.

Murray, B., C. Murray, and S. Brooks. 2001. 'Training Telecentre Managers, Staff and Users'. In *Telecentres: Case studies and Key Issues*, edited by C. Latchem, and D. Walker, pp. 197–212. Canada: The Commonwealth of Learning.

Nair, J. 2000. 'Singapore is not Bangalore's Destiny'. *Economic and Political Weekly* 35 (18): 1512–1514.

Nair, M., and T. M. A. Sharaffadeen. 2009. 'Managing Innovation in the Network Economy: Lessons for Countries in the Asia Pacific Region'. In *Digital Review of Asia Pacific 2009–2010*, edited by S. Akhtar and P. Arinto, pp. 25–42. New Delhi: Sage Publications.

Nalini, R., ed. 2007. *Digital Culture Unplugged: Probing the Native Cyborg's Multiple Locations*. London, New York, New Delhi: Routledge.

Navarria, G. 2006. 'The Three Faces of Government in the Age of the Internet and the Future of Activism Within a Condition of Shared Weaknesses'. *EastBound* 1 (1): 124–152.

Negroponte, N. 1995. *Being Digital*. New York: Alfred A. Knopf.

Ng, C., and S. Mitter (eds). 2005. *Gender and the Digital Economy: Perspectives from the Developing World*. New Delhi: Sage.

Noronha, F. 2003. 'Simputer: Computers for the Poor or an Idealistic Dream?' *Scidev.net*, July 11.

Omvedt, G. 1981. 'Capitalist Agriculture and Rural Classes in India'. *Economic and Political Weekly*, 16 (52): A-140-A-159.

O'Neil, D. 2002. 'Assessing Community Informatics: A Review of Methodological Approaches for Evaluating Community Networks and Community Technology Centers'. *Internet Research* 12 (1): 76–102.

Palackal, A., and W. Shrum (eds). 2007. *Information Society and Development: The Kerala Experience*. Jaipur: Rawat Publications.

PANTLEG. 1999. 'Success Stories of Rural ICTs in a Developing Country'. Report of the PANAsia Telecenter Learning and Evaluation Group's Mission to India, involving visits to the Foundation of Occupational Development and the M. S. Swaminathan Research Foundation, November. http://idlbnc.idrc.ca/dspace/bitstream/10625/35581/1/127462.pdf

Parayil, G. 2005. 'The Digital Divide and Increasing Returns: Contradictions of Informational Capitalism'. *The Information Society* 21(1): 41–51.

Parayil, G., and T. T. Sreekumar. 2004. 'Industrial Development and the Dynamics of Innovation in Hong Kong'. *International Journal of Technology Management* 27(4): 369–392.

Parfitt, T. 2002. *The End of Development: Modernity, Post Modernity and Development*. London and Sterling: Pluto Press.

Parthasarathy, B., and J. Srinivasan. 2008. 'How the Development of ICT Affects ICT for Development: Social Contestation in the Shaping of Standards for the Information Age'. *Science, Technology & Society* 13(2): 279–301.

Parthasarathy, B. 2004. 'India's Silicon Valley or Silicon Valley's India?: Socially Embedding the Computer Software Industry in Bangalore'. *International Journal of Urban and Regional Research* 28(3): 664–685.

Patnaik, U. (ed.). 1990. *Agrarian relations and accumulation: the 'mode of production' debate in India*. Bombay, Oxford: Published for Sameeksha Trust by Oxford University Press.

———— 1971. 'Capitalist Development in Agriculture: A Note'. *Economic and Political Weekly*, 6(39) : A-123-A-13.

Patra, R., J. Pal, and S. Neduvezchi, 2009. *ICTD State of the Union: Where have we reached and where are we headed*. Proceedings of the International Conference on Information and Communication Technologies and Development (ICTD 2009): pp. 357–366, Doha, Qatar.

Peizer, J. 2005. *The Dynamics of Technology for Social Change*. Lincoln, NE: iUniverse.

Pelczynski, Z. A. 1988. 'Solidarity and the rebirth of Civil Society in Poland', 1976–81. In J. Keane (ed.). op. cit., pp. 361–380.

Peterson, C., V. Sandell, and A. Lawlor. 2001. *What Works: TARAhaat's Portal for Rural India*, World Resources Institute. www.digitaldividend.org/pdf/tarahaat.pdf

Petras, J. 1999a. 'Globalization: A Critical Analysis'. *Journal of Contemporary Asia* 29(1): 3–37.

————1999b. 'NGOs in the Service of Imperialism'. *Journal of Contemporary Asia* 29(4): 429–440.

Phillips, R. 2000. 'Approaching the Organization of Economic Activity in the Age of Cross-Border Alliance Capitalism'. In R. Palan (ed.), op. cit: 36–52.

Pick, J. B., and K. Gollakota. 2010. "Technology for Rural Telecenters In India: A Model and Exploratory Study of Diffusion of Information For Telecenter Use and Sustainability". AMCIS 2010 Proceedings.Paper 550. URL: http://aisel.aisnet.org/amcis2010/550

Pickerill, J. 2001. 'Weaving a Green Web: Environmental Protest and Computer Mediate rotest in Britain'. In *Culture and Politics in the Information Age: A New Politics?*, edited by F. Webster, pp. 142–166. London and New York: Routledge.

Pieterse, J.N. 2000. Trends in Development Theory. In *Global Political Economy: Contemporary Theories*, ed. R. Palan, pp. 197–214. London and New York: Routledge.

———— 2005. 'Digital Capitalism and Development: The Unbearable Lightness of ICT4D'. In *Incommunicado Reader*, edited by G. Lovink and S. Zehle, pp. 11–29. The Netherlands: Institute of Network Cultures.

Prahalad, C. K. 2005. *The Fortune at the Bottom of the Pyramid*. Upper Saddle River, NJ: Wharton School Publishing.

Prahalad, C. K., and, A. Hammond. 2002. 'Serving the World's poor, Profitably'. *Harvard Business Review*. 80(9): 48–58.

Pringle, I., and S. Subramanian (eds). 2004. *Projects and Experiences in ICT Innovation for Poverty Reduction*. New Delhi: UNESCO.

Prins, J. E. J., M. M. Eifert, C. Girot, M. Groothuis, and W. J. M. Voermans. 2002. *E-government and its Implications for Administrative Law: Regulatory Initiatives in France, Germany, Norway and the United States*. The Hague: Asser Press.

Putnam, R. 1993. *Making Democracy Work: Civic Traditions in Modern Italy*. Princeton: Princeton University Press.

Putnam, R. 1995. 'Bowling Alone: America's Declining Social Capital'. *Journal of Democracy* 6: 65–78.

Qureshi, I. 2001. 'Simputer to Help Tribals Learn'. Indo-Asian News Service. http://archive.apnic.net/mailing-lists/s-asia-it/archive/2001/09/msg00021.html

Qvortrup, L., C. Ancelin, J. Frawley, J. Hartly, F. Pichault, and P. Pop. 1985. *Social Experiments with Information Technology and the Challenges of Innovation*. Dordrecht: D. Reidel Publishing.

Radhakrishnan, S. 2007. 'Rethinking knowledge for development: Transnational knowledge professionals and the "new" India'. *Theory & Society* 36 (2): 141–159.

Raj, J. V. P. 1998. 'Globalization and its Impacts'. Resource material for the *Strategic Planning Process for the Trocaire Partners in Tamilnadu*, facilitated by ADECOM, Pondicherry and

KSA, Bangalore. Issued by Indian National Social Action Forum (INSAF), Pondicherry Unit.

Rajan, N. (ed). 2007. *Digital Culture Unplugged: Probing the native Cyborg's Multiple Locations*. London, New York, New Delhi: Routledge.

Rajora, R. *Bridging the Digital Divide: Gyandoot Model for Community Networks*. New Delhi: Tata McGraw-Hill Publishing Company.

Ramachandraiah, C. 2003. Information Technology and Social Development. *Economic and Political Weekly* 38(12–13): 1192–7.

Ramachandraiah, C., and V. K. Bawa. 2000. 'Hyderabad in the Changing Political Economy'. *Journal of Contemporary Asia* 30 (4): 562–74.

Ramilo, C. G., and C. Cinco. 2005. *Gender Evaluation Methodology for Internet and ICTs: A Learning Tool For Change And Empowerment*. Melville, South Africa: APC.

Rangaswamy, N. 2006. 'Social Entrepreneurship as Critical Agency: A study of rural internet kiosks'. Proceedings of the 2006 International Conference on Information and Communications Technologies and Development, Berkeley, May 25–26, pp. 143–152.

Ray, A. 2007. *Naked on the Internet: Hookups, Downloads, and Cashing in on Internet Sexploration*. Berkeley, CA: Seal Press.

Remesh, P. B. 2008. 'Work Organisation, Control and Empowerment'. In C. Upadhya and A. R. Vasavi (eds), op. cit., 190–210.

Rheingold, H. 1993. *The Virtual Community: Homesteading on the Electronic Frontier*. Reading, Massachusetts: Addison-Wesley.

——— 2000. *The Virtual Community: Homesteading on the Electronic Frontier (2nd Edition)*. Cambridge, Massachusetts: MIT Press.

Richardson, D., R. Ramirez, and M. Haq. 2000. *Grameen Telecom's Village Phone Programme in Rural Bangladesh: A Multi-Media Case Study*. Canada: Canadian International Development Agency.

Robins, K. 1996. 'Cyberspace and the World We Live In'. In *Fractal Dreams: New Media in Social Context*, ed. J. Dovey, pp. 1–30. London: Lawrence and Wishart.

Robins, K. 1999. 'Foreclosing the City? The Bad Idea of Virtual Urbanism'. In *Technocities*, edited by J. Downey and J. McGuigan, pp. 34–59. London: Sage Publications.

Robins, K., and F. Webster. 1988. 'Athens without Slaves… or Slaves without Athens? The Neurosis of Technology'. *Science as Culture* 3: 7–53.

Robins, K., and F. Webster. 1983. 'Luddism, New Technology and Critique of Political Economy'. In *Science Technology and the Labor Process: Volume 2*, eds. L. Levodow, and B. Young, pp. 9–48. Atlantic Highlands, NJ.: Humanities Press.

Rogers E. M., and P. Shukla. 2001. 'The Role of Telecentres in Development Communication and the Digital Divide'. *Journal of Development Communication* (Special Issue on Telecentres) 12[2]. http://ip.cals.cornell.edu/commdev/documents/jdc-rogers.doc

Roman, R., and R. Colle. 2002. 'Themes and Issues in Telecentre Sustainability'. Paper no. 10, Working Paper Series, Institute for Development Policy and Management University of Manchester, Precinct Centre, Manchester, M13 9GH, UK.

Rosenberg, N. 1976. "Marx as a student of Technology'. *Monthly Review* 28: 56–77.

Rostow, W. W. 1960. *The Stages of Economic Growth: A Non-Communist Manifesto*. Cambridge: Cambridge University Press.

Rothenberg-Aalami, J., and J. Pal. 2005. 'Rural Telecenter Impact Assessments and the Political Economy of ICT for Development'. Berkeley Roundtable on the International Economy (BRIE), Working Paper No. 164, University of California, Berkeley.

Roy, A.1999. *The Cost of Living*. New York: Modern Library.

Roy, S. 2005. *Globalisation, ICT and Developing Nations*. New Delhi: Sage.

Rudra, A. 1970. In 'Search of the Capitalist Farmer'. *Economic and Political Weekly* 5 (26): A-85-A-87.

Sahay, S. 2002. *Tribal Women in the New Profile: Vis-à-Vis their Non-Tribal Twins.* New Delhi: Anmol.

Saith, A. 2008. 'ICTs and Poverty Alleviation: Hope or Hype?' In *ICTs and Indian Social Change: Diffusion, gGovernance, Poverty,* edited by A. Saith M. Vijayabaskar, and V. Gayathri, pp.113–159 Sage, India.

San Miguel, S .2001. 'Connecting Rural India to the Internet: The Challenges of Using VSAT Technology' [Case study from Development Alternatives (DA)]. www.sdcn.org/webworks/cases/vsat_da1.htm

Sandoval, C. 1995. 'New Sciences: Cyborg Feminism and the Methodology of the Oppressed'. In *The Cyborg Handbook.* Edited by C. H. Gray. New York: Routledge.

Sanjay, A. K., and V. Gupta. 2003. *Gyandoot: Trying to Improve Government Services for Rural Citizens in India.* eGovernment for Development- eTransparency Case Study No.11. http://www.egov4dev.org/transparency/case/gyandoot.shtml

Sarukkai, S. 2008. 'Culture of Technology and ICTs'. In *ICTs and Indian Social Change: Diffusion, Governance, Poverty,* edited by A. Saith, M. Vijayabaskar, and V. Gayathri, pp. 34–58 India: Sage Publications.

Sau, R. 1984. 'Development of Capitalism in India'. *Economic and Political Weekly* 19 (30): PE-73-PE-80.

Sawhney, H. 2009. 'Innovations at the Edge: The impact of Mobile Technologies on the Character of the Internet'. In *From telecommunication to Media,* edited by G. Goggin, and L. Hjorth, pp. 105–117. New York: Routledge.

Saxena, A. 2009. 'Gender Evaluation of EgramSuraj (e-good governance) Scheme of Chhattisgarh State', 12th national Conference on e-Governance, Department of Administrative Reforms and Public Grievances, Government of India. Goa: February 12–13.

Saxena, N . 2001. 'Leading Manufacturers in Race for Simputer'. *Economic Times* May 13.

Scholte, J. A. 2000. 'Global Civil Society', in N. Woods (ed.) op. cit., pp. 173–201.

Schön D., B. Sanyal, and W. J. Mitchel (eds). 1998. *High Technology and Low Income Communities.* Cambridge, MA: MIT Press.

Schwittay, A. 2008. 'A Living Lab: Corporate Delivery of ICTs in Rural India'. *Science Technology & Society* 13(2): 175–209.

Scott, A., and M. Page. 2001. 'Change, Agency and Woman's Learning: New Practices in Community Informatics', in *Community Informatics.* Edited by L. Keeble and B. Loader. London: Routledge, pp. 149–94.

Sein, M. K., and G. Harindranath. 2004. 'Conceptualizing the ICT Artifact: Toward Understanding the Role of ICT in National Development'. *The Information Society* 20(1): 15–24.

Sen, A. K. 1989. Food and Freedom. *World Development* 17: 769–81.

———— 1999. *Development as Freedom.* New York: Alfred A. Knopf.

Sen, A.K., and M. Nussbaum (eds). 1993. *The Quality of Life.* New Delhi: Oxford University Press.

Senthilkumaran, S., and S. Arunachalam. 2002. 'Expanding the Village Knowledge Centres in Pondicherry'. *Regional Development Dialogue* 23 (2): 65–88.

Shade, L. R. 2002. *Gender and Community in the Social Construction of the Internet.* New York: Peter Lang.

Shafir, G. (ed.). 1998. *The Citizenship Debates: A Reader.* Minneapolis: University of Minnesota Press.

Sharif, N. 2010. 'Rhetoric of Innovation Policy Making in Hong Kong Using the Innovation Systems Conceptual Approach'. *Science Technology & Human Values* 35(3): 408–434.

Sharma, U. 2003. Women Empowerment through Information Technologies. New Delhi: Authors Press.

Shils, E. 1997. *The virtue of Civility: Selected Essays on Liberalism, Tradition, and Civil Society.* Indianapolis, Ind.: Liberty Fund.

Shiva, V. 1991. *The Violence of the Green Revolution: Third World Agriculture, Ecology, and Politics.* London: Zed Books.

Short, G., and C. Latchem. 2000. 'The Australian Telecentre Experience'. In *Telecenters Around the World*. Edited by W. Murray. Geneva: International Telecommunication Union.

Shrum, W. 2005. 'Social Engineering of the Internet in Developing Areas'. In *Education and the Knowledge Society: Information Technology Supporting Human Development*, edited by T. J. van Weert, pp. 213–221. Boston: Kluwer Academic Publishers.

Singh, A. K., and C. Rajyalakshmi. 1993. 'Status of Tribal Women in India'. *Social Change* 23(4): 3–18.

Singh, N. 2004. 'Information Technology and Rural Development in India'. UC Santa Cruz Economics Working Paper No. 563. SSRN: http://ssrn.com/abstract=523823

Slater, D. 1987. 'On Development Theory and Warren Thesis: Arguments Against the Predominance of Economism'. *Environment and Planning* 5: 263–82.

Smith, P. J., and E. Smythe. 2001. 'Globalisation, Citizenship and Technology: The Multilateral Agreement on Investment (MAI) meets the Internet'. In F. Webster (ed.), op.cit.

Sokolova, M. 2006. 'Improving Quality of eGov Strategies in Belarus, Ukraine and Lithuania through Citizens' Participation in eGov Planning'. Open Society Institute, Center for Policy Studies, Central European University. http://pdc.ceu.hu/archive/00002840039

Solow, R. M. 1956. 'A Contribution to the Theory of Economic Growth'. *Quarterly Journal of Economics* 70 (February):69–94.

Sood, A. D. 2001. *A Social Investor's Guide to ICTs for Development.* Bangalore: Centre for Knowledge societies and Charities Aid Foundation India.

———— 2003. 'Information Nodes in Rural Landscape'. *i4d-Information for Development* 1(1): 14–21.

Sparks, C. 1994. 'Civil Society and Information Society as Guarantors of Progress'. In *Information Society and Civil Society: Perspectives on the Changing World Order*. S. Splichel, A. Calabrese, and C. Spark, 9 (eds), pp. 21–49. West Lafayatte, IN: Purdue University Press.

Spender, D. 1995. *Nattering on the Net: Women, Power and Cyberspace.* Melbourne, Spinifex Press.

Spivak, G. C. 2008. 'Megacity-1997: Testing Theory in Cities'. In *Other Asias*, pp. 161–74. Maiden US, Oxford UK and Victoria, Australia: Blackwell.

Sreekumar, T. T. 2002. 'Civil Society and ICT-Based Models of Rural Change: History, Rhetoric and Practice'. Paper presented at the International Seminar on 'ICTS for Indian Development: Processes, Prognosis and Policies', December 9–11, Bangalore.

———— T. T. 2003. 'De-hyping ICTs: ICT innovations by Civil Society Organizations in Rural India'. *i4d-Information for Development* 1(1): 22–27.

———— T. T. 2006. 'ICTs for the Poor: Civil Society and Cyberlibertarian Developmentalism in Rural India'. In *Political Economy & Information Capitalism in India Digital Divide, Development Divide and Equity*, edited by G. Parayil, pp. 51–87. New York: Palgrave Macmillan.

――――― T. T. 2007a. 'Decrypting E-Governance: Narratives, Power Play and Participation in the Gyandoot Intranet'. *Electronic Journal of Information Systems for Developing Countries* 32, 1–24.

――――― T. T. 2007b. 'Cyber Kiosks and Dilemmas of Social Inclusion in Rural India'. *Media, Culture & Society* 29 (6): 869–889.

――――― T. T. 2007c. 'ICTs for Governance and Development: A Critical Review of Kerala's Recent Experiences'. In *Information Society and Development: The Kerala Experience*. edited by by A. Palackal and W. Shrum, pp. 109–132. Jaipur: Rawat Publications.

――――― T. T. 2010. 'From ICTs to Innovations: Social and Cultural Imperatives in Developing Countries'. (Special Article) *ICT World Today*. Spring: 4–7.

Sreekumar, T. T., and M. Rivera-Sánchez. 2008. 'ICTs and Development: Revisiting the Asian Experience'. *Science, Technology & Society* 13(2): 159–174.

Sriramesh, K., and M. Rivera-Sánchez, 2006. 'E-Government in a Corporatist, Communitarian Society: The Case of Singapore'. *New Media and Society* 8(5): 707–30.

Standage, T. 1998. *The Victorian Internet*. New York: Walker and Company.

Staudenmaier, J. M. 1985. *Technologies Story Tellers: Reweaving the Human Fabric*. Cambridge, Mass.: MIT Press.

Sterling, B. 2001. 'The Year in Ideas: A to Z.; Simputer'. *The New York Times*, December 9.

Sutcliffe, B. 1999. 'The Place of Development in Theories of Imperialism and Globalization'. In *Critical Development Theory: Contributions to a New Paradigm*, edited by R. Munck and D. O'Hearn, pp. 135–154. London and New York: Zed Books.

Tehranian, M. 1990. *Technologies of Power: Information Machines and Democratic Prospects*. Norwood, NJ: Ablex Publishing Corporation.

Terry, A., and R. Gomez. 2010. 'Gender and Public Access Computing: An International Perspective'. *The Electronic Journal on Information Systems in Developing Countries (EJISDC)* 43 (5): 1–17.

Tismaneanu, V. 1990. 'Eastern Europe: The Story the Media Missed'. *Bulletin of the Atomic Scientists* 46 (2) March. www.thebulletin.org/issues/1990/mar90/mar90tismaneanu.html

Tiwari, M., and U. Sharmistha. 2008. 'ICTs in Rural India: User Perspective Study of Two Different Models in Madhya Pradesh and Bihar'. *Science, Technology & Society* 13:2: 233–58.

Thomas, J. J., and G. Parayil. 2008. 'Bridging the Social and Digital Divides in Andhra Pradesh and Kerala: A Capabilities Approach'. *Development and Change* 39(3): 409–435.

Thompson, M. 2004. 'Discourse, Development and the Digital Divide: ICTs and the World Bank'. *Review of African Political Economy* 31(99): 103–123.

Tonnies, F. [1887]. 2002. *Community and Society*. Mineola, NY: Dover Publications.

Townsend, J. 1993. 'Gender Studies: Whose Agenda?' In Shcuurman F. J. (ed.), op. cit: pp. 169–86.

Toyama, K., and K. Keniston. 2008. 'Telecenter Debates'. *Telecentre Magazine* 2 (1): 31–33.

TRAI (Telecom Regulatory Authority of India). 2000. 'Policy Relating to Limited Mobility by Use of Wireless in Local Loop Techniques in the Access Network by Basic Service Providers'. Consultation Paper No. 2000/5FN. www.trai.gov.wllcp.htm

Tripathy, S. N. (ed.). 2002. *Tribal Women in India*. New Delhi: Mohit Publications.

Turkle, S. 1995. *Life on the Screen: Identity in the Age of the Internet*. New York: Simon & Schuster.

UNDP [United Nations Development Programme]. 1999. *Human Development Report 1999*. New York: Oxford University Press.

UNDP. 2000. *Human Development Report 2000*. New York: Oxford University Press.

United Nations.1999. *Economic and Social Survey of Asia and the Pacific 1999*. New York: UN Publications.

Upadhyay, C., and A. R. Vasavi (eds). 2008. *In an Outpost of Global Economy: Work and Workers in India's Information Technology*. Routledge: New York.

Urry, J. 1981. *The Anatomy of Capitalist Societies: The Economy, Civil Society, and the State*. London: Macmillan.

Van Thiel, S. (2001) Quangos: Trends, Causes and Consequences. Aldershot: Ashgate.

Vasagam, R. M. 1999. 'Internet Kiosks: Tamil Nadu leads the way'. *Voices for Change* 3(3): 23–24.

Virilio, P. 1995. *The Art of the Motor*. Trans. Julie Rose. Minneapolis and London: University of Minnesota Press.

————— 1999. *Politics of the Very Worst: An Interview by Philippe Petit*. Translated by M. Cavaliere, edited by S. Lotringer. New York: Semiotext(e).

————— 2000. *The Information Bomb*. New York: Verso.

Visaria, P., and L. Visaria. 1985. 'Indian Households with Female Heads: Their Incidence, Characteristics and Levels of Living'. In *Tyranny of the Household*. Edited by D. Jain, and N. Banerjee. New Delhi: Shakti Books.

Vittal, N. 2001. 'E-Development Enabling Communities to Shape their Future: The Indian Perspective'. In Jayakumar, R. et al., op. cit, pp. 1–30.

Wade, R. H. 2002. 'Bridging the Digital Divide: New Route to Development or New Form of Dependency?' *Global Governance* 8(4): 443–466.

Wajcman, J. 2004. *TechnoFeminism*, Polity Press, Cambridge, UK.

Wajcman, J., and L. A. Pham Lobb. 2007. 'The Gender Relations of Software Work in Vietnam'. *Gender, Technology and Development* 11(1): 1–26.

Walker, A., and C. Walker (eds). 1997. *Britain Divided: The Growth of Social Exclusion in the 1980s and 1990s*. London: Child Poverty Action Group.

Walsham, G. 2010. ICTs for the Broader Development of India: An Analysis of the Literature". *The Electronic Journal of Information Systems in Developing Countries*, 41. www.ejisdc.org.

Walsham, G., and S. Sahay. 2006. 'Research on Information Systems in Developing Countries: Current Landscape and Future Prospects'. *Information Technology for Development* 12(1): 7–24.

Walzer, M. 'The Civil Society Argument'. In Shafir, G. (ed.), op. cit., pp. 89–95.

Webb, J., T. Schirato, and G. Danaher. 2002. *Understanding Bourdieu*. London, Thousand Oaks and New Delhi: Sage Publications.

Weber, S., and J. Bussell. 2005. 'Will Information Technology Reshape the North-South Asymmetry of Power in the Global Political Economy?'. *Studies in Comparative International Development* 40 (2): 62–84.

Webster, F. 1999. 'Information and Communications Technologies: Luddism Revisited'. In *Technocities*, edited by. J. Downey and J. McGuigan, pp. 60–89. London: Sage Publications.

Wellman, B. 2001. Physical Place and Cyberplace: The Rise of Personalised Networking. *International Journal of Urban and Regional Research* 25(2): 227–252.

Wellman, B., ed. 1999. *Networks in the Global Village: Life in Contemporary Communities*. Boulder, Colorado: Westview Press.

Wesolowski, W. 1995. The Nature of Social Ties and the Future of Postcommunist Society: Poland after Solidarity. In Hall, J., ed. op. cit., pp. 110–224.

Williams, M. 2001. Contextualism, Externalism and Epistemic Standards. *Philosophical Studies* 103: 1–23.

Wolmark, J. ed. 2000. CyberSexualities: *A Reader on Feminist Theory, Cyborgs and Cyberspace.* Edinburgh, UK: U of Edinburgh Press.

Woods, N., ed. 2000. *The Political Economy of Globalization.* London: Macmillan.

Woolgar, S., ed. 2002. *Virtual Society? Technology, Cyberbole, Reality.* Oxford: Oxford University Press.

World Bank. 1992. *Governance and Development.* Washington: World Bank.

World Bank. 2000. *Quality of Growth,* New York: Oxford University.

Yates, D. J., G. J. Gulati, A. Tawileh. 2010. *Explaining the Global Digital Divide: The Impact of Public Policy Initiatives on Digital Opportunity and ICT Development.* HICSS, pp. 1–10, 2010 43rd Hawaii International Conference on System Sciences. http://doi.ieeecomputersociety.org/10.1109/HICSS.2010.196

Young, G. 2002. Closing the Gaps: Women, Communications and Technology. *Development* 45(4): 23–8.

INDEX

A

Aarthyas (village elites) 46, 65, 179n; *see also*
    elites
adaptation vs. ground-up innovation 10, 26
Adivasis (aborigines) 42
adoption vs. technology transfer 10
Alavi, H. 175
Albrechtsen, H. 2, 4
all-women centre 110
Amin, S. 128
amoral familism 166
analytical issues 24–7, 163, 166
anecdotes vs. analysis 8, 13, 58–63, 68,
    83, 84
Angel Investors 39
appropriate technology 11, 21, 26, 125–8,
    139, 163, 165
Armitage, J. 19, 168
Arunachalam, S. 44, 55, 97, 115
Association of Nordic Telecottages
    (FILIN) 2

B

Bailur, S. 7
Banaji, B. 175
Banerjee, P. 140
Baran, P. 128
Beniger, J. R. 19
Best, M. L. 61
Bhaduri, A. 175
Bharat Sanchar Nigam Ltd (BSNL) 73,
    90, 147
Bhatnagar, S. 4, 20, 69, 70, 84, 86–7
Bourdieu, 176n
bottom of the pyramid (BoP) markets 125,
    171, 183n, 186n

bureaucracies 16, 18, 38, 71, 91, 95, 133,
    155, 166
bureaucratic structures 166
Businessworld 55
Bussell, J. 19
Byres. T. J. 175

C

Campbell, Colin 2
Canadian Journal of Educational
    Communication 1
caste 6, 11, 13, 31, 51, 65, 91, 97, 103,106,
    115, 122, 123, 160, 184n; elites 42,
    76; forces 42–3, 76; inequality 97;
    oppression 123, 160; upper 90, 156;
    see also Dalits (lower castes)
Castells, M. 19, 36, 38–9, 65, 113, 114,
    118, 133, 180n
C-DAC, Pune 44
Centre for Electronic Governance
    (CEG) 81
Centre for International Development 61
Chakravartty, P. 16–17
Chandhoke, N. 14, 176n
Chaterjee, Partha 15, 16
civil society: capability of 25–6; and
    community 151–5; development
    and democracy 153; elements of
    25; meanings of 16; organizations
    in 17; vs. political society 17; role of
    162; sensitivity to inequities 26; state
    involvement in 14
civil society and cyber-libertarian
    developmentism: cyber-libertarianism
    turn 33–5; expectations and outcomes
    48–56; information village research
    model 40–1; lessons and non-lessons

63–5; social enterprise model
35–40; State vs. CSO relations 56–8;
success anecdotes vs. analysis 58–63;
TARAkendras 45–8
civil society argument: and ICTs 13–19;
questions regarding 162–3
civil society initiatives 25, 97
civil society involvement: in e-governance
projects 92; in innovation 161
civil society organizations (CSOs): see
CSOs (civil society organizations)
Coleman, J. S. 176n
colonial nationalism 16
communities 151; ICT revolution and
3, 151, 164; resources of 48, 113,
162; see also elites; local communities;
marginalized communities; rural
communities
community, studies regarding sense of 7
compact base stations (CBS) 144
computer illiteracy 122, 160
connectivity problems 78, 90
constructivist perspective/views 10, 23, 67,
159, 165
contextualism 24
corDECT system: commercial success 149;
cost and capability of 143; elements
of 144; litigation 147–8
corDECT technology 146–7, 161
corDECT WLL (Wireless Local Loop) 73,
127, 144–9, 161, 165
credit: bank, 79; rural 13, 40, 77,
84, 86
CSOs (civil society organizations):
contributions of 20–1; disjunct
focus 36; expectations and outcomes
64; expectations vs. actual benefits
of 34; failures of 27; ICT-based
development projects 4; kiosks in
155; reasons and goals 23; role of
129; social enterprise and social
movements 112–16; social enterprise
model of 30; and the state 149–50;
and triple helix model 130–4
cyber-kiosks and social inclusion problems:
gender and IT 98–101; gender
divisions 106–9; ICTs and limits of
developmental CSOs 122–3; ICTs
and social change 97–8; knowledge

centres and women's participation
109–12; net-based social action
participation 116–22; rhetoric
and reality of participation 101–2;
TARAkendras 106–9; tribal women
at large 103–6; women and ICTs
101–2
cyber-libertarian developmentalism 4,
168; see also civil society and cyber-
libertarian developmentism

D

DA (development alternatives) 34, 45
Dalit villages 11, 51
Dalits (lower castes) 2, 9, 42, 43, 98, 106,
111, 113, 114, 115, 175n, 179n
Dayanand, Anjali 111
decentralization/decentralizing 2, 20
decentralized delivery system 31, 94, 157
DECT Interface Unit (DIU) 144
demand-side dimensions of ICTs 8
democracy
conflicts with 14–15, 16, 17,
36, 153
strength of 4, 7, 75, 153;
see also local democracy
dependency theory 35, 36, 128
Deshpande, Vinay 135, 136, 137
developing countries 8, 10, 12, 14, 18,
20–1, 25–6, 34, 38–9, 69, 99, 101,
128, 129, 130, 132, 133, 138, 144,
152, 165–8, 170–2
development alternatives (DA) 5, 34, 45
development divide 33, 39
development theory 25, 33, 35, 128, 167
developmental approach 158
developmental thinking 35
digital divide 5, 8, 12, 20, 33, 39, 99, 100,
102, 132, 134, 135, 137, 138, 142,
152, 162
District Rural Development Agencies
(DRDA) 46, 56, 57, 80
donor agencies 14, 18, 34, 58, 155,
156, 162
donor support 61, 119, 156, 162, 164, 172
Dugger, C. 4, 115
Dyer-Witheford, 178n
dynamic information 43

E

economic globalization 37
education model 53
education programmes for illiterate women 107, 108
e-governance 5, 11, 24, 30, 31, 34, 57; early tests of 71; as economic growth tool 94; effect on end users 95; Gyandoot 72–4; and ICTs 93–5; implementation barriers 158; in India 68; narratives of success 82–91; origins in India 68–72; social dynamics of 74; as technical process 156; technology and governance 67–8; *see also* QUANGOs (Quasi-Autonomous Non-Governmental Organizations)
e-governance projects 18, 31, 67, 68, 71, 91, 92, 94, 157, 158, 169
e-governance services 57, 73, 104
electrical supply costs 54, 61, 82
electrical supply problems 47, 77, 80, 162, 172
elites: and bureaucracies 16; caste elites 76; local 6, 11, 42–3, 65, 91; poor vs. 6; rural 81, 109, 172; vs. rural populations 12; village 46, 94, 107, 156
elitist capture 6, 11, 65, 156, 161–2, 172
email 44, 73, 83–4, 103, 134, 142
emancipating technology 102, 161, 172
emancipation precondition 33
embedded autonomy 154
empowerment 5, 7, 13, 20, 25, 31, 35, 36, 76, 101, 102, 118, 169, 251
Encore Software Ltd 138, 141
end users, e-governance effect on 95
English education 64
entrepreneurship and employment 74–7
epithetized phenomena 67
e-topia 22, 65, 67, 127
Evans, P. 153–4
exclusion 11, 14, 17, 20, 24, 34, 63, 99, 100, 104; *see also* social exclusion
expectations and actual benefits 155
expectations and outcomes: about 48–9; Gonniana TARAKendra 53–4; Lehra Mohabbat TARAkendra 54–6; Poornankuppam Centre 50–1; Thirukanchipet Centre 51–3
external support 162, 172

F

failures 12; of CSOs 25, 65, 155, 164, 166, 172; of decolonization 14, 153; as design choice 98; of false hopes 27, 98, 106, 153, 164; of financial resources 162, 172; future research on 167; of groupthink 12, 152, 163; market 164, 172; of the state 16, 18, 27, 57, 65, 78, 155, 164, 166, 172; and successes 18, 24, 26, 48, 78; technology development and implementation 21, 78, 129, 165, 168; *see also* electrical supply problems; elitist capture
Farm Clinics 54, 56, 180n
favouritism 89
Feenberg, A. 67, 151, 159
Fenn, J. 6
Foucault 158
Frank, A. G. 128
Frissen, P. 93
Fukuyama, F. 176n
future research 167

G

Gandhi, M. K. 50, 127, 134, 149, 163, 175n
Gemeinschaft (communities) 151
gemeinschaftlich behaviour 64
gender and IT 98–101
gender divide 99, 100, 104, 105, 106–9, 169
gender inequalities 97, 101, 123, 160
gender separation 108
gender terms 102
Gesellschaft (civil society) 7, 151
global gap 3, 38
Global System for Mobile (GSM) technology 146, 147, 148
globalization 8, 16, 20, 37, 38, 131, 132, 173
Gonniana TARAKendra 53–4
governmentality 24, 31, 70, 93, 156, 157, 158, 159, 168
Government-to-Citizen (G2C) service 72, 74, 75, 81

gradualist neo-liberal paradigm 35
Green, L. 99–101
Green Revolution 12–13, 175n
Grönlund, Å. 7
ground-up innovation vs. adaptation: *see*
    adaptation vs. ground-up innovation
groupthink 152, 163, 164
growth theories 129, 167
Gyandoot information kiosk: see
    soochanalaya (Gyandoot information
    kiosk)
Gyandoot Intranet 68, 85, 89
Gyandoot Project: actual use of kiosk
    services 73; government rollout
    difficulties 80; kiosk employment 77;
    kiosk operations 78; kiosk services
    provided 72; kiosk technology 72;
    services offered by 78; users of
    104–5; *see also* QUANGOs (Quasi-
    Autonomous Non-Governmental
    Organizations)
Gyandoot Samiti 72, 73, 74, 75, 80–2, 85,
    90, 91

H

Habermas, J. 23
Hafkin, N. 4, 98
Hall, P. 36, 133
harassment 99, 100
Haraway, D. J. 169
Hård, M. 26
harmonization/harmony 6, 18, 20, 21, 71,
    110, 150
Harvey, D. 180n
Harvey, F. 138
Hedström, K. 7
Heeks, R. 7, 164, 165, 180n
Hindu: religion 42, 83, 88, 165,
    181n,184n; non-Hindus 43
Hindustan Lever 39, 92
Holloway, S. L. 100
HOPE (Holistic Approach for People's
    Empowerment) 31, 108, 116–18, 119,
    122, 123, 160
human development 8, 36, 37
Human Development Reports (HDR) 37
Human Rights Education Movement of
    India (HREMI) 117

Huyer, S. 101
hybrid agents 11
hype 6, 74, 143, 164
hype cycle 6, 143, 150, 161

I

ICT4D (information communication
    technologies for development) 6, 7, 8,
    11, 12, 128, 151, 152, 164, 165, 170,
    171, 172
ICT-based civil society initiatives 97
ICT-based CSOs 21, 31, 64, 112, 115,
    116, 130
ICT-based e-governance projects 93, 94,
    157
ICT-oriented social movements 160
ICTs (information communication
    technologies): civil society and
    community 151–5; corDECT
    WLL (Wireless Local Loop) 144–9;
    demand-side dimensions of 8;
    for developmental action 107;
    expansion aspects 153; to foster
    communitarianism 151; ICT4D
    and neo-liberal discourse 6–13;
    impact on social hierarchy by 22; to
    improvise developmental planning
    68; innovations 18, 144–50, 171; and
    limits of developmental CSOs 122–3;
    qualities of 20; for restructuring and
    redeployment resources 70; rural
    network society 168–73; and social
    change 97–8; and social development
    10; for social development 126; for
    strengthening arms of governance
    72; structure and agency 155–61;
    technology and sustainability 161–8;
    use and diffusion of 34
ideological tension and ironies 26
illiteracy 5, 100, 102, 106, 107, 122, 137, 160
illiterate women 107
IMF (International Monetary Fund) 14,
    18, 37, 178n
import substitution 68, 69
income enhancement 23
income of participants 9
Indian Institute of Management
    Ahmedabad (IIMA) 81

Indian Institute of Science (IIS) 141
Indian Institute of Technology (IIT) 144
industry, role of 133
industry-university relationship 133
information and communication
technologies (ICTs): *see* ICTs
(information communication
technologies)
information innovation impact 23
Information Technologies Group (ITG) 61
Information Village Research Project
(IVRP): *see* IVRP (Information Village
Research Project)
informational capitalism 35
infrastructure development 171
infrastructure facilities 49, 50, 77
innovation and CSOs in rural ICT 128–30
innovation process models 167
international agencies 18, 70–1
International Development Research
Centre (IDRC) 40
international technology spillovers 10, 38,
132
Internet access 12, 47, 61, 144, 145, 153
Internet kiosks 61, 62, 162
iStation 134
IVRP (Information Village Research
Project) 34, 39, 40–4, 47–8, 53, 55,
63, 110–11, 113, 114, 119, 123;
IVRP kiosks 53, 63, 111

J

James Martin & Co. 39
Jamison, A. 26
Jessop, B. 27
Jha, Satish 57
Jhunjhunwala, A. 146–8

K

Kaviraj, S. 15, 16, 63
Keniston, K. 20, 175n
Kerala 180n, 185n
Khilnani, S. 15
Khosla, Ranjit 57
kiosks: in CSOs (civil society organizations)
155; earnings expectations 82;
economic sustainability 61, 62;

function and organization of 29;
local elites and kiosk management
42–3; operating costs 54; setup costs
55; as social experiments 34; three
kiosks tale 85–91; user assessment of
81; UUA (Uzhavar Uthavi Agam)
56; village 40, 155; *see also* cyber-
kiosks and social inclusion problems;
Gyandoot Project; IVRP (Information
Village Research Project) kiosks
Krikke, J. 146

L

language interface 135, 137
languages 44, 101, 107, 134, 137, 138,
139; *see also* local languages
leapfrog model 170
leftist political thought 15
Lehra Mohabbat TARAkendra 54–6
lessons and non-lessons 63–6
lessons learned 164
Leydesdorff, L. 128
license fees 81
licensing policy 141
limited local participation 48
Linden, A. 6
literacy 36, 101, 107
local communities 3, 28, 162, 172
local democracy 2, 4, 171
local economic regeneration 64, 155
local elites 65, 91; and kiosk management
42–3; vs. the poor 6; social divides 11,
46, 156
local infrastructure 74, 77–8
local languages 44, 54, 55, 73, 135, 165
local resources 48, 64, 82
Lovink, G. 7

M

M. S. Swaminathan Foundation (MSSRF):
see MSSRF (M. S. Swaminathan
Foundation)
Maclay, C. M. 61
Madhya Pradesh 5, 27, 31, 68, 72, 75, 104,
160, 183n
Madon, S. 71, 180n
management training 76

mandis (market) 46, 52, 80, 89, 183n
Mangalam Society 110, 111
marginalization of poor countries 37
marginalized communities 4, 17, 31, 97,
    98, 113, 122, 160, 169
Marx, K. 178n
Marxian economics 130
Marxism Today 33
Mazzarella, W. 6
Mercer, C. 12
Metcalfe's law/effect 63, 156
microcredit 35–6
middle-class NGOs 17
modernization theory 36
Moore, N. 100
MSSRF (M. S. Swaminathan Foundation)
    5, 30, 34, 39, 41, 42, 44, 48, 50, 51, 52,
    55–8, 61, 63–4, 102, 110, 111, 114,
    115, 118, 122, 149, 155, 160, 162
multinational corporations (MNCs) 9, 146,
    147, 161, 165

N

Naramada Bachaao Antholan (NBA) 17
Narmada Dam 17
narratives of success 34, 35, 48, 58–63, 68;
    about 82–5; civil society and private
    sector 91–3; QUANGOS 91–3; three
    kiosks tale 85–91
National Innovation System (NIS) 19, 127,
    131, 150, 165, 167, 168
Nattaimai (village headman rule) 41, 69
Navarria, G. 168
Negroponte, N. 20
net-based social action participation 116–22
network development 70
networked governance 157
networking 20, 31, 63, 68, 94, 95, 114,
    152, 156, 159, 171
new times theory 33
New York Times 2, 114, 115, 138, 139
newly industrialized economies (NIEs) 36–7
newly industrializing countries (NICs) 134,
    154
nonessentialist perspective 67, 159
nongovernmental organizations (NGOs)
    4, 17, 70, 140; critiques of 18; elites
    vs. rural populations 12; ICT-based

development projects 4; limitations of
    123; Small Industrial Development
    Bank of India (SIDBI) 117; social
    experiments 10
non-text-based medium 106

O

One Laptop per Child (OLPC) project 164
Omvedt, G. 175n
O'Neil, D. 7
online networking 114
optimistic projections 53
organization and focus 30–1

P

Page, M. 99
panchayat (local body) 50, 51, 52, 72, 73, 79,
    82, 88–91, 140
Parayil, P. 12, 33, 133
Pham Lobb, L. A. 101
PicoPeta 135, 149; *see also* Simputers
Pierterse, J. N. 8, 35
Pliatzky Report 91
political agenda 36
political and ideological conflicts/tensions
    9, 26, 68, 159
political connections 90
political parties 76
political society 15, 16, 17
politics of technology 145
Pondicherry 5, 22, 27, 30, 31, 34, 39–43,
    55, 56, 58, 59, 60, 63, 64, 102, 110,
    111, 116, 117, 120, 155, 160, 162,
    180n, 184n, 185n
poor vs. local elites 6; *see also* Dalits
    (lower castes); elitist capture;
    social divides
Poornankuppam Centre 50–1
postcolonialism 14–18, 24, 63, 128,
    153, 163, 167, 178n
postcolonial state 14, 16, 17, 153, 163
poverty alleviation 34, 36, 53, 64
poverty-alleviation programmes 9, 11, 20,
    23, 129, 134
power relations 10, 94, 106, 156, 157, 165,
    169, 171
Prahalad, C. K. 78, 171, 183n

private company competition 92
private sector-academic collaboration 145, 149
project benefits 29, 83
project drawbacks 26, 109, 123
public sector driven technology development 69
Punjab 5, 27, 34, 45
Putnam, R. 22, 176n
Pygmy Deposit Scheme 135

Q

quangocratic model 65, 156
QUANGOs (Quasi-Autonomous Non-Governmental Organizations) 5, 13, 14, 18, 20, 21, 23–8, 31, 57, 58, 91–3, 153, 155, 156, 166, 167
Qureshi, I. 139

R

Rajora, Rajesh 72, 104
research questions 19–24, 99
resource constraints 6, 11, 52, 162, 172
resource mobilization 8, 34, 152
Rheingold, H. 151
rhetoric and reality of participation 101–2, 110, 149, 161
Robins, K. 20, 152
Rosenberg, N. 19
rural communities 2, 21, 39
rural elites 81, 109, 161, 172
rural e-topia 65
rural India 113
rural network security 159
rural network society 5, 22, 94, 159, 160; analytical issues 24–7; civil society argument and ICTs 13–19; ICTs, ICT4D and neo-liberal discourse 6–13; organization and focus 30–1; politics of 168–73; research questions 19–24
rural network society innovations: appropriate technology for the masses 125–8; corDECT WLL 144–9; CSOs and the state 149–50; CSOs and triple helix model 130–4; ICT innovations 144–9; innovation

and CSOs in rural ICT 128–30; Simputers 134–43
Rural Participatory Appraisal Techniques 41
rural people, scepticism of 41

S

Saith, A. 178n, 181n
Sandoval, C. 171
satellite communication 39, 47, 139
Sawhney, H. 171
Schwittay, A. 183n, 186n
Scientific American 138
Scott, A. 99
self-sustainable belief 159
Sen, A. 129
Shrum, W. 151
Sikosa, T. 101
simple linear model 21–2, 134
Simputer Trust 135, 138, 141, 142, 149, 161
Simputers 21, 26, 30, 134–43
Small Industrial Development Bank of India (SIDBI) 117
social action 27, 31, 65, 115, 122, 123, 153, 160, 162, 163
social actors' role 23
social barriers 11, 98, 123
social capital 7, 21, 64, 155
social constructivism 10, 23, 67, 159, 165
social development 45, 126, 171; and ICTs 10; techno-determinant models of 65
social divides 11, 55, 65, 102, 103, 106, 109, 118, 151, 169, 171
social dynamics of e-governance: entrepreneurship and employment 74–7; local infrastructure 77–8; sustainability 81–2; user perceptions 78–81
social enterprise model 18, 30, 35–40, 65, 155, 156, 160, 162, 172
social exclusion 33, 71, 98, 100, 122–3, 160
social experiments 3, 10, 27, 34, 115
social groups 78, 151
social hierarchy 13, 106
social inclusion and participation 11, 18
social levelling 101
social movements 13, 15, 17, 98, 112–16, 118, 123, 160, 168

social transformation 4, 33, 36, 97, 113, 116, 126, 128, 172
social venture capital 34
social venture capitalists 39, 125
solar panels 77
soochaks (local kiosk managers) 73, 74, 75, 76, 77, 78, 81, 82, 85, 89, 90, 91, 92, 105, 106
soochanalaya (Gyandoot information kiosk) 5, 73, 74, 78, 81, 82, 85, 89, 90, 92
Sparks, C. 33
Spender, D. 100
Spivak, G. C. 178n
Standage, T. 65
state: ICT project relations 155; influence of agencies 27; involvement in industrial development 154; and patronage 57; projects led by 65; role and effectiveness 153–4; support of 57, 146–7, 150; and universities 133
state-civil society relationships 22, 27, 48, 56–8, 155, 166
state-sponsored QUANGOs 20–1; *see also* QUANGOs (Quasi-Autonomous Non-Governmental Organizations)
static information 43
Sterling, Bruce 139
Stockholm Challenge Award 5, 55, 73, 115
structure and agency 155–61
subaltern publics 17
subsidiaries 92
success anecdotes vs. analysis 58–63
success stories 83, 85
supplementary activities 75
sustainability 28, 29, 37, 40, 43, 48, 58, 61, 65, 74, 81–2, 92, 94, 156, 161, 162, 165, 171
Swedish telecottages 1–2

T

Tamil language software 44
Tamil Nadu 178n, 179n, 185n
TARA (Technology and Action for Rural Advancement) 45, 109
TARAhaat 39, 45, 46, 47, 52, 53, 54, 55, 57, 106, 107, 108, 109, 118, 119, 122
TARAkendras 5, 39, 53, 54, 108, 109; about 45–6; cyber-kiosks and social

inclusion problems 106–9; vs. IVRP 47–8; technology 46–7
techno-determinist models 34, 65, 128, 167, 170
technofeminist approaches 169
technological utopianism 65
technology 43–4, 46–7; diffusion 26; as economic growth tool 70; and governance 31, 67–8; perceptions 19; spillover 36; and sustainability 161–8; transfer vs. adoption 10
Technology and Action for Rural Advancement (TARA): *see* TARA (Technology and Action for Rural Advancement)
technopoles 38, 133
technopolis model 39
techno-social network 148, 157
techno-utopianism 12, 152
Teheranian, M. 19
Telecom Regulatory Authority of India (TRAI) 148
telecottages: in India 2–3; origins of 1–2; *see also* kiosks
The Incommunicado Network (Lovink and Zehle) 7
third sector 14
Third World 15, 138, 139, 153, 157, 168
Thirukanchipet Centre 51–3
Thompson, M. 10
three kiosks tale 85–91
Tiwari, M. 75
Tönnies, Ferdinand 151
trajectory of social innovation 143
tribal districts 103–4
tribal women 103–6
triple helix model 127, 128, 130, 131, 132, 133
Turkle, S. 99

U

United Nations 20, 37, 38
universities 19, 21, 23, 24, 26, 31, 38, 131, 132, 133, 134, 149, 165, 167
untouchability practice 42, 43
urban settings vs. rural India 113
Urry, J. 27
user fees 51–4, 61, 75, 159

user perceptions 74, 78–81
user profile 111
UUA (Uzhavar Uthavi Agam - farmers' support kiosks) 56

V

Valentine, G. 100
village elites 42, 46, 94, 107, 115, 156
village kiosks 40, 155
Village Knowledge Centres (VKCs) 5, 39, 44, 64, 102, 109–12, 155, 160, 162
Virilio, P. 19–20
voluntary agencies 14
VSAT (Very Small Aperture Terminal) technology 47
vulnerability to cyber violence 100

W

Wade, R. H. 4, 8, 9, 12, 152
Wajcman, J. 101, 169

Walker, A. 8
Walsham, G. 6, 7, 20
weather prediction methods 60
Weber, S. 19
Wellman, B. 11
women: and ICTs 101–2; literacy programmes for 107; participation 98, 104–5, 109–12, 160; programmes to attract 106; social exclusion of 100; tribal 103–6; *see also* gender divide
women volunteers 110, 111
women's empowerment 102, 118
women's Self Help Groups (SHGs) 50, 92
Woolgar, S. 67
World Bank 14, 18, 20, 37, 39, 70, 71, 176n, 178n

Z

Zehle, Z. 7

Lightning Source UK Ltd.
Milton Keynes UK
172798UK00002B/2/P